KT-590-049

LIGHT for our PATH

2001

Bible readings with short notes

HBRA

INTERNATIONAL BIBLE READING ASSOCIATION

Cover photograph: 'The Burning Bush' by Paul Koli (India)
from Masao Takenaka and Ron O'Grady: *The Bible
through Asian Eyes* (Pace Publishing in association with
Asian Christian Art Association, 1991)

Editor – Kate Hughes

Published by:
The International Bible Reading Association
1020 Bristol Road
Selly Oak
Birmingham B29 6LB
Great Britain

ISBN 0–7197–0972–5
ISSN 0140–8267

© 2000 International Bible Reading Association

All rights reserved. No part of this publication may be reproduced,
stored in a retrieval system, or transmitted, in any form or by any
means, electronic, mechanical, photocopying, recording or otherwise,
without the prior permission of the International Bible Reading
Association.

Typeset by Avonset, Bath BA1 3AU

Printed and bound in Great Britain by

Omnia Books Limited, Glasgow

CONTENTS

IBRA International Bible Reading Association

Dear Friends

Welcome to this year's *Light for our Path*. The readings in *Light for our Path* are grouped into eleven themes, which are numbered and named in the Contents list on pages 3 and 4. Some of the themes concentrate on one or two books of the Bible, and the names of the books are also mentioned in the Contents list.

Because of our publishing schedule, I am writing this introduction in the middle of our English winter. The hours of daylight are short and often cloudy; the trees are bare; we have a lot of rain to turn the tarmac roads and pavements black – winter in England is dark and can be depressing. As a result, each winter I learn again to value *light*. The electric light which makes my home so welcoming and safe; the flame of the candle which I light at mealtimes; the warm glow of the fire. Sin and the cruelty of human beings to each other can make the world a dark and threatening place, and all of us struggle at times against depression – will human beings never learn to do things differently? In this world, the Bible is a light shining in the darkness. The word of God brings strength, hope and comfort; it warms us and shows us the way; it helps us to 'live as children of light' (*Ephesians 5.8*). I hope that our daily reading of these notes will help us to rediscover that the word of God is truly 'a lamp to my feet and a light to my path' (*Psalm 119.105*).

Kate Hughes (Editor)

Reading LIGHT FOR OUR PATH

- Before reading, be quiet and remember that God is with you. Ask for his Holy Spirit to guide your reading.

- If you do not have a Bible with you, you can work solely from *Light for our Path* by referring to the short Bible passage printed in bold type. (Only the editions printed in English have this.)

- You can begin by reading just the short extract from the daily Bible passage which appears in the notes. Or you may prefer to read the full text of the daily passage from your Bible. The weekly notes use a variety of different Bible translations, which are named at the beginning of the week. You may like to see how the extract in bold type compares with the same passage in your own Bible. And if your Bible mentions parallel passages in other places, comparing these passages can widen your thinking.

- At the beginning of each week's notes there is a text for the week, which can be used as a focus for worship or reflection throughout the week.

- When you finish each day's reading, spend a little time reflecting on it. What does it say to you about God? About yourself? About others? About the world in which we live? Has it changed your thinking? Does it suggest something that you should do? Then use the final prayer (marked with a cross), or any prayer of your own you need to make.

- At the end of each week's notes, there are questions and suggestions for group discussion or personal thought. These are only suggestions – your own reading and prayer may have drawn your attention to other aspects which you would like to explore further. The important thing is that you should let God speak to you through his Word, so that as you read steadily through the year you will be able to look back and see that you have got to know him better and have grown spiritually.

ABBREVIATIONS AND ACKNOWLEDGEMENTS

We are grateful for permission to quote from the following Bible versions:

GNB *Good News Bible*, 4th edition, published by The Bible Societies/HarperCollins, © American Bible Society, 1976.

JB *The Jerusalem Bible*, Students' Paperback edition, published by Geoffrey Chapman, © Darton, Longman & Todd Ltd and Doubleday & Company, Inc., 1968.

NASB *New American Standard Bible*®, © Copyright The Lockman Foundation 1960, 1962, 1963, 1968, 1971, 1972, 1973, 1975, 1977, 1995. Used by permission.

NEB *New English Bible*, © Oxford and Cambridge University Presses, 1970.

NIV *The Holy Bible, New International Version*, Hodder & Stoughton, © International Bible Society, 1980.

NJB *The New Jerusalem Bible*, published by Darton, Longman & Todd, © Darton, Longman & Todd Ltd and Doubleday & Company, Inc., 1985.

NKJV *New King James Version*, © Thomas Nelson & Sons. Used by permission.0

NRSV *New Revised Standard Version Bible*, published by HarperCollins, © Division of Christian Education of the National Council of the Churches of Christ in the United States of America, 1989.

REB Revised English Bible, © Oxford and Cambridge University Presses, 1989.

RSV *The Holy Bible, Revised Standard Version*, published by Thomas Nelson & Sons, © Division of Christian Education of the National Council of the Churches of Christ in the United States of America, 1952.

'Jesus, name above all names' by Naida Hern, © Kingsway Communications. Used by permission.

IBRA INTERNATIONAL APPEAL

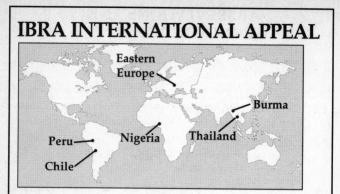

In five continents you will find Christians using IBRA material.

Some Christians will be using books and Bible reading cards translated into their local language, whilst others use English books. Some of the books are printed in the UK, but more and more countries are printing the books and cards themselves. The IBRA International Fund works through churches, Christian groups and Christian publishing houses overseas to make these publications available.

Each year we receive more requests for help from the IBRA International Fund, with greater emphasis on helping our overseas friends to produce their own version of IBRA material.

The only money we have to send is the money you give, so please help us again by giving generously.

Place your gift in the envelope provided and give it to your IBRA representative, or send it direct to:

The IBRA International Appeal

1020 Bristol Road, Selly Oak,
Birmingham B29 6LB, Great Britain

Thank you for your help.

GOD'S NEW WORLD 1
Gospel stories today 1

Notes by Chris Duffett

based on the New International Version

Chris Duffett is an evangelist based at Hoole Baptist Church in Chester; he has a particular concern for young people and those who are homeless. He has a heart for community outreach and seeks to train and equip Christians to reach their local communities with the gospel.

The gospel will only be relevant for today if we, as God's people, try to live it through our everyday lives at work, at home and in our faith communities. If people see how relevant Jesus is in our lives, they will want to live like us. During the next two weeks we shall be looking at readings written hundreds of years ago which challenge us as we apply them to our own contexts.

Text for the week: John 1.10 – 18

Monday January 1   Luke 2.8 – 21

CHRISTMAS EVERY DAY Jewish law regarded the shepherds in today's story as outcasts. As part of their job, they had to sleep rough in order to guard the sheep which were their livelihood. This meant that they were unable to wash and keep clean, and were considered dirty. Yet it was to them that God first chose to announce the birth of his Son, the Saviour of the world, the long-awaited, promised Messiah:

An angel of the Lord appeared to them, and the glory of the Lord shone around them, and they were terrified. But the angel said to them, 'Do not be afraid. I bring you good news of great joy that will be for all the people. Today in the town of David a Saviour has been born to you; he is Christ the Lord.'   (verses 9 – 11)

Just as God chose the outcast shepherds to see his new-born Son, Jesus, we also need to bring the great news of the Messiah to those on the edge of our communities and society. It is important to note from the reading that the angel said it would be good news for *all* people. This includes people who are homeless, lonely, sick, outcast and disabled; God longs for people such as these to hear the gospel so that they, like us, may have 'great joy' (*verse 10*).

✝ *Father, thank you that the Christmas story is for all the people around us that we see every day of the year. Thank you that no one is beyond your love and care and help me to show this in the way I live my life today and every day.*

Tuesday January 2   John 1.1 – 9

YOU ARE THE LIGHT OF THE WORLD   John describes Jesus as with God in the beginning of all time, and as himself God (*verse 1*), but in spite of all this splendour Jesus humbled himself to become one of us. Paul describes Jesus as making himself 'nothing, taking the very nature of a servant' (*Philippians 2.7*). Why did Jesus do this? The world which was in darkness needed a light to come and dwell in it, and Jesus was that light.

> **In him was life, and that life was the light of men ...The true light that gives light to every man was coming into the world.**   (**verses 4 and 9**)

The New Testament uses many names and pictures to describe Jesus: a gate (*John 10.7*), the chief cornerstone (*Mark 12.10*), the shepherd (*1 Peter 5.4*) and living bread (*John 6.51*). However, Jesus himself uses only one picture to describe both himself and his disciples: 'The light of the world'. Just as people were drawn to God through Jesus the light, so people should be attracted to God through us, when we are the light in our communities.

✝ *Jesus, light of the world, help me to walk the walk and not just talk the talk. Help me to live out my faith wherever I am so that I may be a light which draws all people to you.*

Wednesday January 3   John 1.10 – 18

GOD WITH US   Hundreds of years before the 'word became flesh', Isaiah prophesied that Jesus would come to dwell with us. 'The virgin will be with child and will give birth to a son, and will call him Immanuel' (*Isaiah 7.14*). Jesus is Immanuel, 'God with us'. It is so comforting to know that we do not need to work to reach up towards God so that we can be with him. God has reached down with grace, to be with us.

> **The Word became flesh and lived for a while among us. We have seen his glory, the glory of the one and only [Son],**

who came from the Father, full of grace and truth.
(verse 14)

This principle, that Jesus was incarnate, must be at the centre of how we share our faith with people in our communities. We must copy Jesus, who drew alongside people and dwelt with them. Today's reading encourages us to be present where people are and spend time with them, not only to preach, but also to show Jesus to others through our actions. Ken Gnanakan, in his book *Kingdom Concerns* (IVP, 1989, p. 211), writes that 'Fleshing out the gospel makes the message real to the outside world'. I often sit and share friendship with homeless people on the street or in doorways, or sometimes I share my faith with people over a cup of coffee in McDonald's. How can you reach out to people today in ways that put 'flesh on the gospel'?

† *Lord, help me to 'shine as a light in the world to the glory of God the Father' (Alternative Service Book of the Church of England, p. 248)*

Thursday January 4   **Matthew 2.1 – 12**

GOD LOVES THE RICH It is estimated that one in every ten verses in the New Testament refers to 'the poor'. This shows that God has a special concern for the poor. But what about the rich? In today's reading we can see that God also loves the rich. In contrast to the poor shepherds, the second group of visitors to Jesus are traditionally believed to have been elegant and regal. God led three magi (wise men or magicians) from the east, bearing expensive gifts to honour his Son.

On coming to the house, they saw the child with his mother Mary, and they bowed down and worshipped him. Then they opened their treasures and presented him with gifts of gold and of incense and of myrrh. **(verse 11)**

For a moment, picture these three wise men, bowing in worship before an infant and opening their special treasures before him. Then picture yourself as one of the magi, in that humble room with Jesus. What gift have you brought him? We all have gifts that we can bring to Jesus in worship. You may have something of material value that you could give, perhaps to support a missionary. Or perhaps you have a special ability or some time, a special gift which you could freely allow him to use for his will?

11

✝ *Just as the magi bowed in worship before you, I also come before you in worship and offer all that I own. I lay before you the gifts that I possess and freely give all to you, my master and king.*

Friday January 5 Matthew 2.13 – 18

GUARD YOUR FAITH There may be times in our life when we have to run away from situations which are spiritually difficult to a safe place in God. Joseph ran away from Herod to Egypt after God spoke to him in a dream:

An angel of the Lord appeared to Joseph in a dream. 'Get up,' he said, 'take the child and his mother and escape to Egypt. Stay there until I tell you, for Herod is going to search for the child to kill him.' So he got up, took the child and his mother during the night and left for Egypt.
(verses 13 – 14)

Just as Herod searched for Jesus to kill him, so the devil searches for ways to steal, kill and destroy our faith (*John 10.10*). Sometimes it is right to run to a safe place, into the loving protection of our heavenly Father. We need to take time to pray, read the Bible and simply 'dwell' with him so that we can guard our faith from attack by the devil's lies and schemes. There are times when the enemy will try to discourage us, burden us or lie to us. During these times, run to God and try to listen to him. If you can take time off work or from other responsibilities, go on a retreat or quiet day so that you can simply dwell in a safe place and nurture your relationship with God.

✝ *Protecting Father, thank you that I can declare with the psalmist that you are my 'refuge and strength, an ever present help in trouble' (Psalm 46.1).*

Saturday January 6 (Epiphany) Luke 3.7 – 22

EQUIPPED TO LOVE John the Baptist preached some uncompromising and radical lessons to those who flocked to hear him by the River Jordan. He told his hearers that it was essential to share and give to others. This was probably not an easy message for the people to put into practice, and, if we are honest, it is no easier for us today to live a life of giving and sharing.

'The man with two tunics should share with him who has none, and the one who has food should do the same ... I

**baptize you with water. But one more powerful than I ...
will baptize you with the Holy Spirit and with fire.'
(part of verses 11 and 16)**

John points to how we can be equipped for the difficult task of
being people who give continuously: through the Holy Spirit.
Being baptized or soaked in the Spirit means being equipped to
do the will of our heavenly Father, instead of the will of our
'flesh'. The Holy Spirit equips us to love in practical ways; he is
given to us for a purpose, not just for our enjoyment or any
selfish use. The Holy Spirit is a missionary spirit, who equips us
to look beyond our lives to the lives of others, so that we can
share and demonstrate the gospel to all people.

✝ *Jesus, on this day of Epiphany we remember your baptism. May I
be baptized with your Holy Spirit and equipped to live and work for
your praise and glory.*

For group discussion and personal thought

● Think of one new way in which you can 'make the message
real to the outside world'.
● What gift can you bring to Jesus in worship?

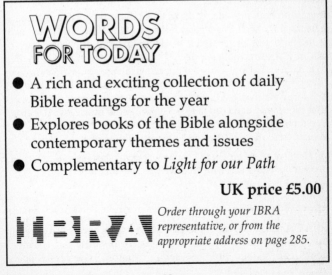

WORDS
FOR TODAY

● A rich and exciting collection of daily
Bible readings for the year
● Explores books of the Bible alongside
contemporary themes and issues
● Complementary to *Light for our Path*

UK price £5.00

*Order through your IBRA
representative, or from the
appropriate address on page 285.*

GOD'S NEW WORLD 1
Gospel stories today 2

Notes by Chris Duffett

based on the New International Version

This second week of readings suggests several ways in which we can reach out to other people in God's name – and challenges us to find ways to put them into action.

Text for the week: Luke 8.40 – 48

Sunday January 7   Luke 7.36 – 50

EXTRAVAGANT LOVE   It would be easy to accuse the woman in today's reading of being a bit 'over the top' in her worship of Jesus. Yet Jesus shows that there was a reason for her over-generous act. She simply wanted to seek forgiveness from him.

When a woman who had lived a sinful life in that town learned that Jesus was eating at the Pharisee's house, she brought an alabaster jar of perfume, and as she stood behind him at his feet weeping, she began to wet his feet with her tears. Then she wiped them with her hair, kissed them and poured perfume on them.   **(verses 37 – 38)**

It was the holy presence of Jesus that caused the local prostitute to gatecrash the well-to-do party. Her act of love towards Jesus, with tears of repentance, kisses of devotion, and the costly act of pouring perfume on Jesus' feet, showed how sincerely she wanted to turn from her sin. Jesus did not cringe at her presence or turn her away; rather, he accepted her act of love and said to her, 'Your sins are forgiven' (*verse 48*). Jesus explained to the critical onlookers that those who need much forgiveness, show much love (*verse 47*). We have all sinned and been forgiven much; therefore, we also should be extravagant in our love towards Jesus.

✝ *Help me to see the depth of your forgiveness for me and to respond to it by loving you with all my heart, soul and mind.*

Monday January 8   Luke 8.40 – 48

REACH OUT AND TOUCH HIM   Jairus was anxious to hurry Jesus back to his home to pray for his little girl who was near death's door; he must have despaired when Jesus spent valuable time asking the crowd who had touched him! The disciples pointed out that it could have been anyone in the large crowd; then a woman who was ritually unclean,

> **seeing that she could not go unnoticed, came trembling and fell at his feet. In the presence of all the people, she told why she had touched him and how she had been instantly healed. Then he said to her, 'Daughter, your faith has healed you. Go in peace.'** (verses 47 – 48)

In spite of Jesus' busy schedule, he took time to find out who had touched him in order to receive healing. He wanted to reassure the woman, to give her his rich blessing of peace. Are there situations in your life that need healing? Reach out to Jesus; he is never too busy to take time for you. Do you have a friend in need of a miracle? Encourage them to reach out to Jesus; he will meet with them and not walk away.

✝ *When my hands are weak, help me to lift them to reach out to you.*
When I am tired, help me to seek after you.
When I feel like giving up, help me to touch your life-giving presence.

Tuesday January 9   Luke 8.49 – 56

THE IMPOSSIBLE MADE POSSIBLE Jairus must have had such hope of seeing his daughter alive when Jesus agreed to go and pray for her – and must have been heartbroken when the messenger announced the sad news of her death. However, before Jairus even had time to weep for his lost daughter, Jesus spoke words of comfort to him, reassuring him that he had the situation under control.

> **While Jesus was still speaking, someone came from the house of Jairus, the synagogue ruler. 'Your daughter is dead,' he said. 'Don't bother the teacher any more.' Hearing this, Jesus said to Jairus, 'Don't be afraid; just believe, and she will be healed.'** (verses 49 – 50)

Jairus's daughter was dead; it was impossible that she could live again. However, what is impossible for us can be possible for Jesus. Many people live in seemingly impossible situations, but we have to look beyond their circumstances to the miraculous. I often meet people who are in need of healing, addicted or scarred from family breakdown. In these situations only Jesus can help, and I can turn only to him. He is the one who can make the impossible possible.

† *Lord Jesus, thank you that when you walked this earth you performed miracles which changed the impossible for people. You can still do this today, so when I am faced with an impossible situation, help me to turn to you.*

Wednesday January 10   Luke 14.7 – 14

FOOD, GLORIOUS FOOD!   Mission is more than proclamation, teaching, social action or healing; it also involves eating and drinking! In the gospels alone, the word 'eat' is found 107 times, and 'drink' some 55 times. A great deal of Jesus' time was spent around the table, eating or drinking with people who were lost and in need of love.

> **Then Jesus said to his host, 'When you give a luncheon or dinner, do not invite your friends, your brothers or relatives, or your rich neighbours; if you do, they may invite you back and so you will be repaid. But when you give a banquet, invite the poor, the crippled, the lame, the blind, and you will be blessed. Although they cannot repay you, you will be repaid at the resurrection of the righteous.'**
> **(verses 12 – 14)**

This passage encourages us to invite all the people who are on the margins of our communities to a meal in our home. Who do you know who is poor, crippled, blind or lame? In this story, Jesus points out the people we should welcome to the heart of our home, around the table where we eat. Ask God whom he would like you to invite for a meal. It may be someone who cannot invite you back, but his promise is that we shall be repaid in heaven.

† *Abba Father, strengthen me to welcome into my home the people who need your love.*
Abba Father, make me bold enough to invite the people I would not usually invite to my home.
Abba Father, help me to be a person who is hospitable in your sight.

Thursday January 11   Luke 14.15 – 24

WE MUST GO The servant in today's story puts me to shame. He is obedient to his master and does exactly what he is commanded to do! There are times when I know that I should share my faith through words and deeds, but I just don't! Laziness and apathy, embarrassment and shame are some of the reasons why I don't share with people what I know to be true. Yet I want to be like the obedient servant who simply fulfils his master's request:

> 'Go out quickly into the streets and alleys of the town and bring in the poor, the crippled, the blind and the lame.' 'Sir,' the servant said, 'what you ordered has been done, but there is still room.' Then the master told his servant, 'Go out to the roads and country lanes and make them come in, so that my house will be full.' (verses 21b – 23)

The reason why many of our churches are empty is simply that we have not obeyed the command of Jesus to 'go out' and 'bring them in' as much as we should. Jesus longs for us to be people who go and 'bring in the poor', as he did.

† *Friend of sinners, help me to love those whom no one else seems to love.*
Friend of the lost, help me to love those who are searching and longing for acceptance.
Friend of the outcast, help me to embrace those who are despised and rejected.

Friday January 12   **John 6.1 – 15**

GIVE WHAT YOU HAVE When I read this story, I often focus on Jesus and the miracle of feeding the multitudes, or on the disciples and how they gathered the leftovers. However, we can also learn an important principle from a very unlikely person, the boy who provided his packed lunch for Jesus to use.

> Philip answered [Jesus], 'Eight months' wages would not buy enough bread for each one to have a bite!' Another of his disciples, Andrew, Simon Peter's brother, spoke up, 'Here is a boy with five small barley loaves and two small fish, but how far will they go among so many?' (verses 7 – 8)

The little boy may have thought he had nothing to offer. But what he did have was freely offered, and it certainly went a long way! We may feel that our gifts or abilities are small and insignificant. Yet when we simply give them into the hands of Jesus, we may see something miraculous happen. Our offering could be multiplied and used to bless many people for the glory of God!

† *'Yours, Lord, is the greatness, the power, the glory, the splendour, and the majesty; for everything in heaven and earth is yours. All*

things come from you, and of your own do we give you'
(Alternative Service Book, p. 129).

Saturday January 13   Matthew 25.31 – 46

LOVE IN ACTION   Jesus teaches us an eternal mystery when
he describes what will happen at the end of the world:
whenever we help someone in a practical way, we actually
minister to Jesus.

> **Then the King will say to those on his right, 'Come, you
> who are blessed by my Father; take your inheritance, the
> kingdom prepared for you since the creation of the world.
> For I was hungry and you gave me something to eat, I was
> thirsty and you gave me something to drink, I was a
> stranger and you invited me in, I needed clothes and you
> clothed me, I was sick and you looked after me, I was in
> prison and you came to visit me.'**   **(verses 34 – 36)**

We do not have to think up extraordinary ways of ministering
to other people, and therefore to Jesus, because in this passage
he suggests some simple things that we can do now. Most
communities have people in jail or in hospital. Most
communities have people in need of clothing, food or water.
Jesus waits for us to minister to him through these people.

✝ *Merciful Father, lead me to minister to your precious Son through
those who are in need.*

For group discussion and personal thought

- In what ways do you minister to Jesus through blessing
  other people?
- How can you and your church 'go out' and 'bring in the
  poor, the crippled, the blind and the lame'?
- Spend some time this week praying (by name if possible) for
  those who are sick or in prison.

GOD'S NEW WORLD 1
Gospel stories today 3

Notes by Ngozi Okeke

*based on the New American Standard Bible
and the New King James Version*

Ngozi Okeke comes originally from Nigeria but now lives in England. Theologically trained, she has been actively involved in Christian work for thirty years. Ngozi now works in the voluntary sector, finding ways to tackle social exclusion among the most disadvantaged groups in our society. She is married to Ken, an Anglican clergyman, and has four children.

People criticize Christianity because it seems to promise much but delivers little. The injustices in the world and the ineffective life and witness of the Church together convince them that God is either impotent or uncaring. However, this week we meet people who thought differently because God touched their lives. The kingdoms of this world are not yet subject to the rule and authority of God, but changed lives are both evidence that God's new world is on the move and also a pledge that the whole earth will be filled with the knowledge of the glory of God as the waters cover the sea (*Habakkuk 2.14*).

Text for the week: John 4.23 – 24

Sunday January 14   **John 1.29 – 42**

COME AND SEE!   We once had a friend who always had the information about everything or knew how to get it. Andrew was like that. He graduated from John the Baptist's inner circle to become one of Jesus' special friends. He was one of two disciples whom the Greeks approached when they wanted to see Jesus (*John 12.20 – 23*) and he discovered the boy who offered his lunch to feed five thousand people (*John 6.8 – 9*). Not surprisingly, he was on the spot when John pointed out Jesus as the Lamb of God. Characteristically, he and his friend went to check it out.

> **Jesus turned and ... said to them, 'What do you seek?' And they said to Him, 'Rabbi ... where are You staying?' He said to them, 'Come and you will see.'   (verses 38 – 39a, NASB)**

Andrew's spiritual curiosity helped him discover the truth, then he went and told his brother. We can learn two lessons from Andrew. First, we should desire to know spiritual truth and share it. Secondly, you never know who you will point in the right direction. Andrew's older brother, Peter, who often spoke and acted rashly, does not immediately strike us as a great evangelist in the making. Yet

his first two sermons converted 8000 people (Acts 2 and 4)! The idea that we might be helping to groom the next Billy Graham should encourage us to lose our inhibitions and speak out for Christ. When did you last say to someone – acquaintance, friend or family member – 'Come and see'?

† *Dear Lord, help us to feel at ease sharing our faith with others.*

Monday January 15 — John 2.1 – 11

WEDDINGS!

> **There was a wedding in Cana of Galilee ... And when the wine gave out, the mother of Jesus said to Him, 'They have no wine.'** (verses 1 and 3, NASB)

I attended a wedding a few years ago where the food contractor kept the guests waiting for over four hours, causing many to leave without refreshments! It was a huge embarrassment for the family. The abiding memory of that wedding is not the beautiful bride or the lovely service, but the failure of the catering arrangements. This was why Jesus' mother was so concerned for the young couple and approached Jesus. This is one of many occasions when Jesus transformed the ordinariness of life with his presence. When we struggle with everyday situations, we often forget that he is interested in *all* areas of our lives. We treat him as God of the gaps, only asking for his help when we have exhausted all other possibilities. However, he is interested in every detail of our lives, however small or unimportant. He loves to share with us, but we have to ask him.

† *Dear Lord, help us to realize how much you care about us and want to share in our lives.*

Tuesday January 16 — John 8.1 – 11

SECOND CHANCE As a child growing up under very strict discipline, 'wait till mother comes home' spelt trouble because I knew I had broken the rules. What an incredible relief to find mother in 'a good mood'. You don't get what you deserve! The woman in our story must have felt the same when she heard Jesus say:

> 'Woman, where are they? Did no one condemn you? ... Neither do I condemn you; go your way. From now on sin no more.' (part of verses 10 – 11, NASB)

She knew with the utmost relief that she would not get what she deserved. Jesus' love contrasts sharply with the bigotry of the religious leaders. Because he had said that he did not come to judge the world but to save it, he did not condemn the woman; neither did he condone her sin. Instead, he offered her a chance to start afresh. Though he loves us as we are, he wants to change us so that we can begin to experience his new life. The cross stands for ever as a reminder of God's offer of a second chance. Like other gifts, it has to be received. Have you received it?

✝ *Dear Lord, thank you for your offer of a second chance through the death of Christ on the cross.*

Wednesday January 17 John 17.20 – 26

UNITY IN DIVERSITY Every society makes laws to regulate people's attitudes and behaviours. The goal is to create harmony and foster 'unity in diversity'. However, 2000 years ago, Jesus instituted a much better code, based not on law but on love. Hours before he died on the cross, he prayed with concern and urgency for his present and future disciples. Among other things, he asked his Father:

> 'That they all may be one, as You, Father, are in Me, and I in You; that they also may be one in Us ... I in them, and You in Me; that they may be made perfect in one, and that the world may know that You have sent Me ... that the love with which You loved Me may be in them.'
> (verses 21, 23 and 26, NKJV)

Christian unity should be based on love – God's love for us in Christ and our love for one another because of it. The fact that Jesus prayed for this unity should have made it possible. However, the Church remains fragmented, sectarian, selfish and apathetic. Unless and until we allow the Spirit of God to light the fire of love in our hearts, transform and reign in our lives, we will never learn to love as Jesus loved us, nor will we ever be truly one as he intended.

21

✝ *Lord, forgive our lack of unity and help us to co-operate with the Holy Spirit so that we may fulfil your will for us and be truly one.*

Thursday January 18   **John 4.5 – 18**

BREAKING DOWN BARRIERS   In Jesus' day, it was improper for a Jewish rabbi to speak to a woman in public. The situation here was further complicated by the fact that this woman, a foreigner, also had a questionable character; five husbands already and now living with a man to whom she was not married. Yet Jesus loved and valued her enough to break down all the barriers in order to bring her into his kingdom. He spoke to her, a fact which the woman recognized:

> **'How is it that You, being a Jew, ask me for a drink since I am a Samaritan woman?' (For Jews have no dealings with Samaritans.)**   **(verse 9, NASB)**

Our society is fragmented by prejudice and discrimination; unfortunately, so is the Church. We care more for our reputation than for the needy people around us. However, if we learn to love as Jesus loved, unconditionally, we will reach out as he did, in a way that breaks down all barriers of race and culture as well as economic and social standing. This should be our only legitimate response if we truly believe that he died to break the barriers that separate us.

✝ *Father, teach us to love unconditionally, just as you have loved us, so that we can reach out to the excluded in our communities.*

Friday January 19   **John 4.19 – 29**

TRUTH IN STRANGE PLACES   Years ago I worked with a boy who had perfected the use of red herrings in conversation. He always changed direction when he felt that the discussion was becoming uncomfortably personal. This made it very difficult to focus on his real needs. The Samaritan woman was doing much the same to Jesus. She responded to every personal challenge with a shift to a general subject. However, Jesus pressed his point:

> **'God is spirit and those who worship Him must worship in spirit and truth.'**   **(verse 24, NASB)**

The real issue is not *where* we worship but *who* and *how* we worship. This is the bottom line for each of us: to recognize

Jesus as Lord of our lives and worship him in sincerity and truth. We also learn from this story that we can encounter 'truth' in the strangest places. In spite of her chequered life, this woman knew that God was sending a Saviour. It is not theology or our knowledge of Scripture that saves us, but the realization that God has sent a Saviour for us, and that he has all the answers we need to live successfully.

† *Thank you, Lord, that you value each of us in spite of our failures. Help us to respond to your love by giving our lives to you.*

Saturday January 20 — Luke 5.31 – 39

CHANGE? WHAT CHANGE?! Most pastors, whatever their denomination, share one frustration: getting their members to embrace wholeheartedly the change that moves them from the familiar into the 'unknown' areas of the Spirit's work. The Pharisees of Jesus' day had the same problems, so Jesus said to them:

> **'No one puts new wine into old wineskins; otherwise the new wine will burst the skins, and it will be spilled out ... new wine must be put into fresh wineskins. And no one, after drinking old wine, wishes for new; for he says, "The old is good enough."'** (verses 37 – 39, NASB)

We love the taste of 'old wine' because it is tried and tested. New wine is too robust, too radical for our comfort. We are not against change or renewal – but not just yet. We are afraid of the unknown outside our comfort zone. We cherish our tried and tested ways of worship and faith almost as an end in themselves. However, the Holy Spirit has his own agenda and timing and only those prepared to change will benefit from his ministry, either as individuals or churches.

† *Lord, help us to be open to any change you may want to make in our lives and in our churches.*

For group discussion and personal thought

- When did you last share your faith with a member of your family or a friend?
- This week we read about the woman caught in adultery and the Samaritan woman with questionable morality. How easily do you cross the barrier of 'respectability' to reach out to those on the margins of society?

GOD'S NEW WORLD 1
Gospel stories today 4

Notes by Jember Teferra

based on the Good News Bible

Jember Teferra is an Ethiopian who has worked for eighteen years in the poorest slums of Addis Ababa. She feels called by the Lord to help alleviate urban poverty, and promotes a philosophy known as the integrated holistic approach.

In this week's Gospel stories, the gift of faith is the key issue, but the holistic ministry of our Lord also comes out vividly. Jesus automatically saw the need to combine physical healing with spiritual ministry. His compassion and love, which were demonstrated both to Jews and Gentiles, labelled him as a radical leader and created constant conflict with the pedantic Pharisees, who criticized him for healing or feeding his disciples on the Sabbath. His teaching was so profound that the narrow-minded and conceited Jewish leaders of his time found it difficult to understand him, even when he referred to the Old Testament which they quoted to discredit him. Even today, some Christians struggle to be 'righteous' without the gift of faith (given through the enabling power of the Holy Spirit) – but without it we cannot be Christlike.

Text for the week: Mark 1.21 – 28

Sunday January 21   Luke 6.1 – 11

LORD OF THE SABBATH: JESUS THE LIBERATOR   When I was a child I used to see things as black and white, just like the Pharisees. Commitment to follow Jesus meant being law-abiding – and I was judgemental if I saw any professing Christian not living 'by the book'. I look back to those days and see this narrow-minded attitude as being 'spiritually immature'. I am grateful to my mother, who repeatedly corrected my failure. However, the anger of the Pharisees was not childlike or naive – it was malicious. When they criticized Jesus for healing the man with the paralysed arm, he did not retaliate in a negative way; instead, he gave them the benefit of the doubt. He said:

'I ask you: What does our Law allow us to do on the Sabbath? To help or to harm? To save someone's life or destroy it?' (verse 9)

It is only through a spiritual maturity which is open to liberation by the Holy Spirit that we can understand the main point and objective of each sentence of the law. If we allow the law to constrain us, we shall continue to miss the point. May the Lord deliver us from being so pedantic and judgemental.

† *Heavenly Father, fill us with your liberating Spirit so that we can recognize the objectives of the law.*

Monday January 22 Luke 8.4 – 8

HOW TO LISTEN, LEARN, UNDERSTAND AND BE FRUITFUL Have you ever taught a class of students or given a talk to a group of people, and watched blank faces staring back at you? When I have experienced such an incident, I have often felt frustrated and disappointed – but, as a human being who can make mistakes, I have also checked whether I could change my approach in order to communicate better with the group. Our Lord seems to feel a similar frustration in the Parable of the Sower, because his values, his mission and his aspirations are never truly understood. His own disciples wanted him to be King of the Jews and get rid of the Roman army of occupation, so that they could have higher positions. Few people understood his higher, greater and more profound spiritual purposes for humankind. If we listen only to what we want to hear, we shall block our ears to what the Spirit wants us to learn. After the seed had been scattered on the path, among the rocks and into the bushes, what a relief when, at last,

'some seeds fell in good soil; the plants grew and produced corn, a hundred grains each.' (verse 8)

As we say today about our computers, sophisticated and clever as they are: you get out what you put in. The Holy Spirit can only make the word of God useful if we are open to hear, learn and be spiritually productive.

† *Help us, greatest of all teachers, to listen to your words and live a life which is fulfilling and worthwhile.*

Tuesday January 23 Mark 1.21 – 28

GOD'S AUTHORITY REPEATEDLY REVEALED This short reading records our Lord's holistic ministry. His authority is shown on several different occasions: when he taught in the synagogue, the audience recognized that he taught with authority. Then the devil who has possessed a man pleads to be left alone, but has to obey the supreme authority and Lordship of Jesus when he orders him to leave the man's body. All in turn recognize his authority:

> The people who heard him were amazed at the way he taught, for he wasn't like the teachers of the Law; instead, he taught with authority. (verse 22)

> 'What do you want with us, Jesus of Nazareth? Are you here to destroy us? I know who you are – you are God's holy messenger!' (verse 24)

> 'What is this? Is it some kind of new teaching? This man has authority to give orders to the evil spirits, and they obey him!' (verse 27)

Those of us privileged to know Jesus as our Lord and Saviour experience his supreme power and authority when we suffer. His holistic ministry to us often deals with our deeper spiritual needs as well as our practical needs. We experience victory. Jesus uses his authority in a positive way, not like the abuse of human authority.

† *O Lord, only you are worthy to possess supreme power and full authority, because you know best how to use it.*

Wednesday January 24   **Mark 2.13 – 17**

JESUS AND THE OUTCASTS   Here again we have conflict over keeping the law. History has many examples of what happens when religious people such as the Pharisees make others outcast in the name of law, or misinterpret the laws in Leviticus so that they ill-treat women during their monthly period or lepers and other sick people. During the Crusades and even today among fanatical Christian sects, atrocities were and still are committed in the name of Jesus. Throughout history, human beings have inflicted suffering and injustice through slavery, racism, class discrimination, fundamentalism and so on. But Jesus said, when he called the outcast tax collector Levi:

> 'People who are well do not need a doctor, but only those who are sick. I have not come to call respectable people, but outcasts.' (verse 17)

Jesus did not write a declaration or call a parliament to pass laws against injustice – he *showed* people what to do. He chose outcasts as his followers. He did not compromise or condone, but went out with open arms to reach, teach, heal and make them his followers. We, as Christians, must examine our actions and reactions. Are we going to set ourselves up as more righteous than Jesus by avoiding and excluding such outcasts? Or are we going to help them to be his followers?

† *Lord Jesus, your life is full of examples for us to follow. Help us to be daring enough, as your followers, to challenge the systems that deliberately reject victims and create outcasts.*

Thursday January 25   **Luke 5.1 – 11**

INADEQUACY REDEEMED BY FAITH   Some Christian experiences have no direct connection with any Bible passage, but we still identify with them. I find myself identifying with Simon, whom Jesus renamed Peter. He might see the great works of Jesus one day, but by the next day he had forgotten all about God's ability to do the impossible. He felt inadequate – and gave the devil an opportunity to shake his faith. When the Lord called me to begin my ministry in the poorest part of Addis Ababa, I saw myself as disadvantaged. I was an enemy of the military Marxist regime then in power and had been a political prisoner for five years. I did not feel confident that the government would agree to make my project a legal organization. My fear even caused problems with some of the donors who supported me. In the same way, when Jesus insisted that he should let down his net to catch some fish, Peter's obedience was half-hearted. What a surprise when they caught so many fish – so many that the net nearly broke! He could not believe this miracle, even though he had seen many in the past. He simply said:

    'Go away from me, Lord! I am a sinful man!'   **(verse 8)**

Then Jesus said to Peter:

    'Don't be afraid; from now on you will be catching people.'
                                                  (verse 10)

All of us have moments of feeling inadequate. I can look back on a ministry to 30 000 very poor members of that Addis Ababa community, for whom I raised about £5 million before our team left to start another ministry in different slums. We left the old area with 52 programmes, which the community now run for themselves. Exactly like Peter and the net which nearly broke.

† *When, like your disciples, we forget what you have done yesterday and feel inadequate today and in the future, don't go away from us, Lord, but stay with us and increase our faith.*

Friday January 26 Luke 7.1 – 10

FAITH BEYOND ALL EXPECTATIONS This Roman officer whom Luke describes so carefully is one of my role models. Looking back to yesterday's notes, here is someone who, to Jews, was an outcast Gentile and a pagan who worshipped the Roman emperor, but who has such faith in Jesus. During the last week of my five years of political imprisonment, some radical Marxists were released. This was a very difficult time for my family and I was having to make some very difficult decisions in order to relieve them of the burden of looking after me in prison. I had read a story about an outcast and his faith and his release from prison – a dramatic miracle which reminded me of Peter's rescue in Acts 12. Releases from my prison, like the 'epidemics of arrests' as we called them, happened from time to time; for the first time in five years I said to the Lord, 'You can still include me with that group of radical Marxists – it is not too late.' I told myself that if the Roman officer in Luke 7 could ask Jesus simply to say the word – don't even come to my house, just give an order and it will happen – then this other outcast, the American one, me, could have the same faith and also see an impossible thing happen. Well, it did happen ... I was released. What did Jesus say about this unique Roman officer's faith?

> **'I tell you, I have never found faith like this, not even in Israel!'** (verse 9b)

Why do we so often only have the total faith that can move mountains when we are desperate (as I was)? Whatever your circumstances, I tell you: try it – it works.

† *Faith is the gift God gives us through the enabling power of his Holy Spirit. Lord, please give us this gift.*

Saturday January 27 Luke 12.23 – 31

FAITH VERSUS MATERIAL VALUES Today, when the gospel of prosperity is spreading like wildfire, we need to pray for integrity and try to understand the true meaning of our Lord's teaching. Before these verses, he warns us that the value of our lives does not lie in what we own (*verse 21*). When Ethiopia experienced a Marxist revolution in 1974, my husband was arrested and our bank account was frozen. By 1976 our house, our car and my jewellery had been confiscated and we were forbidden to sell any of our belongings. We came from a privileged class and had lived quite comfortably; now, we had four children under eight years old, I was also in prison and we were completely penniless – you can imagine how difficult life was. It was a true test of faith, and it was not easy. Learning to separate ourselves from material possessions was only possible through God's gift of complete faith, and the lesson completely changed our values, for ever. Such lessons must be even harder for those who, taught by the prosperity gospel, believe that to be a follower of Jesus Christ means to be materially rich all the time! Jesus tells us not to worry, but to look around and observe nature and all the good things which he gives us so freely. What a great verse for those of us who know this to be true:

> **'Your Father knows that you need these things. Instead, be concerned with his Kingdom, and he will provide you with these things.'** (verses 30b – 31)

We should pray for those who believe that being a Christian is a short cut to being wealthy. God gives to those who will give to others – and the devil gives his followers many opportunities to make money in illegal ways.

† *Heavenly Father, you own the whole universe and you know our needs; you will provide as you know best. Give us faith to depend on you and to know what is most important in our lives.*

For group discussion and personal thought

- What does it mean to you, in terms of cost and value, to follow Jesus?
- Think about all your prejudices and those people whom you see as 'outcast'. Using the Bible for guidance, discuss how you should deal with those labelled as outcasts.
- Reflect on all your experience of lack of faith; how do people grow in faith? Use Peter as a case study.

GOD'S NEW WORLD 2

Psalms for today 1

Notes by Paul Duffett

based on the New Jerusalem Bible

Paul Duffett was ordained in 1959 and worked in the Diocese of Zululand for sixteen years. Returning to England, he was rector of two Hampshire villages and then spent almost eleven years as rector of Papworth and chaplain to a major organ transplant hospital. He retired in 1998 and now lives near Cambridge.

The Psalms are poetry, often passionate poetry. Many were intended to be sung and are therefore hymns as well. Some of the hymns in our hymn books are based on or inspired by psalms. The Psalms are also prayers and often deeply personal, bringing to God just about every emotion we can think of. That's why they are relevant for us today. They say what we feel about God, ourselves and others, as well as about nature and the universe.

Text for the week: Psalm 1.3

Sunday January 28   **Psalm 1**

NARROW IS THE GATE TO LIFE – BROAD THE ROAD TO DESTRUCTION The title of today's notes comes from Matthew's Gospel (*see Matthew 7.13 – 14*). Perhaps Jesus was meditating on this psalm when he said these words. He was also doing what the psalm suggests: 'murmuring [God's] law day and night' (*verse 2*), a sign of love and delight in it.

> **Such a one is like a tree planted near streams;**
> **it bears fruit in season**
> **and its leaves never wither,**
> **and every project succeeds.**   **(verse 3)**

We have had a very dry summer in England and the plum tree in my garden only just survived! Its leaves fell almost as soon as the fruit was ripe. Jesus refers to the Holy Spirit as life-giving water (*John 7.38 – 39*) and the trees in the perfected world portrayed in Revelation 22.2 bear fruit every month and have leaves for healing. When the harvest is ripe, then comes the harvesting and, even with today's sophisticated methods, there is plenty of dust. The wicked, says the psalmist, are:

> like chaff blown around by the wind ...
> [their] path ... is doomed.   (verses 4 and 6)

Totalitarian political regimes were a feature of the twentieth century – but where are they now? There may still be a lot of them around but how long will they last? Delighting in God is the secret of *true* success.

✝ *Help me, Lord, to want true success in your way and give me grace to find it.*

Monday January 29   Psalm 2

PLOT AND COUNTERPLOT   This psalm may have been written to celebrate King David's enthronement. It is patriotic and rather triumphalist!

> He who is enthroned in the heavens laughs,
> Yahweh makes a mockery of them [other nations],
> then in his anger rebukes them,
> in his rage he strikes them with terror.
> 'I myself have anointed my king
> on Zion my holy mountain.'   (verses 4 – 6)

Let's face it, this attitude has been a temptation to the Church throughout the ages. Yahweh/God is on *our* side! Indeed, it could have been part of Jesus' temptation in the desert (*Matthew* 4):

> [God] said to me, 'You are my son ...
> Ask of me, and I shall give you the nations as your
>   birthright,
> the whole wide world as your possession.
>   (verses 7b and 8)

To be a mighty king over the world, all-powerful, not powerless – what a temptation! Of course the way of sacrificial love *appears* weak but it is the strongest power in the world. The cross and resurrection lead to ascension. The wisdom of the ages tells history and kings:

> In fear be submissive to Yahweh ...
> How blessed are all who take refuge in him!
>   (verses 11 and 12b)

The uproar among nations struggling to be the best *is* impotent (*see verse 1*).

✝ *We come to you, King of all, with reverence and love.*

Tuesday January 30   **Psalm 6**

REAL PRAYER FOR REAL NEED There have been many
believers in God who have been imprisoned, persecuted by brutal
enemies. Think of the horrors of the Holocaust. The hostage in
Lebanon, Terry Waite, was just one of many in isolation for years.
How does it really feel to be in such terrible circumstances?

> Yahweh, my bones are shaken,
> my spirit is shaken to its very depths ...
> I am worn out with groaning,
> every night I drench my pillow
> and soak my bed with tears.   (verses 2b, 3 and 6)

The psalmist is honest with God, himself and us. 'How long
will this go on?' he cries. This prayer can be echoed by many
Christians, not only those who are persecuted but also those in
painful sickness, bereavement or depression and loss of faith.
Honesty is the best policy! And hopefully others too will be able
to say with the psalmist,

> Yahweh has heard the sound of my weeping,
> Yahweh has heard my pleading.
> Yahweh will accept my prayer.
> Let all my enemies be put to confusion.
>   **(verses 8b, 9 and 10a)**

✝ *Help me not to be afraid to identify my true feelings and tell you,
Lord, who understand everything.*

Wednesday January 31   **Psalm 29**

LORD OF THE STORM I am writing this on the day a
terrible cyclone is approaching the east coast of the USA and
not long after ravaging earthquakes in Turkey and Greece. The
power of nature is indeed awesome. If this is so, then what must
the Creator be like?

> Give Yahweh his due of glory and strength ...
> adore Yahweh in the splendour of holiness ...
> Yahweh's voice shatters cedars ...
> Yahweh's voice carves out lightning-shafts,
> Yahweh's voice convulses the desert ...
> strips forests bare.   (part of verses 1, 2, 5, 7, 8 and 9)

There is much we need to learn about the transcendence and omnipotence of God. God is not a cosy God and we need to stretch our faith and our worship to acknowledge that fact. Glorious, awesome, but merciful.

> **Yahweh will give strength to his people,**
> **Yahweh blesses his people with peace.** (verse 11)

The psalmist helps us to look God in the face from our knees!

† *Bless, Lord, all those caught up in natural disasters with the strength they need.*

Thursday February 1   Psalm 33

SING AND SHOUT I remember well a confirmation in the Diocese of Zululand. I was standing to the left of a visiting bishop who was perhaps not very familiar with Zulu singing and harmony. To the right of the bishop stood our evangelist, and my goodness! did he sing (or shout)! The bishop obviously thought he was shouting and his face was pained and indignant as he turned to look at the undaunted singer. Perhaps he was being deafened! However, we could do with a bit more shouting for God. There are thousands who shout about their football team or a gambling win – anything which really moves and thrills them.

> **Shout for joy, you upright;**
> **praise comes well from the honest.**
> **Give thanks to Yahweh on the lyre,**
> **play for him on the ten-stringed lyre.**
> **Sing to him a new song,**
> **make sweet music for your cry of victory.** (verses 1 – 3)

Worship in a large congregation with a big organ or band, or even without any accompaniment, is an uplifting experience. Singing your heart out for God is a way of showing thanks, praise, and love.

> **A large army will not keep a king safe ...**
> **But see how Yahweh watches over those who fear him,**
> **those who rely on his faithful love.** (verses 16a and 18)

Next time you sing, don't worry about your voice (tuneful or untuneful!) or who is listening. You are addressing God.

† *Give me grace, O Lord, to worship you with all my heart, mind, soul and strength.*

YOU ARE CHRIST'S AND CHRIST IS GOD'S   The New Jerusalem Bible has a curious introduction to this psalm. It says that David composed it when he had escaped death in battle by pretending to be mad (*see 1 Samuel 21.11 — 22.4*)! The psalm is also written like a song, with different people singing alternate verses, rather as we sing the psalms today in some churches. The verses balance each other: the meaning of one verse is repeated in a different way by the next. In that way it becomes a reflective meditation.

> **Fix your gaze on Yahweh and your face will grow bright,**
> **you will never hang your head in shame.**
> **A pauper calls out and Yahweh hears,**
> **saves him from all his troubles.**
> **The angel of Yahweh encamps**
> **around those who fear him, and rescues them.**
> **Taste and see that Yahweh is good.**
> **How blessed are those who take refuge in him.**
>
> **(verses 5 – 8)**

God is a God of unconditional love. We are called upon to boast only in him and his love. As St Paul tells us, 'Let us boast only in the Lord'. All we are and all we have which is really worthwhile is from him and by him, for, in the words of today's title, also from St Paul, we are Christ's, and Christ is God's.

✝ *Thank you, Lord, that you make my life so worth living as I serve you and others.*

THE BIG ROCK CANDY MOUNTAIN   This is the title of an old song which I came across the other day. It tells of a 'travelling' man:

> As he roamed along, he sang a song
> Of the land of milk and honey,
> Where a bum can stay for many a day
> And he won't need any money...

I can remember hearing it sung to a guitar by an American folk-singer. Of course, it is a dream of 'the buzzing of the bees in the cigarette trees, The soda water fountain' and it doesn't come true: 'they never arrived at the lemonade tide On the Big Rock Candy Mountain'. Psalm 36 gives us a different vision of the God who is our Rock and our strength:

Yahweh, your faithful love is in the heavens ...
your saving justice is like towering mountains ...
how precious, God, is your faithful love ...
in you is the source of life,
by your light we see the light.   (part of verses 5, 6, 7 and 9)

Many churches sing a hymn based on these verses. It includes these words:

Thy justice like mountains high soaring above,
Thy clouds which are fountains of goodness and love.

and ends:

O help us to see
'Tis only the splendour of light hideth thee.

Our 'source of life' is grace and strength for our daily living.

† *Glory to God, Source of all being, Eternal Word and Holy Spirit; as it was in the beginning, is now and shall be for ever.*

For group discussion and personal thought

● What picture do the psalms we have used this week give you of God?
● Have they helped you to express personal prayer and worship? If so, how?
● If you were asked to write a psalm yourself, what would you write?

GOD'S NEW WORLD 2
Psalms for today 2

Notes by John Grover

based on the Psalter of the Book of Common Prayer
of the Church of England

John Grover is a priest working in the Scottish Episcopal Church. Previously he was vicar of a parish in England for twenty years, and spent another seven years as warden of a retreat house.

This week's readings show how the writers of the Psalms faced similar situations to ours today. They write of joys and sorrows, faith and doubt, danger and happiness. We discover how their faith and trust in God sustained and encouraged them. The translation of the Psalms in the *Book of Common Prayer* is designed for use in worship; psalms, like today's hymns, use poetry to speak about trust in God.

Text for the week: Psalm 138.7

Sunday February 4 **Psalm 46**

OUR HOPE AND STRENGTH Psalms have been part of the worship of God for nearly 3,000 years. They have stood the test of time because they speak about intense personal feelings. Here the writer expresses confidence in God, faith and trust in particular times of danger.

> **God is our hope and strength; a very present help in trouble.**
> **Therefore will we not fear, though the earth be moved: and though the hills be carried into the midst of the sea ...**
> **The Lord of hosts is with us: the God of Jacob is our refuge.**
> **(verses 1, 2 and 11)**

Earthquake, flood, persecution, war: these disasters are part of human experience. The Psalmist lists them all and proclaims his faith that God is present to help in *all* times of trouble. Countless believers in God have said these words in times of distress and danger and still say them today. It is God who brings peace, hope, comfort and safety. Knowing that he is present and having faith in him can bring a trustful serenity to his people.

† *O God, make speed to save us: O Lord, make haste to help us.*

Monday February 5   Psalm 71.1 – 6

HELP! MAYDAY! SOS! It is often suggested that people turn to God for help only when they are in great difficulty. Then they remind him of their former faith and ask him to rescue them. There may be an element of this here.

> **In thee, O Lord, have I put my trust, let me never be put to confusion: but rid me and deliver me in thy righteousness, incline thine ear to me and save me ...**
> **For thou, O Lord God, art the thing that I long for: thou art my hope, even from my youth.**
> **Through thee have I been holden up ever since I was born: thou art he that took me out of my mother's womb; my praise shall be always of thee.**   **(verses 1, 4 and 5)**

It is said that the following verse was written on the wall of a cell in Changi jail in Singapore when the Japanese occupied it during World War 2: 'Only one life – 'twill soon be past. Only what's done for Christ will last.' Perhaps these were the last words written by a man about to die. In times of calamity and distress, many discover their need to place their hand in the hand of God. We need him every hour.

† *Lord, when we go out into the darkness, may we put our hand into your hand, and know that this is better than holding a light and safer than knowing the way.*

Tuesday February 6   Psalm 72

GOD OF ALL THE EARTH This is a prayer that an endless dynasty of perfect kings will reign in Jerusalem, and that the blessings of justice and peace, care for the poor and plentiful harvests will bring all nations to worship God. We hear this again in the words of Jesus: 'Thy kingdom come, thy will be done in earth as it is in heaven' (*Matthew 6.10*).

> **In his time shall the righteous flourish: yea, and abundance of peace, so long as the moon endureth.**
> **His dominion shall be also from the one sea to the other: and from the flood unto the world's end ...**
> **All kings shall fall down before him: all nations shall do him service.**   **(verses 7, 8 and 11)**

God's perfect kingdom is a kingdom of peace and love, where swords are made into ploughshares and spears into pruning hooks, where each man sits under his own vine or fig tree, with none to cause alarm (*Micah 4.1 – 4*). Jesus teaches us that this kingdom is here. It requires from us honesty, justice, care for others and forgiveness – and that we make our own his prayer that this kingdom may be established on earth and God's will be done.

✝ *May our Lord Jesus Christ reign in our hearts as king, now and for ever.*

Wednesday February 7 — Psalm 96

REVERENCE   This psalm was sung as the Ark of the Covenant was brought into Jerusalem by King David (*1 Chronicles 16.23 – 33*). We can picture the joyful procession, with the blowing of horns and trumpets, the clash of cymbals, the sound of lutes and lyres, the king making sacrifices and distributing bread, meat and cakes – a brilliant and exciting event.

> **Ascribe unto the Lord the honour due unto his name: bring presents and come into his courts.**
> **O worship the Lord in the beauty of holiness, let the whole earth stand in awe of him ...**
> **For he cometh, for he cometh to judge the world, and the people with his truth.** (verses 8, 9 and 13)

Sometimes our worship in church is exciting and lively, at other times it is quiet and contemplative. It always, however, needs to be reverent, allowing us to think and listen. The fourteenth-century English writer Julian of Norwich, who lived a life of prayer, wrote that being 'at home' with the Lord did not mean 'being casual and forgetting our manners' – the difference between the two attitudes is one of reverence. Even the most informal service should maintain dignity and an awareness of God's presence.

✝ *Teach us to see your hand in all your works, and to serve you with reverence and thanksgiving.*

Thursday February 8 — Psalm 135

COUNT YOUR BLESSINGS   This psalm was addressed to those who served in the Temple in Jerusalem. It lists some of God's mighty saving acts which affect all his people.

> **O praise the Lord, laud ye the name of the Lord: praise it, O ye servants of the Lord;**

Ye that stand in the house of the Lord: in the courts of the house of our God.

O praise the Lord, for the Lord is gracious: O sing praises unto his name, for it is lovely. (verses 1 – 3)

In the Bible we read of God's saving acts throughout the history of his chosen people. This psalm lists creation, the Passover and the conquest of Canaan. We could add Noah's ark, the rescue of Isaac, Moses and the children of Israel at the Red Sea, the return of the exiles from Babylon ... and then the coming of the Messiah, the final, complete act of salvation through the death and resurrection of Christ. For all these blessings we praise and thank God continually.

† *We bless you for our creation, preservation, and all the blessings of this life; but above all for your immeasurable love in the redemption of the world by our Lord Jesus Christ.*

Friday February 9 **Psalm 138**

COURAGE AND CONFIDENCE This psalm could have been sung by the young Jewish men in the book of Daniel as they proclaimed their faith in God and defied those who believed in foreign gods (*Daniel 3*).

For though the Lord be high, yet hath he respect unto the lowly: as for the proud, he beholdeth them afar off.

Though I walk in the midst of trouble, yet shalt thou refresh me: thou shalt stretch forth thy hand upon the furiousness of mine enemies, and thy right hand shall save me. (verses 6 – 7)

Here we find confidence that our God will triumph over everything. In the words of Julian of Norwich (see notes for Wednesday), 'all shall be well, and all shall be well, and all manner of thing shall be well'. Christians have every reason to be optimistic, because we believe that the resurrection of Jesus has achieved a total victory over sin and death. This is our assurance in times of danger, in pain, or at the approach of death.

† *Risen Lord Jesus, thank you for the courage and confidence that your victory gives us.*

Saturday February 10 **Psalm 147.12 – 20**

A CHOSEN PEOPLE God does more than give us confidence and maintain our morale. His work is revealed in the world around us. I often tell the story of two people looking out of a window: one says, 'What a glorious view!'; the other says, 'This window is dirty!' It is so easy to complain about trivial things instead of glorying in the wonder of creation!

> **He maketh peace in thy borders: and filleth thee with the flour of wheat ...**
> **He giveth snow like wool: and scattereth the hoar frost like ashes ...**
> **He hath not dealt so with any [every] nation: neither have the heathen knowledge of his laws.   (verses 14, 16 and 20)**

The Old Testament often tells us of the power and wonder of God in creation. This psalm reminds us of the story of the creation in Genesis, or chapter 38 of the book of Job. God shows his care for his people by the gifts he gives through his created world. Gifts such as beauty, which we can so easily spoil; the new life of a child, which God calls us to protect and nurture; the harvest, which God commands us to share with the hungry. These gifts which God gives to us, his chosen people, bring with them responsibilities towards our brothers and sisters in God's new world.

✝ *Merciful God, you have prepared such good things for those who love you that they are beyond human understanding. Pour into our hearts such love for you that we may obtain what you have promised us.*

For group discussion and personal thought

● How can I use the Psalms in my own worship of God?
● In my relationship with God and with his creation, do I see the beautiful view – or the dirty window?

DARE TO BE DIFFERENT 1
Live simply

Notes by Kate Hughes

based on the New Revised Standard Version

In the past, Kate Hughes has been an Anglican nun for 20 years and then spent 14 years working with the Church in Southern Africa. Today, she works from her home in an Urban Priority Area council estate, editing books and writing and editing distance learning courses in theology. Currently she edits *Light for our Path* and the *Preachers' Handbook* for IBRA.

The poverty which is spoken about in this week's readings is not necessarily material poverty – lack of the necessities of life such as adequate food and clothing. It is more the lack of possessiveness – not clinging to things or using them as a barrier against God. Putting God at the centre of our life is not easy, and these readings suggest some of the dangers we need to watch out for.

Text for the week: Luke 12.34

Sunday February 11   Luke 6.17 – 21

HANDS EMPTY TO RECEIVE I watched some children playing. They were fighting over who should have which toy and one of the boys grabbed two cars and held them tightly in his hands to make sure no one else got them. Then I offered each of them a sweet. The boy with the cars could not take a sweet because both his hands were full. He could only accept the sweet I offered if he put down one of the cars so that his hand was empty to receive what I gave him.

> 'Blessed are you who are poor,
>   for yours is the kingdom of God.   **(verse 20b)**

Like the boy with the toy cars, we are often so busy making sure we get what we think is our rightful share of the good things of life that we have no time for God, no space in our lives to notice that he is offering us a share in his kingdom. There is nothing wrong in accepting good things; the things that we need and enjoy are gifts from God. But we should not clutch them so hard that we have no room left for more important things. It is those who know that they need God and leave a space for him in their lives who are the poor who will receive his kingdom.

✝ *O God, help me to leave space in my life for you.*

Monday February 12   Luke 6.22 – 26

PUTTING THINGS IN THE RIGHT PLACE   Material possessions are not wrong in themselves; it is not money which is evil, but the *love* of money (*1 Timothy 6.10*), allowing money to become too important in our lives, so that there is no space left for God. If we focus too much on what we possess, thinking how rich we are, listing in our minds the things that we have – the good education, the good job, the car, the TV, the annual holiday abroad, the fine house, the fashionable clothes – that is all we shall ever have. That will be our consolation in this life. But in the next life there will be – nothing. We shall not be able to take all these things with us, and unless we have made time and space for God in this life, we shall be left with nothing for eternity.

> **But woe to you who are rich,**
> **for you have received your consolation.**   **(verse 24)**

✝ *O God, thank you for all the material gifts you give us; help us to keep them in their right place, so that there is plenty of space left in our lives for you.*

Tuesday February 13   Luke 12.32 – 34

REAL TREASURES   For the first time in my life, I have a burglar alarm in my house. Part of me feels that I should trust God, rather than a burglar alarm, to look after my house; but another part of me does not want to make it easy for a thief to break in and steal in order to buy drugs. However, a burglar could not steal the things which make my house precious – the presence of God who found the house for me six years ago; the love of the friends who have visited me here; the joy I get from my garden.

> **Make purses for yourselves that do not wear out, an**
> **unfailing treasure in heaven, where no thief comes near**
> **and no moth destroys. For where your treasure is, there**
> **your heart will be also.**   **(verses 33 – 34)**

When I turn the corner at the top of the street and see that the light on the alarm box on the front of my house is still red and not flashing blue, I always thank God for looking after my home while I have been away. This very ordinary house is not special because it contains expensive things, but because it is a symbol of God's loving care for me. And no burglar can steal that.

✝ *Thank you, Lord, that no one can take our real treasure away from us – your love and care.*

Wednesday February 14   **Matthew 11.25 – 30**

HANDING OVER OUR BURDENS   It is not only material possessions which can become so important in our lives that they leave no space for God. We can also become so tired, worried, anxious and frightened that we have no time or energy left for God. Many of our burdens are so heavy that we cannot carry them on our own or sort out the problems ourselves. We need the honesty and humility to admit that they are too much for us.

> **Come to me, all you that are weary and are carrying heavy burdens, and I will give you rest.**   **(verse 28)**

If we are willing to hand our burdens over to God, he will carry them for us. If we are willing to listen to him, he will tell us what to do. If we are willing to rest in him, we shall have the energy to tackle the difficulties in our lives as he leads us gently through them.

✝ *Lord, help me to hand my burdens over to you and not try to take them back, because I need the rest that only you can give.*

Thursday February 15   **Jeremiah 17.5 – 10**

STRONG ROOTS   A few years ago, I planted a tree in my garden. While it was small, I had to support it with a wooden post, so that the strong winter winds would not pull it out of the ground, and make sure it had plenty of water. This year I was able to remove the post because the tree had developed such a strong and deep root system that it could support itself without help. It will sway and bend in the wind, but its roots are deep enough to hold it firmly in the ground.

> **Blessed are those who trust in the LORD,**
>   **whose trust is the LORD.**
> **They shall be like a tree planted by water,**
>   **sending out its roots by the stream.**   **(verses 7 – 8)**

Learning to trust in God is like the tree developing strong roots. He helps and supports us while we are learning to trust him; and as we trust him to lead us, guide us and help us, we become firmly rooted in the soil of his love. Once our roots are deep, we shall be able to stand up to the strong winds of life without being uprooted.

✝ *O Lord, help me to put down strong and deep roots of trust in you.*

Friday February 16   **Ephesians 5.1 – 20**

GREED AND IDOLATRY An idolater is someone who worships idols. We usually think of an idol as a statue or object made of wood or stone, or something natural like a mountain or a tree. But an idol is anything to which we give power – the power which rightfully belongs to God. God, as our creator, has the right to ask us for time, attention, co-operation, love. If we give too much of any of these things to someone or something else, there is a danger that that person or thing will become an idol. The writer of the letter to the Ephesians makes an interesting point about idolatry:

One who is greedy (that is, an idolater).   **(verse 5)**

Greed is taking more than we need. We are greedy if we continue to eat after we feel full. We are greedy if we have two cars to impress the neighbours when we really only need one car to take the children to school or travel to work. We are greedy when, instead of enjoying sport as a healthy pleasure, we allow it to fill our lives so that playing for our team or going to every football match becomes more important than God. Greed is linked to not trusting God to provide for us; not believing that his love is enough for us; not giving him his rightful place at the centre of our lives.

✝ *Forgive me, Lord, when I misuse your gifts, so that greed turns them into idols which draw me away from you.*

Saturday February 17   **Philippians 4.10 – 20**

STRENGTHENED AND SATISFIED BY GOD God has been at the centre of all our readings this week. If he is at the centre of our lives, we have no need to worry or be anxious; we shall get our priorities right, and not be greedy for other things and experiences. If our roots go deep into God's love, it will not matter so much what happens above the ground.

In any and all circumstances I have learned the secret of being well-fed and of going hungry, of having plenty and of being in need. I can do all things through him who strengthens me. (verses 12 – 13)

Putting God at the centre of our life requires work from us. There are some things we shall have to give up and do without. Other things will need to be kept firmly in their rightful place. We have to give time and effort to getting to know God and listening to him, so that we can live up to his expectations for us. But in all this, God is there beside us, strengthening us so that through him we can do everything he has planned for us.

And my God will fully satisfy every need of yours according to his riches in glory in Christ Jesus. (verse 19)

✝ *O God, you ask me to put you at the centre of my life, and I do not find this easy. Thank you that at the same time you give me the strength to do it.*

For group discussion and personal thought

● What are your real treasures?
● What burden do you need to hand over to God?
● How can you help your roots to grow deep and strong?
● What is the thing in your life which makes you greedy? How can you stop it becoming an idol?

DARE TO BE DIFFERENT 2

Be peacemakers

Notes by Philip Wadham

based on the New Revised Standard Version

The Revd Philip Wadham is employed by the Anglican Church of Canada as a Mission Co-ordinator on the Partners in Mission programme. He has worked with Indian communities in Ecuador, with the USPG in England and in an Anglican/United Church parish in western Canada. He continues to travel regularly in Latin America and the Caribbean.

The Hebrew word for 'peace' is '*shalom*'. In John's Gospel Jesus says of his mission, 'I came that they may have life and have it abundantly' (*John 10.10*). This is what *shalom* is: abundant life. Peacemakers are those who work to make *shalom* real for people, or at least as real as possible, given the brokenness of this world. Stories this week feature Pedro and Marga, an Indian couple who live in a town in eastern Ecuador. He is a priest serving both the local Anglican church and some communities further down the river. Neither he nor Marga is a saint, at least in the way the word is popularly used. Pedro occasionally drinks too much and Marga doesn't always love her neighbour. But they do, in their own way and to the best of their ability, work for *shalom*/peace.

Text for the week: Luke 6.45

Sunday February 18   Luke 6.27 – 31

GOOD FOR BAD   Of course Pedro had his identity papers with him. He knew how unwise it was during this present time of civil unrest to travel without them. But the army sergeant, noting his dark skin and Indian features, was suspicious of him and told him to leave the bus to answer some further questions. Although the sergeant was satisfied that Pedro was no threat, he nevertheless set him the task of cleaning around the check point, a punishment for being Indian.

> [Jesus said] 'But I say to you ... Love your enemies, do good to those who hate you, bless those who curse you, pray for those who abuse you ... Do to others as you would have them do to you.'   **(verses 27, 28 and 31)**

Pedro would be hours late getting home, perhaps delayed overnight; Marga and the children would worry. The sergeant's suspicion and hatred were punishing them also. His task finished, Pedro was free to continue his journey. While he waited for a bus, he decided to continue his cleaning, going beyond his 'punishment'. Though the sergeant showed no appreciation, this was an inner cleansing for Pedro. Hatred can be contagious but he had refused to let this particular act of ill-will infect him.

† *Loving God, who through your Son taught us to care for all people, work in us to love even those who hate us.*

Monday February 19   **Luke 6.32 – 36**

GIVING AND RECEIVING Pedro and Marga had three children, two girls aged six and eleven and a boy of eight. Though school was free, books and uniforms were not – another expense from Pedro's small monthly wage. So when a neighbour, Rosa, a single mother, asked him for a loan so that her daughter Sandra could attend school he did not know how to respond.

> [Jesus said] 'If you lend to those from whom you hope to receive, what credit is that to you? Even sinners lend to sinners, to receive as much again. But ... lend, expecting nothing in return ... and you will be children of the Most High.'   **(verses 34 – 35)**

Pedro said he needed to think about it. That evening he talked with Marga. 'She'll never be able to pay us back from the small, uncertain wages she earns. There will simply be more requests, if not from her then from others.' Marga agreed. She also knew that school was important, not just because it gave greater hope for the future but for Sandra's dignity and self-esteem now. 'If other requests do follow, we'll have to say, "No". But if we cut back on some things we could help Rosa.' Though, to be honest, Marga was not certain where they could 'cut back'.

† *Generous God, you have said that it is more blessed to give than to receive. May we believe this and act on it.*

Tuesday February 20   **Luke 6.37 – 42**

JUDGING OTHERS In the 'Ecuatel' office the clerk told Pedro that his call was in booth No. 2. He picked up the phone and heard the bishop's voice from his office in Quito. They exchanged greetings and then got to the point of the conversation. 'It's been reported to me, Pedro, that you drank too much two weekends ago. Is that true?' Pedro recoiled and then remembered the celebration that he and Marga had attended, the fourteenth birthday of a niece which marked her entry into adulthood in a poor family where others had died in childhood. 'Yes,' he confessed, he had.

> **[Jesus said] 'Why do you see the speck in your neighbour's eye, but do not notice the log in your own eye? Or how can you say to your neighbour, "Friend, let me take out the speck in your eye," when you yourself do not see the log in your own eye?'** (verses 41 – 42a)

The bishop warned that such behaviour was unacceptable from a church leader and that he would 'be watching the situation'. That evening Pedro and Marga wondered who had told the bishop. There were a number of possibilities, some of them people whose lives were much worse, but this was not the place for counter-accusations and judgements. Marga spoke for both of them. 'Jesus told us not to judge but to love our neighbour. But it isn't easy, is it Pedro?'

† *Patient God, we are quick to make judgements on others but slow to see our own failings. Forgive us.*

Wednesday February 21   Luke 6.43 – 45

LIVING THE GOOD NEWS One week each month was reserved for the river trip, five days away from home visiting mission stations. In one community, there was a wedding. In another, sad news of the death of one of the elders. In the village furthest down river good progress had been made on a new church. Pedro had learned to expect the unexpected and this trip was no exception. At Bella Vista two people from another village urged Pedro's group to visit them.

> **[Jesus said] 'The good person out of the good treasure of the heart produces good, and the evil person out of evil treasure produces evil; for it is out of the abundance of the heart that the mouth speaks.'** (verse 45)

This village was about the same size as Bella Vista and it seemed as if the whole community wanted to meet Pedro. Speaking for all of them, one person said, 'We've seen what the Church is doing. You haven't just come to preach but you've helped build a school. Our children need to learn also and we'd like the Church to come here and help build us a school.' Pedro explained that he couldn't give an answer straight away. He would need to consult, prepare a budget, see what was possible. But he would definitely be in touch soon.

† *Determined God, whose will for all people is dignity and hope, may our actions always be consistent with our words of love.*

Thursday February 22   Luke 6.46 – 49

TESTING TIMES   When Pedro was out of town the people of Paushiyacu frequently consulted with Marga on urgent matters, both pastoral and spiritual. This showed the confidence they had in her and she was grateful for this trust. She listened carefully and with respect to their concerns, responding as she thought right. Some stories she heard severely tested her faith: poverty and misfortune, 'Christian' employers who swindled their workers, husbands unfaithful to their wives.

> **[Jesus said] 'I will show you what someone is like who comes to me, hears my words, and acts on them. That one is like a man building a house, who dug deeply and laid the foundation on rock; when a flood arose, the river burst against that house but could not shake it, because it had been well built.'**   **(verses 47 – 48)**

At such times Marga thought of the One she followed and assumed that Jesus too was tested: by religious people who were malicious towards him (*Luke 11.53 – 54*), a close friend who betrayed him (*Luke 22.3 – 6*), a frightened disciple who denied he knew Jesus (*Luke 22.54 – 60*). Yet through all this he remained faithful. Jesus' faithfulness was a strength to Marga.

† *Strong God, when we face circumstances that shake us, remind us that we are built on Christ, an immovable rock.*

Friday February 23   Luke 12.57 – 59

CONFLICT AND RESOLUTION?   There was tension down river. The small Indian community of Babaco, established many years ago and following a life of farming and hunting, was afraid of the new community nearby. The people in Colonia Cuenca had lived as tenant farmers in the south of Ecuador until their land was repossessed by the owner. Establishing

Colonia was their hope for the future. Unfortunately, many people in Babaco saw Colonia as the first of many new non-Indian communities that would threaten their way of life. Though both communities were mission stations of the Church, disputes arose between them, tempers flared and bad feelings grew.

> [Jesus said] 'And why do you not judge for yourselves what is right? Thus, when you go with your accuser before a magistrate, on the way make an effort to settle the case.'
> (verses 57 – 58a)

Pedro called the leaders of both communities together. He listened as they talked about their fears and he added his own thoughts. These included respect for traditional ways of life, the importance of welcoming the stranger, and that, despite racial differences, they were still all children of one God, brothers and sisters in Christ. They agreed that they needed to keep talking together. Pedro hoped they would, because they still needed to share a great deal.

✝ *God of reconciliation, give us eyes to see not just our own point of view but that of others and to see all people though the eyes of your love.*

Saturday February 24   Matthew 10.34 – 39

SPEAKING TRUTH IN LOVE 'The trouble with being a Christian', said Marga, 'is that people don't always like what you say.' It was supper time and she was talking with Pedro about their visitor that afternoon. He was a member of the town council and unhappy that the Church opposed a new housing development in Paushiyacu. At a meeting earlier in the week the people had protested that families would be displaced to make room for homes that none of them could afford to buy. 'It's not right. This land was given to us and now they want to take some back to make money.' Pedro, with others from the community, had said this to the council. The angry visitor that afternoon accused Pedro of making trouble.

> [Jesus said] 'Do not think that I have come to bring peace to the earth; I have not come to bring peace, but a sword ... Whoever does not take up the cross and follow me is not worthy of me.'
> (verses 34 and 38)

'The trouble is that they want the Church to keep quiet, but when something is wrong we can't remain silent. To do so would be to deny the One we follow.' For Pedro, Marga and numerous other poor Christians in our world, working for *shalom*/peace (see the introduction to this week) is a heavy cross to bear. As brothers and sisters in Christ we are called to share some of its weight.

† *Demanding God, make us outspoken on behalf of your truth and justice, yet gentle towards those with whom we disagree (Matthew 10.16).*

For group discussion and personal thought

● Pedro and Marga would not think of themselves as saints. Are they right?
● What does it mean to 'love your neighbour as yourself'?
● What would '*shalom*/peace' be for you and for the community in which you live?

DARE TO BE DIFFERENT 3
Let God be seen in you

Notes by Helen Van Koevering

based on the New Revised Standard Version

Helen Van Koevering was involved in mission work in Southern Africa from 1986 to 1997, and out of that experience wrote her Master's dissertation in 1999 on the women of Northern Mozambique. She now lives in an Urban Priority Area in South Wales and works with women in an ecumenical parish. She is married with three children.

God is at work in our lives as Christians. This he does for love of his Son, his people and his creation. By turning to God, seeing the example of Jesus and knowing the Holy Spirit's activity and life within us, we are able to understand something of the mystery and glory of the Father, Son and Spirit. The passages this week point to the ways in which God's life is seen in us, transforming and involving us in his mission to the world.

Text for the week: 2 Corinthians 3.18

Sunday February 25   **Exodus 34.29 – 35**

RADIANCE   Faces reveal the life going on inside. Today's passage is about the radiant face of Moses, the man and lawgiver who spoke directly with God. The Israelites saw this radiant face as evidence that Moses had seen and spoken to God.

> **Whenever Moses went in before the LORD to speak with him, he would take the veil off, until he came out; and when he came out, and told the Israelites what he had been commanded, the Israelites would see the face of Moses, that the skin of his face was shining; and Moses would put the veil on his face again, until he went in to speak with him.**
> **(verses 34 – 35)**

Moses' face radiated the openness and boldness of his relationship with God, but he veiled his face in awareness of the sin and humanity which separated the Israelites from God. Yet it is in the unveiled face of Moses that we catch a glimpse of what God intends for humanity. Our relationship with God will be seen in the life that we radiate to others.

✝ *Lord, may I be so aware of your presence today that your life will shine through me to touch others.*

Monday February 26   **2 Corinthians 3.12 – 4.2**

FREEDOM   The history of the world is full of stories of struggles for freedom. Nations and tribes have fought foreign threats, refugees have fled danger in their homelands, husbands and wives have left their marriages and families, teenagers have left home – all for freedom. Yet violence, insecurity and estrangement continue and increase. Real, life-changing freedom for humanity, the Bible says, is to be found in recognizing our sin and separation from God and in seeing the glory of the Lord in the life of Jesus, his Son.

> **When one turns to the Lord, the veil is removed. Now the Lord is the Spirit, and where the Spirit of the Lord is, there is freedom. And all of us, with unveiled faces, seeing the glory of the Lord as though reflected in a mirror, are being transformed into the same image from one degree of glory to another; for this comes from the Lord, the Spirit.**
>
> **(verses 16 – 18)**

Moses' boldness with God is now available to us all. Turning to the Lord and the indwelling Holy Spirit frees us to know, and be known by, God, ourselves and others. God cannot change our histories, but the Holy Spirit can change us from the inside out by opening up new possibilities of survival, resistance and transformation.

✝ *Thank you, Lord, for the freedom I have by knowing you, and for all that you are doing in my life. Help me to be more and more open to your Spirit so that I can become more and more like Jesus, and that you may be seen in me.*

Tuesday February 27   **Luke 9.28 – 36**

UNDERSTANDING

> **Peter said to Jesus, 'Master, it is good for us to be here; let us make three dwellings, one for you, one for Moses, and one for Elijah' – not knowing what he said. While he was saying this, a cloud came and overshadowed them; and they were terrified as they entered the cloud. Then from the cloud came a voice that said, 'This is my Son, my Chosen; listen to him!'**
>
> **(verses 33 – 35)**

Peter's understanding was obviously far from complete, though we cannot fault his enthusiasm! In recognizing the glory of what he saw, he wanted to contain the experience in buildings. In the shadow of the cloud, God spoke to these men. From then on they knew that Jesus was God's Son, and that he had the anointing and authority of his Father. Full understanding of God's purpose and mission had to wait until Jesus had completed his work of the cross. Our understanding of God will increase as we take time to listen to Jesus in prayer, in study of the Bible and in fellowship with other Christians. Being open to hear the wisdom of God is the first step to living out the wisdom and understanding of God that others will see in our lives.

† *Teach me, Lord, to listen for your word of wisdom for my life and for those around me.*

Ash Wednesday February 28   Isaiah 58.1 – 12

PARTICIPATION   How we live out our religion, spend our energies and respond to needs around us is vital. It will show whether we have listened to Jesus and begun to understand the glory and power of God. Today's passage spells out how God expects us to share his activity in the world. As we share in meeting the needs of others, God can include them in his loving embrace and they can know the light, healing and glory of God.

> **Is not this the fast that I choose:**
> **to loose the bonds of injustice,**
> **to undo the thongs of the yoke,**
> **to let the oppressed go free,**
> **and to break every yoke?...**
> **Then your light shall break forth like the dawn,**
> **and your healing shall spring up quickly;**
> **your vindicator shall go before you,**
> **the glory of the LORD shall be your rear guard ...**
> **your light shall rise in the darkness**
> **and your gloom be like the noonday.**
>
> **(verses 6, 8 and 10b)**

Preaching and doing the word of God go hand in hand with the mission of the Church, particularly in poorer areas of the world. The practical involvement of skilled Christians in health, education and development, working alongside evangelists, teachers and preachers, demonstrates God's concern for the wholeness of human life. In this way, Christians can show that

God truly shares in the real concerns of people, and the Church grows.

✝ *Jesus, bring your light and healing to this world, and use our sharing in the work of your Church to bring glory to God.*

Thursday March 1   Joel 2.1 – 2, 12 – 17

ATTITUDES

> The day of the Lord is coming, it is near –
> a day of darkness and gloom,
>   a day of clouds and thick darkness! ...
> Yet even now, says the LORD,
>   return to me with all your heart,
> with fasting, with weeping, and with mourning;
>   rend your hearts and not your clothing.
> Return to the LORD, your God,
>   for he is gracious and merciful,
> slow to anger, and abounding in steadfast love,
>   and relents from punishing.
>
> **(verses 1b – 2a, 12 – 13)**

When God begins to touch our lives, it can be difficult, painful, even frightening, as we recognize the majesty and judgement of the Lord God. This is the fear of the Lord. But God's summons to judgement is primarily an opportunity for repentance and renewal. Our humility and broken hearts are signs of true repentance for our veiled lives: attitudes, issues and actions closed to God's life. Returning to God opens up new perspectives as God's Spirit renews and heals our lives. Humility, trust and fear of the Lord allow God to work, and be seen, in our lives.

✝ *Lord, I kneel before your Majesty and ask forgiveness for the parts of my life which I have kept veiled from you. May others see in me what I have seen in you.*

World Day of Prayer
Friday March 2   Ephesians 3.14 – 21

COMMUNITY

> I pray that you may have the power to comprehend, with all the saints, what is the breadth and length and height and depth, and to know the love of Christ that surpasses knowledge, so that you may be filled with all the fullness of God.   **(verse 18)**

Today is a day for focusing on the unity and fellowship of Christian men and women around the world, particularly praying for the women of Western Samoa who are responsible for preparing today's service. Our readings this week have highlighted ways in which God can be seen in individual Christians and the local church, but today Paul's prayer gives us a much broader vision of our part in the community of saints. The vastness and intimacy of the loving embrace of the Father, Son and Spirit are reflected in the Christian community – both those in our local church and around the world, but also those who have gone before. Together we are the Body of Christ. We pray better for one another when we know about each other's situations and contexts, and our prayer helps us to show by our actions that we value and support one another. In prayer we discover what we are already – co-workers sharing in God's life in this world. When we recognize that we belong to each other, we take a step away from suffering, poverty, tears and isolation and towards the sharing of love, joy, peace and the world's resources. In this renewed community, others will see that God is our companion, refuge and friend.

† *Thank you, Lord, for enabling us to be part of your community of saints. What support, comfort and encouragement that brings!*

Saturday March 3   **2 Corinthians 5.20b – 6.10**

TRANSFORMATION

> **As servants of God we have commended ourselves in every way ... by purity, knowledge, patience, kindness, holiness of spirit, genuine love, truthful speech, and the power of God.** (verses 4a, 6 – 7a)

Jesus has made the power of God available to us by his work on the cross, and we are now privileged to be part of the activity of God as we respond to the transforming, indwelling Spirit. Paul and Timothy confidently list the characteristics that point to the grace of God in their lives and encourage others, like the Corinthians, to be reconciled to God. Do people see the activity of God in our lives, as individuals and the community of the Church? Transformation takes time – time spent in prayer, study of the Bible and living in the community of the Church – and we are urged not to give up, 'not to accept the grace of God in vain' (*verse 1*). Let God be seen in our lives, for the glory of God the Father, God the Son and God the Holy Spirit.

† *God, I have seen something of your grace and love. May I more and more reflect your life, so that I can help to transform the world around me and bring glory to you.*

For group discussion and personal thought

● How does reflection on the Trinity affect how you see God and understand your life as a Christian?
● Consider the life of a saint known to you, alive or dead, and thank God for his life seen in that person.

Finding Our Way
TOGETHER

● A series for leaders of house fellowships, Bible study groups and worship groups
● An opportunity to explore world issues and modern themes in the light of the Bible
● Includes background notes, ways of leading groups, contemporary stories, activities for adults, questions for discussion, suggestions for prayer and ideas for action
● Uses the same passages and themes as *Light for our Path*

Books 1–4 UK price £6.50 each/£20 for the set

IBRA *Order through your IBRA representative, or from the appropriate address on page 285.*

LENT – JOURNEY WITH CHRIST 1
Which way?

Notes by Supriyo Mukherjee

based on the New Revised Standard Version

Supriyo Mukherjee is an Anglican priest. He was ordained in the Church of North India in 1975. Since 1979 he has been living and working in England. At present he is the Diocesan Adviser for Community Relations and Inter-faith for Coventry, and Team Vicar of Coventry East Team Ministry.

During Lent we focus on the humanity of Jesus. This human Jesus was tested as we are (*see Hebrews 4.15*), he went through the agony in the garden of Gethsemane and at the end he suffered rejection, humiliation and death on the cross. This is the Jesus we try to follow – a humble and human Jesus, a suffering Jesus, yet a victorious Jesus. We cannot imitate the almighty and immortal God, but we can follow our brother Jesus because he was human, and when we follow Jesus we also become victorious like him.

Text for the week: Philippians 2.5 – 7a

Sunday March 4   Luke 4.1 – 13

SON OF MAN According to Luke, Jesus is Son of God because he is son of Adam (*see Luke 3.38*: 'son of Enos, son of Seth, son of Adam, son of God'). By creation we are all children of God, and Jesus the Messiah, the second Adam, frees us from the slavery of Adam's sinfulness by his act of righteousness and obedience. 'Therefore just as one man's trespass led to condemnation for all, so one man's act of righteousness leads to justification and life for all' (*Romans 5.18*). This concept is vital for our salvation – but we are not simply saved by the death of Jesus on the cross. We also have to follow the way of Jesus.

> **Jesus, full of the Holy Spirit ... was led by the Spirit in the wilderness, where for forty days he was tempted by the devil.** (verses 1 – 2)

Jesus was tempted just as any human being is tempted in his or her everyday life. However, Jesus overcame his temptations. This gives us courage to believe that we too can overcome our temptations – we can follow the Son of Man.

✝ *O God our heavenly Father, we thank you for our Lord Jesus who became one of us. Give us grace to follow in his footsteps, so that we too can be victorious over our temptations.*

Monday March 5   Luke 9.18 – 27

DIFFERENT VIEWS OF JESUS

[Jesus] asked them, 'Who do the crowds say that I am?' They answered, 'John the Baptist; but others, Elijah; and still others, that one of the ancient prophets has arisen.' He said to them, 'But who do you say that I am?' Peter answered, 'The Messiah of God.'   **(verses 18b – 20)**

It was important for Jesus to know what the others thought about him. It should also be important for us to know the Muslim view, the Hindu view, the Sikh view or the Buddhist view of Jesus. Even the different authors of the New Testament understood Jesus differently. Respect for other views of Jesus helps our own ideas to mature. Dependence on a certain creed will not save us. Jesus says, 'Not everyone who says to me, "Lord, Lord," will enter the kingdom of heaven, but only the one who does the will of my Father in heaven' (*Matthew 7:21; compare Luke 6:46*). Faith in Jesus is not the same as beliefs about the person of Jesus – it is our trust in Jesus as Guru who reveals the will of our heavenly Father and shows the way to act on it. Real Christians are not a group of people who belong to a religious group called Christianity; they are the followers of Christ, although they may hold a variety of personal opinions about the person of Jesus.

✝ *O Lord, graft in my heart true religion and release me from the bondage of religiosity.*

Tuesday March 6   Luke 9.51 – 56

DISCIPLESHIP In Ezra and Nehemiah we read about the hostility between Jewish people and Samaritans. Probably the seed of enmity was sown between these two races when Zerubbabel rejected the offer from the Samaritans to help rebuild the Temple (*Ezra 4.1 – 5*). Samaritans worshipped the same God, but did not believe that Jerusalem was specially holy. Here, Jesus is going to Jerusalem and so the Samaritans reject him. We can see how James and John hated this:

> When his disciples James and John saw it, they said, 'Lord, do you want us to command fire to come down from heaven and consume them?' But he turned and rebuked them. Then they went on to another village.

(verses 54 – 56)

But Jesus rebuked them. If we wish to follow Jesus, we cannot be racists – we cannot even hate our enemies. Christians often quote from the Old Testament to justify violence or war. However, you cannot mix old and new rules. Jesus' new rule of love is not compatible with many Old Testament ideas. Jesus said, 'New wine must be put into fresh wineskins' (*Luke 5.38*).

✝ *May my life be guided by your rule of love.*

Wednesday March 7   Luke 9.57 – 62

FOLLOWING A PAUPER?

> Foxes have holes, and birds of the air have nests; but the Son of Man has nowhere to lay his head.   (verse 58)

Jesus gave up everything to become one of us. He was born in a manger and brought up as a carpenter. At the beginning of his ministry he might have had ambitions to be famous and powerful (remember his temptations). Yet he chose to identify with the poorest of the poor and become a homeless person. However, in Jesus' day people were generous to a holy man, so Jesus did not have to beg for his food and clothing. He was even able to support twelve disciples beside himself (and he had Judas as his treasurer). Some Christians have a vocation to give up everything to live in a community; for most of us, however, it is enough that we do not get too attached to our material possessions. 'You cannot serve God and wealth' (*Luke 16.13*). But many people in today's world find security and comfort in their material possessions and do not seem to *need* God any more.

✝ *Lord, help me to follow your way and free me from all false senses of security.*

Thursday March 8   Luke 11.29 – 32

FOLLOWING FOR THE RIGHT REASON   People followed Jesus everywhere, so that he often had to use a boat to escape the crowd. Most of the people followed Jesus to receive material benefits: some wanted to be healed, some wanted to watch him perform miracles, others followed him to eat the bread he produced by his miraculous power.

> **This generation is an evil generation; it asks for a sign.**
> **(verse 29)**

In our consumer society many people do exactly the same. In the past, in many parts of the world, people converted to Christianity in order to receive material benefits. Even today, many people become Christians to raise their standard of living or their social status, and some missionary organizations support this view. However, the religion of Jesus teaches us to give more than receive. And Jesus came to reveal the Fatherhood of God – his miracles were indeed outward *signs* of that revelation – Fatherhood of all people, not just Christians. The Church also has to work for the Kingdom of God – for equality, fairness and justice for the whole community, irrespective of religion or race, irrespective of whether people are Christians or not. We should learn from Jesus to say 'No' to people who come to Christianity for the wrong reasons.

✝ *May I be more happy in giving than in receiving.*

Friday March 9   **Luke 13.22 – 30**

THE NARROW DOOR

> **'Strive to enter by the narrow door; for many, I tell you, will try to enter and will not be able ... Indeed, some are last who will be first, and some are first who will be last.'**
> **(verses 24 and 30)**

At the last judgement, people who claim to know Jesus will not be saved, but other people from all over the world will be saved. Why? On Monday we saw that real Christians are those who follow Christ. Some people like to follow the teachings and way of Jesus but do not want to belong to a Christian community, and perhaps would not call themselves Christians. Gandhi was one such person. He did not think that Christians were better people than Hindus and baptism did not transform them. We often claim to know Christ but some others know Christ better because they follow the way of Christ. The way of Jesus is difficult – it is the way of sacrificial love, the way of the cross. Christianity spends a lot of time maintaining the traditions and customs of its fabric, forgetting its real role as

Church: to serve as the instrument of God's reconciliation with the world.

✝ *Lord, help me choose the narrow door of self-giving and lead me to your heavenly peace.*

Saturday March 10   Philippians 2.5 – 11

THE MIND OF JESUS Christianity is often regarded by others as an arrogant religion because we claim to know the only truth and regard all others as ignorant. However, we bear the name of the humble Jesus. We cannot spread the good news by shouting out our claim to knowledge; like Mother Teresa of Calcutta, we do this by *living* the gospel. Jesus showed us how to live the good news by obeying the will of the Father.

Let the same mind be in you that was in Christ Jesus.

(verse 5)

We can understand what God wants us to do by looking into the mind of Christ, which was fully made known to us on the cross. During Lent we meditate on the cross so that we can understand better the mind of Christ – and follow him more closely on his way.

✝ *Merge my mind with yours so that I have the knowledge of your divine will.*

For group discussion and personal thought

● How often do you remember that Jesus was a human being like us? Do you find this helpful?
● Jesus showed us the way: do you walk in it?
● Do you waste time arguing about the person of Jesus? Would you be a better person spiritually if you tried more to live the gospel of Christ instead? What one step could you take today to follow Jesus more closely?

LENT – JOURNEY WITH CHRIST 2

The cost

Notes by David Huggett

based on the Good News Bible

David Huggett is a Baptist minister who is involved in adult Christian education. Currently he is also Secretary of the Western Baptist Association in South West England.

Getting 'something for nothing' is a common enough human ambition. But deep down in our hearts we know it doesn't often happen that way. The mother who rejoices in the birth of her baby, the student who celebrates the passing of his exams, the rescuers who drag a victim from the rubble of an earthquake, know that there is a price to be paid and they are prepared to pay it. So it is no surprise that during this season of Lent we are being invited to reflect on what cost may be involved for us in following Jesus. That cost is likely to be different for each one of us. But whatever it is, it needs to be faced in the light of the price Jesus paid for us.

Text for the week: Luke 14.27

Sunday March 11   **Jeremiah 22.1 – 9, 13 – 17**

THE COST OF BEING A LEADER Here it is the king of Judah, but it could equally well be someone else with leadership responsibilities – in the home, in the workplace, in the school, in the church. The principle is always the same – leadership brings responsibility. You are not a leader for your own benefit or advancement, but for the benefit of the people you lead.

> **'I, the Lord, command you to do what is just and right. Protect the person who is being cheated ... Do not ill-treat or oppress...'**   **(part of verse 3)**

Verses 13 – 17 have a sad ring of truth about them. People in leadership can be so busy building up their own bank balance, providing for their own retirement, careful about their own status and reputation, that they forget the well-being of those who depend on them. But it works both ways. It is not easy being a good leader and those who are led have their own particular responsibility of prayer support for their leaders (*1 Timothy 2.1 – 2*). How often do you pray for the leaders of your church, community and nation?

✝ *Lord, in every situation help me to do what is just and right.*

Monday March 12   Luke 12.51 – 53

CONFRONTING THE WORLD

'Do you suppose that I came to bring peace to the world?'
(part of verse 51)

The first answer that springs to mind may be, 'Yes, that's exactly what we thought you had come to bring.' After all, isn't Jesus given the title of 'Prince of Peace'? Didn't he himself promise 'Peace is what I leave with you' (*John 14.27*)? But that is only part of the truth. When Christ's rule is accepted by individuals and communities, peace is certainly one of the beautiful consequences. But as we know, Christ's rule is not always accepted, and when the standards of truth which Christ taught and for which he died challenge the commonly accepted standards of our world, there is often conflict. Jesus himself was increasingly opposed by those whose authority and status he challenged. In the end they hounded him to death. Jesus never suggested that his followers should live in a fool's paradise. Journeying with Christ during this Lent may well mean that we too will have to confront some of the evils of our age – and pay the price.

✝ *Give us courage, mighty Lord, to stand up for what we know to be true, and give us wisdom to do so with grace and tenderness.*

Tuesday March 13   Luke 13.31 – 35

THE COST OF CARING Jesus didn't mince his words! Herod was utterly opposed to him. He needed to be confronted, but also to be reminded that he had no ultimate power over the Christ. But if Herod had put himself beyond hope, there were others for whom Jesus yearned deeply.

'Jerusalem, Jerusalem! ... How many times have I wanted to put my arms round all your people, just as a hen gathers her chicks under her wings, but you would not let me!'
(part of verse 34)

Sometimes we may be in danger of rejecting people whom God has not rejected. We can dismiss as hopeless those who don't see things the way we do. Perhaps our stand for Christian principles has led to opposition and so we try to defend ourselves by withdrawing from the very people who need our caring and compassion. Anger, shrugging our shoulders, withdrawing – none of these are fitting reactions, because in reality it is not we who are being rejected but the one who went to the cross for the people of Jerusalem and everyone like them.

† *Lord, give me the kind of concern for people that you had.*

Wednesday March 14   Luke 14.25 – 33

COUNTING THE COST   At this point in his ministry Jesus was very popular. His teaching and miracles had given him 'star' status, and the crowds that followed him were expecting great things of him. Then came the bombshell:

> **'Those who do not carry their own cross and come after me cannot be my disciples.'**   **(verse 27)**

Of course Jesus was using strong language in order to force the crowd to think carefully about what they might be letting themselves in for. The point he was making was that even the most precious of human relationships must be subordinate to the disciple's relationship to the Lord. Human ties are very precious and hopefully there will be no conflict of interests, but if there is, then we have to bear that cross and put the claims of Christ first. It would be irresponsible not to face up to the possibility of such pressure on some of our human relationships before we agree to become a disciple. Otherwise we would be like the rash builder or the rash king.

† *Lord, I know that following you isn't simply a matter of giving up things for the sake of it. But help me to be ready to sacrifice anything that spoils my relationship with you.*

Thursday March 15   Luke 10.5 – 15

BEING VULNERABLE   Every Christian has the responsibility to share the good news of Jesus Christ, both by the way we live and by the words we say.

> **Say to the people there, 'The Kingdom of God has come near you.'**   **(part of verse 9)**

Only part of the mission of the seventy-two was to preach. They were also to allow people to minister to them. Generous hospitality was very important to the Jews, and it can play a significant part in our mission strategy. But the way we receive hospitality is as important as the way we give it. That too can be a significant part of our mission. In our zeal to give to people, we may forget that often the best way into their hearts and minds is first to receive from them – in other words, to make ourselves vulnerable. Along with vulnerability must go sensitivity. These seventy-two disciples were eager to share the good news of the kingdom, but they had to know when it was right to back off and withdraw.

† *Lord, I want to be zealous in serving you. But I want to be wise too. Help me to know when to hold back, and help me to be humble enough to receive, even from people who have much less than me.*

Friday March 16   **Philippians 3.12 – 21**

IN TRAINING   No one could have blamed Paul if he had decided at this point in his life to take things easy. He had spent long hard years in the service of Christ. Now in prison, he could be nearing the end of his life. But it appears that nothing was further from his mind.

> **The one thing I do ... is to forget what is behind me and do my best to reach what is ahead. So I run straight towards the goal in order to win the prize, which is God's call through Christ Jesus to the life above.**
>
> **(verses 13b and 14)**

'Forgetting what is behind' may suggest that Henry Ford was right to say that 'History is bunk'. But history is important because we can learn from it. Your own personal history is important, whatever it may have been. Yet the Christian life is fundamentally a forward-looking affair. We are thankful for the past, especially for all that God has taught us about himself. But we look to the future because we are a pilgrim people – or, to use Paul's picture, we are in a race. And if the end is in sight for some of us, that is all the more reason to put in a last sprint for the tape. Even when Jesus looked forward and saw only the cross, he kept his face forward – and paid the price.

† *Lord, whatever I face today I know that you will be in it with me. Give me the grace to persevere and to run with determination the race that lies before me.*

A GOOD SOLDIER   Suffering is an inescapable part of being human. Because we live in a broken world where relationships are easily fractured, we suffer the results in our personal lives and communities. This is true for everyone, but particularly so for Christians. Because of our loyalty to Christ and our commitment to his way of life, we find ourselves from time to time in conflict with our society.

> **Take your part in suffering, as a loyal soldier of Christ Jesus. A soldier on active service wants to please his commanding officer and so does not get mixed up in the affairs of civilian life.**   **(verses 3 – 4)**

A man or woman who joins the army hopes that it will never be necessary to face the dangers of battle. But they know they may have to, and they are trained accordingly. The suffering that we may have to endure as Christians could come from many different sources — physical, mental or spiritual. The difference is that Christians know what the ultimate outcome is going to be (*verse 12*). That makes all the training and discipline worthwhile.

† *Teach us, good Lord,*
to serve you as you deserve,
to give and not to count the cost,
to fight and not to heed the wounds,
to toil and not to seek for rest,
to labour and not to seek for any reward
save that of knowing that we do your will.

(St Ignatius of Loyola)

For group discussion and personal thought

● What issues need confronting in your community? How would you go about making the Christian point of view known and understood in a firm yet gracious way?

● As an enlisted soldier of Jesus Christ, are there any areas of your life that would not bear inspection? What disciplinary measures could you take to remedy the situation?

LENT – JOURNEY WITH CHRIST 3

Time for God

Notes by Tom Arthur

based on the New Revised Standard Version

Tom Arthur, an American Presbyterian, was recruited from his home denomination to serve three churches in Cardiff. He is now minister of Weoley Hill United Reformed Church in Birmingham, England, where he lives with his Dutch wife Marieke and their three children, adopted when in Wales.

Taking time for God is not escaping from life, but entering more fully into it. We are bombarded by invitations to 'the good life' which cost us the world because they cost us our relationship to others and our own integrity. The invitation to journey with Christ gives us a relationship with others, the world and ourselves which is deep and rich in meaning.

Text for the week: Isaiah 55.6

Sunday March 18   Isaiah 55.1 – 9

WHAT IS THE CATCH?   Our Lord offers free food and drink to the thirsty and the penniless. Who would hesitate to step into the queue with open hands? Or is it too good to be true? Is there a catch? The urgency in Isaiah's verses sounds too much like the words of a salesman. Don't let the moment of opportunity pass you by, he says:

> **Seek the LORD while he may be found,**
> **call upon him while he is near.**   **(verse 6)**

This appeal reminds me of the one the seventeenth-century poet Andrew Marvell made in his poem 'To his coy mistress', who was teasing him and playing 'hard to get':

> Had we but world enough, and time,
> This coyness, lady, were no crime.

What is the catch? How much is it going to cost me, really? Or could it be true that God's totally free offer of 'an everlasting covenant' and 'steadfast, sure love' (*verse 3*) is genuine? Is there really such a thing as a 'free lunch'? Can it really be true that his ways are not like our ways?

† *Lord, save me from cynicism, that I may rejoice in your gifts.*

Monday March 19   **Genesis 28.10 – 19a**

IMPORTANT PLACES   While Jacob was on his way from Beersheba to Haran, the sun set, so he stopped, found a stone for a pillow, and slept. It was a place with nothing there, without significance for anyone. But Jacob had a dream there that changed his life, and then this empty place became an important place:

> **Then Jacob woke from his sleep and said ... 'This is none other than the house of God, and this is the gate of heaven.'**
> **(verses 16 – 17)**

The ordinary stone used as a pillow is set apart for holy use in a rock cairn to mark a sacred event. Rambling across the hills of rural Wales I often came across small standing stones or cairns marking holy places like this, and wondered what life-redeeming visions had taken place there. Sacred moments become sacred places. Old Saxon stone crosses mark places where angels descended and ascended on people whose stories are now lost. It is perhaps enough to know that such places exist. We have our own life-transforming dreams and awakenings in empty places between this important place and that important place. For us the centre of the world is not where they say it is, in monuments to magnificence, in stately homes or towering office blocks, but in those moments when God touched us, and our lives and our world were turned upside down. It is good to see that we are not crazy, that others have marked such moments as well.

† *May I never forget the moments when you, my Redeemer, have opened my eyes to your grace.*

Tuesday March 20   **1 Corinthians 10.1 – 13**

HIGH RISK   I honestly don't know why Christianity isn't any more popular than it is these days. I have read much about the contemporary fashion for high risk sports and Paul, here, promises a way of life steeped in risk. In a world that is weary of safety nets and couch potatoes, we are called to strip off our securities and go with the Exodus people into the wilderness. Paul says that most of the people of Israel didn't survive their journey, but we will:

> **God is faithful, and he will not let you be tested beyond your strength.** (part of verse 13)

Anyone who has ever dieted knows how common it actually is to be tempted beyond our strength. We are even familiar with the temptation to deny Christ – and all too often give in to it. But although Paul is exaggerating here, he is also saying something important. He goes on to say that the cup of blessing we share is a communion in the blood of Christ. Christian commitment to the world is fully real. It does not shirk suffering, not even death, because it knows God's grace is paramount. It is a bit like bungee jumping – scary, but with a spiritual tether attached, a leap of faith which defies death even while it does not escape it. We shall not ultimately fail because God is with us even in death.

† *Lord, take away my fear, that I may be carried by faith to risk all for your glory.*

Wednesday March 21   **John 1.43 – 51**

COME AND SEE   Jesus calls Nathanael 'a true Israelite' and Nathanael asks with childlike astonishment,'

> **Where did you get to know me?' Jesus answered, 'I saw you under the fig tree'... Nathanael replied, 'Rabbi, you are the Son of God!'**
> **(part of verses 48 – 49)**

Nathanael is amazed by the Rabbi's mysterious powers of perception. But Jesus is teasing him. The real difference between Jesus and Nathanael does not lie in their powers of perception. When he had first been told about Jesus, Nathanael had said, 'Can anything good come out of Nazareth?' The difference between Jesus and Nathanael is the difference between Nathanael's cynicism and the readiness of Jesus to greet someone with a compliment. Is Nathanael too ready to believe? Some people say the Church is in decline today because in our scientific, technological age the capacity for belief has disappeared. That is only half true. In our flat spiritual landscape the need to believe in something deeper than ourselves gnaws at our souls with an increasingly painful hunger, until we are willing to believe in almost anything. We are like Nathanael. We are cynical and credulous by turns, lacking in spiritual maturity. Nathanael will grow up. His faith will not stay at the level of hero worship for ever. He has been invited to take a journey, to 'come and see' (*verse 46*), to set out on a path of discovering the identity of Jesus by discovering his own identity, so that Christ can live in him as sap lives in the vine (*John 15.4*), and he himself can be nothing less than the child of God (*John 1.12*). Then he will see as Jacob saw, able to see 'angels ascending and descending' (*verse 51*) with insight and understanding.

† *Lord, call me to walk with you, that I may know you in my own heart.*

Thursday March 22   Luke 6.12 – 16

A COMPANY OF TWELVE   A German theologian once said, 'Ein Mensch ist kein Mensch': a single person is no person at all. There is a gregarious spirit deep in human nature that brings us into companionship with others. Think of the partnerships you have known: Batman and Robin; the three Musketeers Athos, Porthos and Aramis; the four Beatles Paul, John, George and Ringo. It is always better when we do things together. The list of those Jesus called out of his disciples (the word means something like 'apprentices') to be apostles ('delegates', those who are sent out to get the job done) is one of the best known partnerships:

> **Simon, whom he named Peter, and his brother Andrew, and James, and John, and Philip, and Bartholomew, and Matthew, and Thomas, and James son of Alphaeus, and Simon, who was called the Zealot, and Judas son of James, and Judas Iscariot.   (verses 14 – 16)**

In our familiar marketplace world our leaders are chosen for their power to compete and win. These apostles, however, represent what it meant for God's people, the twelve tribes of Israel, to be chosen from among those who lose. The twelve apostles are chosen to represent Jesus before they are ready. Too full of themselves, they try to perform solo high wire acts and fail, try again and fail again. What will it mean to represent the one who lived for others (*Mark 15.31*)? Only after Jesus has given himself completely to them on the cross will they understand why they are not called to be single individuals, but a company of twelve.

† *Thank you, Lord, that I do not have to walk alone, for with you I am in good company.*

REAL PRAYER   Christian discipleship, like all discipleship, is a learning process. My father, a Presbyterian minister, taught me to write out the Lord's Prayer and tape it on to the lectern when I led worship. 'You never know when you will draw a blank,' he said. But now that I have been a minister myself for some twenty years I never have a problem. I can rattle off the Lord's Prayer like those 'empty phrases' of Gentile prayers (*verse 7*). To be sure, even the Lord's Prayer can become empty when it is recited from habit, in a formal and ritualistic way. Jesus seems to be asking his disciples to throw away everything they know about prayer and get real. Prayer is to be an embodied spirituality, something we *do* as much as something we *say*. Words and actions complement each other; both are necessary. We are to bring heaven to earth by working in partnership with God, opening our minds, our hearts, our very souls to what God wants for the world. We are to pray:

> **'Forgive us our debts as we also have forgiven our debtors.'**
> **(verse 12)**

What we pray for is to be embodied in what we do. God's care for us can never be separated from how we care for our neighbour. This is repeated at the end, in case we have missed the point:

> **For if you forgive others their trespasses, your heavenly Father will also forgive you; but if you do not forgive others, neither will your Father forgive your trespasses.**
> **(verses 14 – 15)**

Praying in the way that Jesus taught is not a matter of liturgical conformity, nor is it a ritualized means of bending the mind of heaven to our needs. It is having the mind of Jesus (*Philippians 2.5*), having a deep, heart-transforming care for the world, a longing for the way things happen on earth to change, and a longing to be part of that change. Thus our prayers are not empty, but full of grace and truth.

† *Lord, teach me to pray.*

ABIDE IN HIM   'Abide with me' is a fine hymn. Its words speak importantly of God's unfailing presence just when that presence may seem most absent. But like much of Christian piety, it misses the point, if the point has anything to do with the scripture reference made here. There is no question that Christ abides in us. It is he who asks us to abide in him:

> **'Abide in me as I abide in you. Just as the branch cannot bear fruit by itself unless it abides in the vine, neither can you unless you abide in me.'** (verse 4)

An adult-to-adult mutuality needs to be central to the relationship. He abides in us as we abide in him. Thus we are called to something more than a merely child-like faith. Sin, here, is not characterized as disobedience to external authority but as withering on the vine. We are those in whom Christ abides as we are 'rooted and grounded in love' (*Ephesians 3.17*). To change the picture, it is as if our driving skills are no longer a matter of obeying the rules of the drivers' manual, but have become a part of who we are, a matter of response that is the fruit of long practice. The time has come for the Father to hand over the keys.

✝ *Lord, I have seen your dwelling place. It is within me. And I have found mine in you.*

For group discussion and personal thought

- What sacred moments and sacred places have you experienced in your own life?
- How can you help your prayer to be 'embodied spirituality, something we *do* as much as something we *say*?

LENT – JOURNEY WITH CHRIST 4
New beginnings

Notes by Carol Mouat

based on the Jerusalem Bible

Carol Mouat is a Roman Catholic Dominican Sister who has been involved in Theological Education by Extension in South Africa for the past ten years. Currently she is on the staff at Hawkstone International Pastoral Centre in Shropshire, England.

The readings this week speak to us of God's unconditional love and forgiveness. The key words are love, trust, covenant, forgiveness and hope.

Text for the week: 2 Corinthians 5.17

Sunday March 25   Isaiah 40.27 – 31; 41.8 – 13

DO NOT BE AFRAID   God's love for us is unconditional and everlasting. We have no need to fear because the Lord gives us his strength and power.

> **Do not be afraid, for I am with you;**
> **stop being anxious and watchful, for I am your God ...**
> **For I, Yahweh, your God,**
> **I am holding you by the right hand;**
> **I tell you, 'Do not be afraid,**
> **I will help you'.**   **(verses 10a and 13)**

People often feel the need to lean on God when there is a crisis in their lives. We tend to seek his strength when we need to rely on him. But God wants us to call on him at all times, to allow him to shower us with his love in both the good and bad moments of our lives. And his perfect love will drive away all fear.

✝ *Loving Father, we call on you to be very close to us at all times, to protect us from all harm and to help us put our complete trust in you.*

COVENANT   In this reading we experience a very loving God who binds his relationship with Noah and his two sons by forming a covenant with them. The covenant is sealed with a promise of blessing.

> **[God said,] 'When the bow is in the clouds I shall see it and call to mind the lasting Covenant between God and every living creature of every kind that is found on the earth.'**
>
> **(verse 16)**

Promise is the key word in this passage. We are weak human creatures who often fail to keep our promises. People have let us down in the past and we do the same. But the Lord does not break his divine promise and will never let us down. Although there are times when we may experience him as distant, he never leaves us; he remains faithful to us at all times.

✝ *Faithful God, help us to remain faithful to you, and to all whom we meet in our daily lives.*

LEAVE YOUR COUNTRY

> **Yahweh said to Abram, 'Leave your country, your family and your father's house, for the land I will show you.'**
>
> **(verse 1)**

How many of us are prepared to let go of our security? Do we even hear the voice of God calling us to leave all and follow him? This is not an easy task. A very deep faith, trust, willingness to take risks and a lot of courage are required if we are to let go of all our security. Letting go could mean many things: leaving your homeland and moving to a new cultural environment; giving up your job in order to move into full-time ministry in the Church; selling up the family farm and moving into the city – God's call takes many forms. Giving up what is known and familiar usually involves a lot of pain. It is not easy to say goodbye to the 'known' and move on to the 'unknown'. Many of us have experienced the pain of 'letting go' our securities and moving on to a life in which we trust in God alone. When we respond generously to his call, the risk we take is accompanied by peace and inner freedom.

✝ *Help us, Lord, to hear your call and have the courage to respond. Help us to find someone who can guide and support us in our decision-making.*

FORGIVENESS AND LOVE   This is a remarkable story with three main characters: the father, his older son and his younger son.

> **The father said, 'My son, you are with me always and all I have is yours. But it was only right we should celebrate and rejoice, because your brother here was dead and has come to life; he was lost and is found.'**   **(verses 31 – 32)**

Do you recognize yourself in any one of the characters, or even in all three of them? The elder son had worked hard and lived a good life, seeking only to please his father at all times. He experiences rejection when his father welcomes home the lazy and selfish younger brother who has lived a life of debauchery and squandered all his money. He is portrayed as self-righteous and jealous. It is the younger son – the sinner – who is the hero of the story. The father is a man of patience who waits and longs for the return of his weaker younger son. He shows his love by embracing the sinner and celebrating his return – although the question of why he gave his inheritance to his sons before his death is never answered!

† *Forgiving Father, sometimes I find it very difficult to forgive people who hurt me or hurt someone close to me. Help me to forgive with your compassionate love and forgiveness.*

SAVING SINNERS   Jesus came to save sinners. This was his ministry.

> **'It is not those who are well who need the doctor, but the sick. I have not come to call the virtuous, but sinners to repentance.'**   **(verses 31 – 32)**

In this story we are confronted by the extraordinary behaviour of Jesus. He approaches a tax collector called Levi and invites him to follow him. Levi responds by inviting Jesus to a great reception in his home. Jesus sits down with the tax collectors and enjoys a good meal. When the Scribes and Pharisees question his behaviour his reply is straightforward: his concern is not with the righteous but with sinners. His dealings with Levi show us how to empower people. Do we do the same?

† *Jesus, help us to empower the weak and the sinner rather than avoid them and criticize their bad behaviour.*

Friday March 30   **2 Corinthians 5.16 – 21**

NEW CREATION   Paul is appealing to the people of Corinth to be reconciled to one another and to Christ.

God in Christ was reconciling the world to himself, not holding men's faults against them, and he has entrusted to us the news that they are reconciled.   **(verse 19)**

Reconciliation is closely connected to peace and justice. If we are reconciled with ourselves and forgive ourselves in our daily lives, and forgive others who have hurt us in the past and the present, we shall experience peace. Peace spreads like ripples on a pool and our love and forgiveness will enable others to love and forgive.

✝ *Heavenly Father, we live in a world where violence seems to be the norm in the daily news. We pray for peace in our world, that people at war with one another may be reconciled and united in love.*

Saturday March 31   **Isaiah 43.16 – 21**

NEW LIFE   The prophet Isaiah puts us in touch with the beauty of creation and the signs of hope. God is making a road in the wilderness and paths in the wild (*verse 19*). Many of us have experienced life in the wilderness, where everything seems dark and gloomy and we often cannot see the light. The pain we feel at times leaves us depressed, but God offers us a chance to turn away from the past and experience new life.

No need to recall the past,
No need to think about what was done before.
   See, I am doing a new deed.   **(verses 18 – 19a)**

This is what our Christianity is all about! It is a deep faith in God, especially when the road is tough. It is believing in his great love for us. It is knowing that we shall experience the 'water in the wilderness' (*verse 20*).

✝ *Jesus, help me to be a prophet of hope, not 'doom and gloom'.*

For group discussion and personal thought

● With which of the characters in the story of the Prodigal Son do you most identify: the father, the older son or the younger son?
● In what ways have you experienced both the wilderness and God's water in the wilderness?

LENT – JOURNEY WITH CHRIST 5

Knowing what lies ahead

Notes by Mike Pennington

based on the Jerusalem Bible

Michael Pennington, married with two children and two grandchildren, was a naval engineer before ordination as an Anglican priest. He has served in some deprived areas in the North of England and has been both a school and a hospital chaplain. Now retired, he is still active in churches on Tyneside. Ships and the sea are his great interest.

In worship and study, Christians follow the life of Jesus and find words and ideas – sometimes hundreds of years old – which point towards him. Looking back, and knowing about his life and death, we can often give deeper meanings to what was said and done than people could at the time. Their understanding may have developed later. This week's readings remind us of what lies ahead. Such knowledge may be painful, even though we know of the glorious end.

Text for the week: Psalm 69.35 — 36

Sunday April 1   John 12.1 – 8

BETHANY This story of the meal at Bethany is full of tensions. Beautiful scent fills the house, and yet the presence of the eternal Lord of life reminds us not only of holiness and glory, but also that the poor will always have a claim on us. Even here our thoughts are thrown forward as Jesus relates the costly ointment to his burial.

> **Lazarus ... whom he had raised from the dead ... was among those at table. ... Jesus said, '... you will not always have me [with you].'**   **(part of verses 1, 2, 7 and 8)**

Lazarus was at the meal, full of life. Jesus had recently raised him from death. In a few days' time, Jesus would be at another meal, the Last Supper, speaking of giving his body and blood. Iscariot, whom John tells us used to steal money given to the apostles, would also be there, with his own evil purpose in mind. Mary's lovely act of devotion contrasts sharply with the selfish aims of Judas.

† *Richness and poverty, life and death, devotion and betrayal, the divine and the human – Lord, you know them all and hold them together in your being. Help me to find your healing presence in those things in my life which seem to pull me in different directions.*

Monday April 2   Isaiah 50.4 – 11

A MYSTERIOUS FIGURE Although these words were written hundreds of years before the birth of Jesus, the 'Servant' whom Isaiah describes has a strange resemblance to Jesus and his deeds. What vision and understanding did Isaiah have of the one who was to come? After his arrest, Jesus was put through a pretence of a trial. He was insulted and beaten. Yet in the end, his oppressors came to nothing, and the Servant looks forward to a more hopeful outcome, even though there are some who will not accept his guidance.

> **Lord Yahweh is coming to my help,**
> **who dare condemn me?**
> **They shall all go to pieces like a garment**
> **devoured by moths ...**
> **Whoever walks in darkness,**
> **and has no light shining for him,**
> **let him trust in the name of Yahweh,**
> **let him lean on his God ...**
> **But you, you are all setting light to a fire ...**
> **Then in with you to the flames of your fire ...**
> **you shall lie down in torments.**   **(part of verses 9 – 11)**

† *Heavenly Father, holy men and women of old knew of your love for your children. You strengthen those who call upon you and are faithful to you. May I lean on you in times of trouble and find your guiding light and supporting arm.*

Tuesday April 3   Psalm 69.13 – 21, 29 – 36

A VISION OF GOOD AND BAD POWER Two years ago, the holiday weather was very, very hot. I had to keep in the shade, wear a hat to keep the sun off my bald head, and drink a lot. This was nothing compared to that Friday afternoon in Jerusalem when Jesus hung on the cross. He didn't get much refreshment or shelter.

When I was thirsty they gave me vinegar to drink.

(verse 21b)

Someone who feels that what is happening to him is like a flood threatening to drown him, knows that he can call to God, whose saving power will be in vivid contrast to the terrors of the moment. Pains, insults, even the deep waters of death, give way to the love of God. This psalm seems to be like a vision of the future, as Jesus comes to the end of his life.

✝ *Reach down your hand from above, save me, rescue me from deep waters, from the power of aliens who tell nothing but lies, who are prepared to swear to falsehood! (Psalm 144.7 – 8)*

Wednesday April 4   **Psalm 122**

UP TO JERUSALEM Jerusalem was always a place of longing, of pilgrimage – the sort of thing of which dreams are made. Here was the symbol of God's presence – the Ark in the Temple. Here lasting peace and harmony would eventually be found. The vision of St John looks even further: 'I saw the holy city, and the new Jerusalem, coming down from God out of heaven, as beautiful as a bride all dressed for her husband' (*Revelation 21.2*). No wonder the pilgrims sang songs like this psalm when they went there.

How I rejoiced when they said to me,
  'Let us go to the house of Yahweh!'
And now our feet are standing
  in your gateways, Jerusalem.   **(verses 1 and 2)**

When Jesus went up to the city, people cheered and shouted. Their cries echoed the ancient words of the psalm. But there were hard and sinister things to follow before the great mystery of Easter Day. Those early pilgrims could never have imagined the true glory of the risen Lord that was to be revealed in Jerusalem hundreds of years later.

✝ *Lord Jesus, your destiny was to be fulfilled where the steps of millions of pilgrims had gone before. Help us to be faithful pilgrims of our own age, seeking you in our own holy places. There we shall find and know you, worship you and proclaim you.*

Thursday April 5   **Luke 19.41 – 44**

DESTINY REJECTED My father was a great collector of things. Nothing of great value, just odd bits of this and that. He threw nothing away, including old papers. When he died many years ago I had to clear his house, the office of the family business and a huge warehouse. It was a long, boring and tiring job and I threw away much of what he had collected. Years later, I now realize that I threw out some things which I regret – especially some old diaries telling of family experiences. I just didn't look carefully enough, or think about their future interest to my own children and grandchildren. I did not recognize the opportunity when I had it – it was hidden from my eyes. Jesus wept as he thought about how Jerusalem had failed to understand and fulfil its destiny.

> **If you ... had only understood ... you did not recognize your opportunity when God offered it!**
>
> **(part of verses 42 and 44)**

Within a lifetime his words came true, as the city was reduced to ruins.

† *Lord, I have missed many chances in the past to do good things, to help people, to tell of your love. Sometimes I have been careless, or not thought, or not kept my eyes open. Forgive me, Lord, for my failures, and in the future make me more sensitive to the situations in which I find myself.*

Friday April 6   Luke 21.20 – 24

THE SIEGE   The world has been used to scenes such as Jesus described. Violence and brutality have continued through the centuries, and millions of ordinary people have struggled to escape, often finding themselves in terrible situations. 'Knowing what lies ahead' suggests that Jesus was very well aware of what human beings will do to reach their goals. They build their cities with strong buildings, reliable services and organizations and see them as places of safety and refuge. But they may not be, and people may have to rethink quickly how they organize their lives.

> **Those inside the city must leave it, and those in country districts must not take refuge in it.**   **(verse 21)**

This is another of those frequent reminders that human achievement lasts only a short time. If it pulls us away from our relationship with God and our eternal destiny, then we may find that things go very wrong. Read in Genesis 11 the story of the building of the famous Tower of Babel.

† *Lord, help me to look at my life in the light of your holiness. Am I relying on things which are not truly strong? Show me where I can really put my trust. Perhaps I should be thinking more about you, your power and your love.*

Saturday April 7   Luke 19.28 – 40

SHOUTING ALOUD FOR GOD Here Jesus fulfils what people had expected for a long time – they knew what lay ahead. The prophet Zechariah (*9.9*) had written very similar words over 500 years earlier. It all seemed so wonderful: the palms, the cheers, the shouting.

The whole group of disciples joyfully began to praise God at the top of their voices for all the miracles they had seen. (verse 37)

Some of these voices, threatened by the chief priests and the elders (*Matthew 27.20*), might have shouted something very different on the following Friday. Yet Jesus knows that if human voices cannot be heard, then the stones of the city will bear witness that the King of Glory passed this way.

† *What sort of Lord are you if the very stones will proclaim your glory? You, the Master, ride in humility as humble people praise you. Lord, when I think about the last days of your life, I find I cannot put my thoughts into order. Perhaps that is just as well, Lord, for you cannot be contained by human thought – or anything else.*

For group discussion and personal thought

● We have seen this week how words and actions may prove to be significant many years later. What things that you say and do today could turn out to be significant in time to come? (In a group, other people may see you more clearly than you do yourself.)

● What have you brought into the present from deeply-felt past experiences?

LENT – JOURNEY WITH CHRIST 6

Who cares?

Notes by Paul Duffett

based on the New Jerusalem Bible

This week is sometimes called 'Holy' because it is the week when the most solemn events of Jesus' life take place. We are called and confronted by these events, drawn into these dramatic days. The New Jerusalem Bible calls them 'The Passion', which means 'suffering' – suffering of a very special kind. Jesus' whole passionate ministry is focused on this last complete offering of himself to God.

Text for the week: Psalm 118.22

Palm Sunday April 8　　　　　　　　　**Psalm 118.1 – 2, 8 – 29**

THE LORD'S DOING　　Things are not what they seem on this first Palm Sunday. There are the large crowds shouting 'Hosanna, blessings on him who comes in the Lord's name' (*verse 25a*) and there is 'him' – riding on a donkey. What is going on? Perhaps only 'he' knew. The crowds seem to have got the wrong idea, and on Friday many of them turned against him. They thought that this 'king' was on a victory procession – but was he? Was the donkey a clue? A donkey is no proud steed of war but a humble beast of burden. Jesus chose to quote different verses from this psalm to those shouted by the crowd:

> **The stone which the builders rejected**
> **has become the cornerstone;**
> **This is Yahweh's doing,**
> **and we marvel at it.**
> **This is the day which Yahweh has made,**
> **a day for us to rejoice and be glad.**　　　　　**(verses 22 – 24)**

This is the way God intended it. Rejected, but victorious and glorious. A modern prayer book, *Celebrating Common Prayer*, has a misprint in this psalm (*verse 28*): the word God has the 'd' missing: 'You are my Go and I will thank you'! This Holy Week can we go with God and afterwards go for him?

Monday April 9   **Luke 22.14 – 30**

RELATIONSHIPS AND RECONCILIATION   When I was one of five children at home, the behaviour which earned the worst punishment was quarrelling at the table! But here are twelve of the most privileged people, who have spent three years with the greatest spiritual leader the world has produced, all arguing at once! Jesus, compassionate and patient, remains faithful to his calling. This Passover is for him the most important meal of his life, an event for which he has longed (*verse 15*). Now he will leave his will and testament in bread and wine. This cup is the new covenant in his blood.

> **He took bread, and when he had given thanks, he broke it and gave it to them, saying, 'This is my body given for you; do this in remembrance of me.' He did the same with the cup after supper, and said, 'This cup is the new covenant in my blood poured out for you. '**   **(verses 19 – 20)**

The old covenant has been superseded for ever. God saw the blood of a lamb on the doorposts of the Israelite homes in Egypt and passed over them, allowing the Israelites to go free from slavery. The blood now is the blood of the Lamb of God, sacrificed for the forgiveness and freedom of sinners. Then suddenly there is Judas with his betrayal and all the apostles quarrelling about who should be 'greatest'! Jesus, however, remains consistent. He, the leader and host at the meal, is serving them all – Judas included. Those who follow faithfully inherit God's Kingdom.

† *Lord, give me grace to work out your reconciliation in my relationships.*

Tuesday April 10   **Luke 22.39 – 46**

ALONE WITH GOD   There are times when we have to do things alone. No one else can do that exam or have that operation and certainly we shall be all alone at the time of death. Jesus knew that his terrible ordeal was about to begin. He wanted to be with his father and ask for his help, just as we might do. Verse 39 says he made his way 'as usual' to the Mount of Olives, in order to pray. He prays the prayer we might all do with the mental pain of facing something we dread, unknown.

> 'Father,' he said, 'if you are willing, take this cup away from me. Nevertheless, let your will be done, not mine.' ... In his anguish he prayed even more earnestly, and his sweat fell to the ground like great drops of blood.
>
> **(verses 42 and 44)**

Jesus' sweat was nothing to do with the warmth of the garden of Gethsemane on a spring evening. It was the result of the intensity, the urgency and energy of his prayer. Faced with what was about to happen, I think I would find myself acting like the disciples: 'sleeping for sheer grief' and failing the test (*verses 45 – 46*). How can our prayer become more intense and authentic, like the prayer of Jesus?

† *Lord, strengthen me in mind and body to pray with my whole being.*

Wednesday April 11   **Luke 22.47 – 62**

KISSING AND CRYING   This passage is full of emotion and drama. The deceiving kiss, a scuffle with swords, an arrest, a friend's denial, a look of love, and bitter tears when the cock's crow pierces the night like an air-raid siren. Who is in charge of this human shambles? Jesus says, 'This is the reign of darkness' (*verse 53*) but in fact he is still the leader. He challenges the chief priests, the police and civil authorities. 'What are you afraid of? Am I a bandit?' He knows about Peter and finds a brief moment to look at him with love and pain and judgement. Peter had never before experienced such a moment of truth and his 'conversion' goes deeper than ever before:

> The Lord turned and looked straight at Peter, and Peter remembered the Lord's words when he had said to him, 'Before the cock crows today, you will have disowned me three times.' And he went outside and wept bitterly.
>
> **(verses 61 – 62)**

When we make a mess of things, it is the Lord who can give us wisdom and pick us up and set us straight. How much we need to listen and learn!

† *We have deceived and denied you. Thank you that you still look at us lovingly.*

Thursday April 12   **Luke 23.1 – 25**

TRUMPED-UP CHARGES   I once heard someone damning the World Council of Churches by association. Russian priests were members, Russia was communist and so the WCC must be communist! The Archbishop of Canterbury had visited a Hindu temple, Hindus were not Christian, therefore the Archbishop was not a Christian and the Archbishop was a President of the WCC ... and so on! It is so easy to attack people with vague, emotional, half-true accusations.

> **We found this man [Jesus] inciting our people to revolt, opposing payment of the tribute to Caesar and claiming to be Christ, a King ... He is inflaming the people.**
>
> **(verses 2 and 5a)**

It is so easy to dehumanize people by taking away their rights. Then you can treat them as things, as less than human. So King Herod 'together with his guards, treated [Jesus] with contempt and made fun of him' (*verse 11*). Under terrible provocation, Jesus is dignified and silent in the face of Herod's curiosity (*verse 9*). Even Pilate, that hardened and self-seeking politician, did his best to free Jesus. We would all like to wash our hands of this travesty of justice – but we can't, because we know that the same temptations and tendencies can be found in our own hearts.

† *Lord, we need your grace constantly to avoid our all too human responses to critical situations.*

Good Friday April 13   **Luke 23.26 – 49**

FRIDAY THE THIRTEENTH   In some cultures Friday the thirteenth is considered 'unlucky'. Why is this? The number thirteen stands for Judas, the thirteenth in the group of Jesus and the apostles, and Friday is crucifixion day. So put the two together and you have unlucky Friday the thirteenth. It was indeed a dark moment in history. We have all become aware of 'man's inhumanity to man' through terrible pictures on our TV screens, but the older I get, the more difficult it becomes for me to think about this act of barbarism inflicted on Jesus. Yet out of it come these marvellous words:

> **Daughters of Jerusalem, do not weep for me; weep rather for yourselves and for your children.**   **(verse 28)**

> **Father, forgive them; they do not know what they are doing.**   **(verse 34)**

> **In truth I tell you, today you will be with me in paradise.**
>
> **(verse 43)**

I know a man whose son was murdered. He said, 'I can't be churchwarden any more, because I can't forgive the murderer.' I asked him to give himself time. A year later he said, 'On Good Friday I could ask God to forgive him, because that is what Jesus asked – not "*I* forgive you".' He was getting there! Why? Because God had been there and was with him in the darkness, anger and grief. We can never be anywhere where God is not.

† *Thank you, God, that you understand the depths of human suffering. Help me to hold on to you always.*

Holy Saturday April 14   John 19.38 – 42

'NOWHERE TO LAY HIS HEAD' Jesus' poverty was complete. He had abandoned his life to his Father and sheer faith had brought him through. He depended on friends who looked after him (*Luke 8.1 – 3*) and disciples who abandoned him and then enemies tortured and killed him. Now what? Two people were in positions of authority:

> Joseph of Arimathea, who was a disciples of Jesus – though a secret one because he was afraid of the Jews – asked Pilate to let him remove the body of Jesus ... Nicodemus came as well, the same one who had first come to Jesus at night-time ... They took the body of Jesus ... Since ...the tomb was nearby, they laid Jesus there. (part of verses 38 – 42)

The time had come for Joseph and Nicodemus to come out and openly take a stand. Even when he was dead, Jesus was leading people closer to God. His head was laid at last in a borrowed tomb, but that is always how he works. He knocks at the door of our lives and asks if he can use us for his service, then comes in to be with us for ever.

† *We mourn, O Lord, when we think of the violence you endured, but thank you that it was for us and that now you live with and in us.*

For group discussion and personal thought

● Is your love for God 'passionate'?
● How do we learn to forgive and love those who betray us?
● How do you understand that Jesus suffered and died 'for us'?

LENT – JOURNEY WITH CHRIST 7

Emptiness and triumph 1

Notes by Lloyda Fanusie

based on the Revised Standard Version

Lloyda Fanusie is a Methodist Local Preacher, Circuit Tutor and Family Life Education Trainer, currently engaged in racism awareness workshops in Britain. Previously, she was a teacher and Head of the Bible Knowledge Department at the Albert Academy in Sierra Leone and also lectured at the Sierra Leone Theological Hall and Church Training Centre and the Simon of Cyrene Theological Institute in London.

As we continue our journey with Christ, we need to stand on the authority of Scripture as it records the key events in his life. We can understand the doubts and fears of those who try to make sense of the historical reality of the bodily resurrection of Jesus. Nevertheless, the empty tomb, the fact that no one has ever produced Jesus' corpse and the accounts by witnesses of his resurrection appearances all point to his triumph over death. Our unique Christian faith accepts the presence of the living Christ, the saviour of the world.

Text for the week: Luke 24.5

Easter Sunday April 15   Luke 24.1 – 12

OUR RISEN HEAD   Christians continue to find strength in the fact of the Resurrection. To the fearful in hiding, those with burdens, the strong, the weak, the marginalized, Jesus is the Messiah, the saviour of the world, the upholder of womanhood, the promoter of culture, the remover of stumbling blocks, the protector of all. He even understands the doubting and works things out with them. Today we recall details about burial clothes, burial rites, the rhythm of life, death and resurrection.

> But on the first day of the week, at early dawn, they went to the tomb, taking the spices which they had prepared. And they found the stone rolled away from the tomb, but when they went in they did not find the body.   **(verses 1 – 3)**

This passage draws attention to the difference between the presence of the Risen Lord and the significance of presence in human culture. It is natural that we are concerned about the dead, the living, and the unborn – past, present and future generations – but the Lord is both part of all of these and at the same time beyond them. So it was appropriate that the women who came to fulfil the burial obligation were questioned by the strange men, the angels (*verse* 5): 'Why do you seek the living among the dead?' These women who saw the empty tomb first shared their experience with the menfolk, who gave a completely stereotypical response: the women were prattling, telling idle tales. How wrong they were! Eventually doubt would turn to implicit faith.

† *Our glorious risen Lord, thank you for your precious gift of life and your eternal presence with us.*

Monday April 16   **John 20.1 – 18**

BELIEF THROUGH SEEING AND HEARING   In spite of the rather confusing sequence of events, the truth of the resurrection appearances still prevails. Jesus is alive! What a privilege for the early witnesses! Mary must have gone with the other women who found the stone at the entrance of the tomb missing. She uses the plural – we – to tell Peter and John what they had seen (*verse* 2). But they could not simply believe her words – they had to run to the tomb to see for themselves. John, the younger and faster man, arrives first followed by Peter, who enters the tomb. They do not see any dazzling men, simply the burial clothes, the silent witnesses to the real, dead human being who is no longer there. The body is absent! Jesus' earlier prophecies about his death and resurrection had not been fully grasped by the disciples.

> **Then the other disciple, who reached the tomb first, also went in, and he saw and believed; for as yet they did not know the scripture, that he must rise from the dead.**
>
> **(verses 8 – 9)**

Mary, concerned about the whereabouts of the body, hovers around the tomb and so becomes the first person to see the risen Christ. She recognizes his voice and, although she cannot understand what has happened, his presence drives out her fear and dries her tears.

† *Open our eyes and ears, O Lord, to recognize your presence with us even when we do not completely understand it.*

OUR REDEEMER LIVES God's incalculable love for humankind (*John 3.16*) embraces both the universe and the individual. The New Israel has no boundaries, Jew and Gentile alike belong to God's Kingdom. Part of the Old Israel's witness was to be an example to other nations. Israel's relationship with God was depicted symbolically as that of husband/wife, father/son, parent/child, and rulers – priests, judges, prophets, kings – were sent as deliverers, saviours and champions. But God's support for Israel against other nations, which Isaiah describes in this passage, is not unconditional. Elsewhere in the Old Testament, God uses the nations as a rod of correction against Israel. Old Israel's history was often a cycle of transgression-disaster-repentance, followed by God's mercy and deliverance. New Israel journeys with Christ who, like God in this passage from Isaiah, calls us by name, identifies us individually and gives us self-worth. We share Israel's story and Israel's dependence on the mercy and deliverance of God, reinforced for us by the divine role of Christ our Redeemer.

> **'I, I am the LORD, and besides me there is no saviour ... I am God, and also henceforth I am He; there is no one who can deliver from my hand; I work and who can hinder it?'**
>
> **(verses 11 and 13)**

✝ *Merciful God, upholder of old and new, teach us to trust your love and power both for ourselves and for your world.*

RAISED WITH CHRIST Paul's references to the Resurrection in 1 Corinthians are the earliest written account of this great Christian truth. Those who witnessed to the risen Christ had no doubt about what they saw, once they realized that they were not hallucinating. They saw Jesus going through closed doors and heard his voice. They spread the news of God's saving work. Paul points out that if we do not believe in the Resurrection, then Christ's work is incomplete and our religion is false. If our hopes for life only relate to the present, we are missing out on the realities of God's plan. The full cycle of life and death is what makes humanity complete. So we come to appreciate how Christ/Emmanuel is, within history, the first fruits of the dead.

For as in Adam all die, so also in Christ shall all be made alive. But each in his own order: Christ the first fruits, then at his coming those who belong to Christ.   (verses 22 – 23)

By his death, Christ has triumphed over the enemy. Now in faith we are raised with him who shares with us the outpouring of the Holy Spirit.

† *Risen Lord, may your presence remain with us as we continue to unravel the mysteries of life. May the Holy Spirit rule us now and always.*

Thursday April 19   **John 20.19 – 23**

BEHIND CLOSED DOORS   'Talking with God' goes on! Ten disciples and some others were in hiding, away from the Jewish authorities, when Jesus entered the room from nowhere! This was their opportunity to see the Risen Lord and they were glad (*verse 20*). He offers them peace and a mission.

Jesus said to them again, 'Peace be with you. As the Father has sent me, even so I send you ... If you forgive the sins of any, they are forgiven; if you retain the sins of any, they are retained.'   **(verses 21 and 23)**

'Walking with God', the journey, continues. The disciples are sent out with the assurance that they are filled with the Holy Spirit which Jesus has breathed on them. Those on the margins are given power. As we, the inheritors of the faith, continue that pilgrimage, we take with us the freshness of the Holy Spirit, and we hold on to the hope that we too can forgive or retain sins. What an exaltation! Our moral judgement is called into action. Jesus warns us, however, to beware of double standards. We must be fair, tempering justice with mercy.

† *Merciful God, thank you for revealing yourself to us. Direct us when we are called to affirm or question other people's standards.*

Friday April 20   **John 20.24 – 31**

LIFE IN CHRIST'S NAME   The appearances of Jesus enabled the ten disciples and some of the women to testify that they 'saw' and 'heard'. This time, Thomas, who has been absent, also has his chance. Why do we criticize him so much as unbelieving, sceptical, a doubter, too analytical, one who demands proof? He was indeed forthright (*verse 25b*). Like the others, he felt the need for personal experience. When the glorified body of the Risen Christ appeared again, Thomas was challenged and invited to see and feel for himself. Jesus encouraged him to believe what he saw – he did not need to touch as well in order to know the truth. What a mighty God we serve! Jesus goes beyond the present by offering blessings to those who have not seen and yet believe.

Now Jesus did many other signs in the presence of the disciples, which are not written in this book; but these are written that you may believe that Jesus is the Christ, the Son of God, and that believing you may have life in his name. (verses 30 – 31)

This includes us, past and future generations.

✝ *Lord, strengthen our faith when we are beset with doubt and anxieties in this troubled world, so that we may believe and trust even when we cannot see and touch.*

Saturday April 21   **Isaiah 52.13 – 53.12**

MAN OF SORROW AND OUR TRIUMPHANT INTERCESSOR Like the Old Testament prophets before him, Christ prophesied his Resurrection. Events and occurrences in the New Testament are seen by those who described them as the fulfilment of Old Testament prophecies. Isaiah could not have known when his words would be fulfilled, but the God of yesterday, today and tomorrow knows and synchronizes the right times and events, revealing the good news of salvation to each generation.

For that which has not been told them they shall see, and that which they have not heard they shall understand.
(part of verse 15)

Isaiah spoke about the Servant of the Lord, lifted high on the cross, startling many who looked at the sorrowful scene of a grief-stricken righteous man placed between transgressors. This was God's plan. The Saviour was led, silent, like a sacrificial lamb to be slaughtered, only to rise victorious over death. Just as the Servant was lifted up to suffer, so our Risen Lord was raised in exaltation and power, interceding for us as he sits in glory, upholding humankind, making us right before God.

✝ *Thank you, Lord, for words of prophecy and insight – and for your glorious fulfilment of them.*

For group discussion and personal thought

● Discuss or think about some of the views put forward by scholars either in support of the Resurrection or questioning it. What do you think of these ideas? And do you agree with Paul's claim that we are raised with Christ?

SHARING GOD'S WORD

(Previously *Preachers' Handbook*)

● A resource for everyone involved in preparing sermons and talks

● Suitable both for the experienced but busy, and for those who are less experienced

● Provides basic structures for sermons and talks, plus suggestions for developing themes to suit your own context

● Based on the same passages and themes as *Light for our Path*

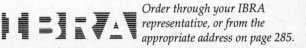

Order through your IBRA representative, or from the appropriate address on page 285.

LENT – JOURNEY WITH CHRIST 8
Emptiness and triumph 2

Notes by Isaiah Gaddala

based on the New International Version

Isaiah Gaddala has had a teaching ministry in Bible colleges and seminaries for 26 years and is currently an Assistant Professor of Homiletics at Union Biblical Seminary, Pune, India. He has also travelled widely in India conducting revivals for churches and retreats and workshops for pastors and lay people of all denominations.

The resurrection of Christ from the dead is the heart of Christianity. Christmas climaxes in Easter. The tragedy of Good Friday is replaced by the triumph of Easter. As we journey with Christ this week, we enter into the phase of his earthly life when he transcends all human barriers to make contact with the disciples. They are confused by the events of the previous days, but the appearances of Jesus after the Resurrection prove to them beyond all doubt that he is alive and is the same person who was crucified and died. May you also know the glory of the presence of the risen Lord as you read and think about these passages!

Text for the week: Revelation 1.5b – 6

Sunday April 22   **Luke 24.13 – 35**

DASHED HOPES – DIVINE PRESENCE Frustrations are part of human life. We are frustrated when what we hope for does not materialize or someone does not live up to our hopes. Place yourself in the shoes of these frustrated disciples walking to Emmaus after an eventful week in which their expected Messiah had suffered a humiliating death at the hands of their hated enemies, the Romans. What happened to all his claims? He said he would usher in a 'kingdom', establish a righteous 'regime' and make them his 'co-rulers'.

'But we had hoped that he was the one who was going to redeem Israel ... They [the women] went to the tomb early this morning but didn't find his body ... Then some of our

companions went to the tomb ... but him they did not see.'
(part of verses 21 – 24)

These statements summarize their frustrations: no political deliverance for Israel, no body, no meeting with Jesus in person. But in the midst of their dashed hopes on that dusty road away from Jerusalem towards Emmaus, in walks a 'stranger' – in fact, the very same, long-expected Messiah (recently dead but now alive). He clarifies their doubts and confirms his promises through his divine presence. Do not let your frustrations cloud your vision of the ever-living presence of God on your journey of life! Make him your 'fellow-traveller' when the going gets tough!

† *Thank you, Lord, for being my Emmanuel in all the moments and situations of my earthly journey. Help me to walk with you hand in hand each day of my life.*

Monday April 23   **Luke 24.36 – 43**

THE NATURE OF LIFE AFTER DEATH   There is life beyond the grave! This is not the pious wish of a few disgruntled religious folk here on earth. There truly is a life beyond death and the grave. Proof? The resurrection appearances of Jesus of Nazareth, who once lived on this earth, was crucified, rose again on the third day, walked with some real disciples and made himself known to them once again. What would our life be like if we believed in that kind of existence – life beyond the grave?

'Look at my hands and my feet. It is I myself! Touch me and see' ... he took [a piece of broiled fish] and ate it in their presence.   **(part of verse 39 and verse 43)**

A real person eating real food! A real person – but a glorified personality, for he could walk through 'closed doors' and appear in any place he wished. In his resurrected and glorious body Jesus assures us beyond any doubt that we can face life beyond the grave and that it will be his kind of life. His presence clarified the shape of our future resurrected bodies and he brought them 'shalom', the complete peace of God and the joy of his eternal presence.

† *Thank you, Lord, for the promise of life beyond the grave. Help me to face this day with the certainty that you are always with me.*

LIFE WITH CHRIST AND WITHOUT CHRIST Frustration always leads to disorientation! Peter and the other disciples had obeyed the first call of Jesus to come and follow him. That call included the promise to make them 'fishers of men'. But their hopes had been shattered by the crucifixion and death of Jesus, who did not fulfil their political ideals. In the face of this disorientation, they took their own steps for survival and decided to go back to their old profession of fishing. A life and profession without Christ? Yes, but look at the disastrous results.

> 'I'm going out to fish,' Simon Peter told them, and they said, 'We'll go with you.' So they went out and got into the boat, but that night they caught nothing.   **(verse 3)**

That night they caught nothing! They decided to depart from Christ and his mission (*cf. John 20.21*) but Christ did not leave them. He came back and restored them. This is the power of resurrection – God's supreme power to restore what is broken. Jesus appeared to them with the dawn, talked to them lovingly, told them where to catch fish and even gave them breakfast! Jesus did not give up on them when they had given up on him. He had high hopes for them and had literally invested his life in them.

✝ *Lord, I confess that like the disciples I have often tried to ignore your expectations for my life. Forgive me and enable me to stay faithful to you.*

LOVE'S TRUE RESPONSE How can we tell if we truly love someone? Love cannot be measured by emotional and verbal expressions alone. Love is tested and proved by the acts of obedience. Having restored the 'backsliding' Peter and his companions, Jesus spoke to them about more serious issues. Look at the beauty of Jesus' approach: he gains their confidence through endearing conversation and early morning breakfast! He then tests Peter's loyalty by repeated questions:

> 'Simon, son of John, do you truly love me?'
> **(part of verses 15 – 17)**

Why ask the same question three times? To make sure that Peter truly understands him and the implications of his answers. When Peter makes a positive response, Jesus spells out these implications – a practical demonstration of love by accepting twin responsibilities for two groups of people: feeding and taking care of lambs and sheep. These are the two important responsibilities of both shepherds and pastors: feeding the lambs and sheep by leading them to green pastures and taking care of the lambs and sheep by defending them from attacks by wolves. Did Peter live up to these expectations? Yes, he did, but only because the Holy Spirit empowered him on the day of Pentecost.

† *Dear Lord, thank you for the privilege of serving you. Help me to love you more even as I serve you.*

Thursday April 26   **Philippians 1.12 – 26**

LIVING ABOVE THE CIRCUMSTANCES OF LIFE Paul's letter to the Philippians is an outstanding example of life lived not 'under' circumstances but 'above' them. Paul wrote this letter when everything was going against him; he was falsely accused, beaten up, framed and imprisoned. In the Roman prison he was constantly guarded by soldiers. But his heart was free and so he writes this letter with the exuberance of Christian joy. He looks at his present life from a divine perspective.

> **Now I want you to know, brothers, that what has happened to me has really served to advance the gospel ... what has happened to me will turn out for my deliverance.**
>   **(verses 12 and 19b)**

The restrictions placed on him only helped to advance the gospel and imprisonment would lead to his deliverance. What a perspective on life! Nothing happens to us that is not allowed by the permissive will of our Heavenly Father. Paul saw everything from this perspective. Nothing in life or in death can deter him from being faithful to the risen Lord. Look at his famous words in verse 21: 'For me, to live is Christ and to die is gain.' How do we look at life's changes and chances? If Christ is in us, we shall be for him in all walks of life. Make sure that today you live not 'under' life's circumstances but 'above' them.

† *Risen Lord, grant that nothing in my life or my death will prevent me from being faithful to you.*

Friday April 27   **Revelation 1.4 – 8**

THE NAME ABOVE ALL NAMES What's in a name? Everything, according to Jewish thinking. For a Jew, a person's name is not an identity but an indication of his or her character. So, in these few verses, look at the number of names that are given to Jesus: the source of grace and peace (a greeting which combines Greek (*charis*, grace) and Jewish (*shalom*, peace) forms); the one who was and is and who is to come (repeated again in verse 8); Jesus Christ; the faithful witness; the firstborn from the dead; the ruler of the kings of the earth; the one who loves us; the one who has freed us from our sins by his blood; the one who has made us to be a kingdom and priests; the one who is coming with the clouds; and, to top them all,

'I am the Alpha and the Omega.'   (part of verse 8)

Altogether eleven names in five short verses. The rest of the book of Revelation has many more names and titles for Jesus. How many names of Jesus do we know? Apart from a few familiar ones like God, Father and Jesus, many Christians hardly know the many other names and titles that the Bible uses for him. Next time you pray, why not use some of the names for Jesus, perhaps in alphabetical order, and spend time in worship of him!

† *Jesus, name above all names,*
beautiful Saviour, glorious Lord,
Emmanuel, God is with us,
blessed Redeemer, living Word.
      Naida Hearn (Hymns Old and New, *Anglican edition, 273*)

Saturday April 28   **Psalm 16**

TRUE SECURITY   Where can we find it and who can give it to us? Security is undoubtedly one of the basic needs of humanity. Some put their trust in riches, others in fame and popularity and still others in people whom they regard and trust. But all of them will fail one day or another. This psalm tells us who can give us true security. In verses 1 – 3 David claims the Lord as his security, the only source of all good things. But along with trusting God, David also trusts God's people (*verse 3*). Trusting false gods is vanity; they can only give untold misery, not security. But those whose hearts are set on the Lord, who trust him, receive safety, security and sound counsel.

> **I have set the Lord always before me.**
> **Because he is at my right hand,**
> **I shall not be shaken.**   **(verse 8)**

Of course, making the Lord our security does not mean that we are immune to problems. Problems are bound to come as long as we live in this world. But because we have set the Lord always before us, we shall not be shaken. Verse 10 is applied to Jesus the Messiah, whose body did not experience decay and decomposition. All those who believe in him can claim these promises if they are found in him and him alone.

† *Help me, O Lord, to make you my source of total security. I know I can face all life's problems with your presence and power!*

For group discussion and personal thought

- How would you try to convince someone who is not a Christian that there will be a future resurrection of all the dead?
- Try to speak to a non-Christian this week in a friendly way and share with them your experience of the Resurrection in your daily Christian life.

NEW ROADS AHEAD 1
Change of direction

Notes by Val Ogden

based on the Good News Bible

Val Ogden worked in training and broadcasting before becoming a Methodist minister. She served in the United Church of Zambia and is now based in the UK as a minister in the Wolverhampton Trinity Circuit.

Take a moment to reflect on your journey of life and faith up to this point. Can you identify certain life-changing moments? People, places or events which made an impact on your life and caused you to think differently or even change direction? This week's stories from Acts 9 and 10 show something of Saul and Peter's faith journeys, and in particular how certain extraordinary events altered the course of their lives for ever. As we reflect on them, we too may be inspired to face the life changes and faith challenges that still lie ahead of us, and to explore the new directions God offers to us through them.

Text for the week: Acts 9.15 – 16

Sunday April 29   **Acts 9.1 – 9**

A GOOD INTRODUCTION Mrs Thompson travelled to another town and attended the local church on Sunday morning. Her own minister had given her a letter of introduction which she handed to the Secretary in the vestry. He read it and smiled. 'Ah, I see you are a very committed Christian in your home church, and even an Elder. You are most welcome. It's a blessing that God has brought you here.'

In the meantime Saul kept up his violent threats of murder against the followers of the Lord. He went to the High Priest and asked for letters of introduction to the synagogues in Damascus, so that if he should find there any followers of the Way of the Lord, he would be able to arrest them, both men and women, and bring them back to Jerusalem.   **(verses 1 – 2)**

I wonder if the synagogue officials were smiling when they read Paul's letter of introduction. Did they see his visit as a blessing – a chance to be rid of these disruptive Christians? Or as a curse – heralding fear and violence and attracting unwanted attention from the Roman authorities? Saul clearly saw his letter of introduction as written authority to pursue evil. Most of us at some time are introduced into a new situation – perhaps a new workplace or a new church community. What letter of introduction would we like to take with us? And are we the kind of newcomers who bring blessings or troubles?

† *Lord, through being introduced to me, may people be introduced to you.*

Monday April 30   Acts 9.10 – 20

A FEARFUL REPUTATION   Saul had been struck blind and helpless, but his reputation as a persecutor went before him. Ananias understandably hesitated when he was told to find Saul and lay hands on him.

> **Ananias answered, 'Lord, many people have told me about this man and about all the terrible things he has done to your people in Jerusalem. And he has come to Damascus with authority from the chief priests to arrest all who worship you.'**   **(verses 13 – 14)**

When I was seventeen, I had to be interviewed by a highly respected Professor of Theology for a place at university. People warned me that he asked very tough questions and enjoyed frightening young students. I entered his room trembling from head to foot. You can imagine how surprised I was when he smiled, told me to relax, and offered me a chocolate biscuit! People's reputations do go before them, but it is up to us as Christians whether we accept those reputations and allow them to prejudice us. Just as the hard shell of an insect or sea creature hides the soft flesh underneath, so the hardness of someone's outward personality can hide the soft heart beneath which is aching for kindness. Saul in his blindness and weakness needed God's touch through Ananias to restore him. Perhaps God is calling you and me to give the Ananias touch to someone we fear.

† *Help me, Lord, to ignore reputation and seek reality, swallow fear and speak comfort, trust your call and touch hearts. Amen*

Tuesday May 1 Acts 9.21 – 31

THE PERILS OF CHANGE Saul, who has been doing the killing, now finds that he himself is in danger. Four times in these ten verses it is recorded that the Jews, both those who spoke Greek and those from Jerusalem, wanted to kill him. Even those who didn't want to kill him could not believe that he had changed.

> **'Isn't he the one who in Jerusalem was killing those who worship that man Jesus? And didn't he come here for the very purpose of arresting those people and taking them back to the chief priests?' ... Saul went to Jerusalem and tried to join the disciples. But they would not believe that he was a disciple, and they were all afraid of him.**
>
> **(verses 21 and 26)**

Prison Fellowship is an international Christian organization which can tell many stories about prisoners who have committed their lives to Christ and are determined to be changed people. But once outside the prison, they face the same problems as Saul. Criminals they knew in prison want them dead. Family, friends and possible employers don't trust them. It was Saul's powerful preaching and personal testimony which 'proved' that he had changed (*verse* 22). We need to be open to the testimonies of those who claim they have been changed by Christ and, instead of doubting them, look positively for the proof.

✝ *I am a new creation.*
No more in condemnation.
Here in the grace of God I stand.

Wednesday May 2 Acts 10.1 – 16

DIFFERENT THINKING For the rest of this week we examine the amazing story of Peter in Acts 10. He certainly had some changes of direction to face – changes in outlook, understanding and belief. The learning process begins with a vision which comes when Peter is feeling hungry.

> **He saw heaven opened and something coming down that looked like a large sheet being lowered by its four corners to the earth. In it were all kinds of animals, reptiles, and wild birds. A voice said to him, 'Get up, Peter; kill and eat!' But Peter said, 'Certainly not, Lord! I have never eaten anything ritually unclean or defiled.'** **(verses 11 – 14)**

As the book of Acts progresses we see that the new believers joining the Church were a very mixed bunch indeed – just like the animals in Peter's vision. Jews who followed strict laws about washing and eating were suddenly mixing with non-Jews who knew nothing about such things. There were uncircumcised Gentiles alongside circumcised Jews who claimed that circumcision was a necessary requirement for joining the Church. Who was right? The issues were becoming heated and complex! So when God urged Peter to get up and eat and not to regard anything or anyone as unclean (*verse 15*), he seemed to be saying, 'New Church – new thinking!' And that change of direction challenges Peter personally, as we shall see tomorrow.

† *Lord, help me to be open towards new thinking in the life of my Church.*

Thursday May 3   **Acts 10.17 – 33**

DIFFERENT BEHAVIOUR Peter, still full of his vision, responds to an invitation from Cornelius who is a Roman army captain and therefore a Gentile. Before the vision Peter would have wanted to avoid him, but now...

> **Cornelius met him, fell at his feet, and bowed down before him. But Peter made him rise. 'Stand up,' he said, 'I myself am only a man ... You yourselves know very well that a Jew is not allowed by his religion to visit or associate with Gentiles. But God has shown me that I must not consider any person ritually unclean or defiled. And so when you sent for me, I came without any objection.'**
> **(verses 25 – 26 and 28 – 29)**

Changing traditional thinking and behaviour which is contrary to God's way, can be very hard indeed. An African Christian may know in his heart that 'all are one in Christ' but still find himself saying to his daughter, 'You can't marry a man from that tribe – they're not good people!' Perhaps the clue to changing behaviour lies in Peter's words 'I myself am only a man'. Peter's vision has made him recognize and celebrate the fact that God created us primarily as human beings. Religious, cultural and physical differences are far less important in the Creator's eyes. Have today's Christians really grasped that truth? To know it is one thing. To show it is another.

† *Christ from whom all blessings flow, perfecting the saints below,*
Hear us who thy nature share, who thy mystic body are.
(*Charles Wesley*, Hymns and Psalms, 764)

Friday May 4   **Acts 10.34 – 43**

A SERMON FROM THE HEART   Acts records a wonderful
sermon given by Peter. He speaks, not as a trained preacher, but
from his own experience of knowing Jesus (*verse 39*) and shares
the new truths he has learned through the vision.

> 'I now realize that it is true that God treats everyone on the
> same basis. Those who worship him and do what is right
> are acceptable to him, no matter what race they belong to.'
> **(verse 34)**

Trainee preachers in the British Methodist Church take a course
called 'Faith and Worship'. It can be hard work, with lots of
reading and assignments to complete, but it is well worth it. At
the end of the course, people have a much better understanding
of the Scriptures and how to prepare worship and sermons. But
of course trainee preachers need more than the course to equip
them. Like Peter, they need to preach from their own, personal
experience of following Jesus and keep alert for the messages
that God may want to communicate through them. Peter's
personal vision was not for him alone. It held a vital message
for the whole Church. What have you seen that should be
shared?

† *May my mind and my mouth be channels for your truth, O God.*

Saturday May 5   **Acts 10.44 – 48**

A SERMON WITH SPIRIT!   Before Peter had even finished
speaking, the truth of his words was confirmed in a most
wonderful way.

> The Holy Spirit came down on all those who were
> listening to his message. The Jewish believers who had
> come from Joppa with Peter were amazed that God had
> poured out his gift of the Holy Spirit on the Gentiles also.
> For they heard them speaking in strange tongues and
> praising God's greatness.   **(verses 44 – 46)**

The Jews from Joppa had heard the words and now they saw
the proof. Truths preached in words need to be confirmed by

evidence if they are to take root. That's why one minister preached the same sermon to the same congregation every Sunday for six weeks. When one member found the courage to ask why, he was told, 'I keep preaching it because I haven't yet seen any proof that you're acting on it!' By all means say 'Thank you' to a preacher after the service if he or she has done a fine job. But the greatest thanks a preacher can have, and the thing God wants most, is to see the truths that have been spoken confirmed in our lives.

✝ *O God, help us to put into action what we hear preached in church.*

For group discussion and personal thought

● What changes of direction have you faced in the past, or are you facing today in (a) your own life and (b) your church community? How do the stories of Saul and Peter inspire and help you?

NEW ROADS AHEAD 2
Crossing new boundaries

Notes by Rodney Dreyer

based on the New International Version

Rodney Dreyer is an Anglican priest from South Africa working in the Church of England. Before coming to England, he worked in the Diocese of Pretoria in the Church of the Province of Southern Africa. He is currently Vicar of Hawkhurst in Kent and also works as a facilitator/consultant in the field of theological education. He is married to Sandra and they have two teenage children.

Thresholds, crossroads, boundaries: these are all very much part of our being and our becoming as people of God. As we grow in understanding the purpose of God, we are often brought face to face with the changes and challenges he asks of us. This was true in the Early Church and is also true in the Church of this new millennium.

Text for the week: Acts 14.21 – 23

Sunday May 6   **Acts 11.1 – 18**

A TURNING POINT   The baptism of the centurion Cornelius is the turning point of the Acts of the Apostles, a decisive moment when he was filled with the Spirit in baptism. He was a Gentile!

> **'God has even granted the Gentiles repentance unto life.'**
> **(verse 18)**

God had touched the life of a person who was not one of the chosen people of God! Do I share God's openness of heart or do I regard myself as privileged? Do I feel possessive of the faith or am I open and surrendered to it? Today let us pray for the people of our world and for the Christians already active in the Church. We pray that they may be open to the world and that their way of life may present to all the authentic Word of God in the power of the Spirit.

† *Lord, open our hearts to the riches of your grace. Amen*

Monday May 7

GUIDED BY THE SPIRIT The Church is founded in Antioch, the capital of Syria, which in those days was a totally Gentile country. The Spirit directs, 'pushes', the Apostles towards the influential and important places in the world of those days.

The Lord's hand was with them, and a great number of people believed and turned to the Lord. (verse 21)

The Church finds its way when it allows itself to be guided by events and by the Holy Spirit. It is persecuted in Jerusalem, chased from its birthplace there. The Christians were dispersed and everywhere they went they founded new communities. Those who persecuted them had not expected this result when, for example, they killed Stephen and the other Christians. Do I put my trust in the Church? Do I acknowledge deep down in my being that its present difficulties are not beyond the grasp of God's hands and that they may lead to a greater missionary expansion? Do I believe that God is guiding history? Lord, I ask you to help me go beyond appearances.

✝ *Lord, open our hearts to the riches of your grace. Amen*

Tuesday May 8

THE SPIRIT SPEAKS From the beginning the communities had some structure. There were various roles such as prophets, evangelists, teachers and pastors. We are told that

while they were worshipping the Lord and fasting, the Holy Spirit said... (verse 2a)

It is interesting that their worship, which included both the reading of the Word of God and the celebration of the Eucharist, has an extra dimension to it, that of fasting. The first Christians regularly made fasting a part of their daily lives. It was while they were doing this that the Holy Spirit spoke. Because Christian communities are different from all other groups, they are conscious of possessing the Lord Jesus Christ in their midst, alive, risen from the dead, at work in the church community through the power of his Spirit. Of course, the Church contains men and women who are human, who are fallible, but these men and women are bearers of God. They listen to God and are animated by him and so they are ready and responsible to be sent out to proclaim the Word of God. Am I prepared to travel new roads in order to proclaim the Word of God in word and deed?

† *Lord, open our hearts to the riches of your grace. Amen*

Wednesday May 9   Acts 13.13 – 16, 26 – 33, 38 – 39

GROWING   The mission of Paul and Barnabas from now on will fill the pages of the book of the Acts of the Apostles. In the story, the names of many provinces and cities will be landmarks which we can check on a map. They went down to Seleucia and from there they sailed to Cyprus. They set sail from Pathos and came to Perga in Pamphilia. They went on from Perga and came to Antioch of Pisidia. In Antioch of Pisidia, which is in present Turkey, the Jewish community met together every Saturday. They sang psalms, read the Law and any of the members present could be asked to comment on the reading. This is what Jesus did on every Saturday throughout his life, attending the synagogue wherever he happened to be. Here, we see Paul doing the same, reading the Law and expounding it:

> **Standing up, Paul motioned with his hand and said: 'Men of Israel ... listen to me!'**   **(verse 16)**

Do I, like Jesus and Paul, regard the Old Testament as the plan of God? Do I believe that this plan has been achieved in the new covenant in Jesus Christ, not simply thrown out? How much do I love the Bible and the Jewish people? In line with the great prophetic tradition, Paul knows that God is present in all this, God has a stake in whatever is human. Indeed, God became incarnate in the human, in history, in geography, in a culture and a tradition. So the glory of God is a person growing and becoming and loving. And that is our calling: to help people to grow, to encourage the growth of one person or an entire human group. How can I share in this great and godly work, even in small ways? In my family? In my relationships?

† *Lord, open our hearts to the riches of your grace. Amen*

Thursday May 10   Acts 13.42 – 52

THE JOY THE SPIRIT GIVES   The Good News is spread around the city of Antioch in Pisidia, in the market places, the streets, the shops, in homes, from neighbour to neighbour. The people gather around Paul, and Paul and Barnabas speak out boldly.

> **Many ... followed Paul and Barnabas.**   **(part of verse 43)**

The people of the Old Testament were chosen first, it is true, but they could not keep the salvation of God for themselves alone. God's choice had to spread to all peoples, as indeed the prophets had foreseen and announced. The God of the created order loves everyone and it is wrong to try to keep God's grace to yourself. This applies to us also. So how do I feel about the efforts of the Church to reach out more and more to the people outside? We are told that the disciples were filled with joy. Do I experience this joy in the depths of my heart as I share the Good News with others – a joy which no failure can stop? Am I easily discouraged? Joy and the Holy Spirit go together, so let me reflect on the fact that God makes use of any instrument for his plans, including those instruments that seem to be most useless.

✝ *Lord, open our hearts to the riches of your grace. Amen*

Friday May 11   Acts 14.1 – 18

THE USELESS IDOLS OF OUR LIVES   We are told that Paul and Barnabas fled to Lystra and Derbe and preached the gospel there.

> **The Jews [at Iconium] who refused to believe stirred up the Gentiles and poisoned their minds against the brothers.**
>
> **(verse 2)**

Paul and Barnabas do not turn back in the face of persecution or difficulty. Instead, this trial becomes an opportunity to spread the Good News to more people, in other cities, to cross new boundaries. At Lystra Paul heals a man who was crippled from birth. He works the same wonders as Jesus and as Peter, who healed the paralysed beggar near the temple. But the man Paul healed was a Gentile, and so we see God showering his blessings on all those who do not yet know God. We need to ask God to broaden our hearts, so that we can live with our contemporaries without any feeling of being superior and bring people Good News so that they will turn from idols to a living God. We can make idols out of even the best things: love, profession, work, leisure, rest, health, beauty, comforts which are given absolute value. The characteristic of an idol is that it is empty, idle and ultimately disappointing, incapable of really giving us what we ask it for. So we ask the Lord to help us not to make anything more important than it really is and to give us the grace to rely on God alone for what is essential. Is God an idol or an icon for me?

✝ *Lord, open our hearts to the riches of your grace. Amen*

Saturday May 12   Acts 14.19 – 28

RETRACING OUR STEPS   Today we focus on the last part of the first missionary journey of St Paul. Paul and Barnabas go back along the way that they came, in order to strengthen the communities they have founded:

> **Paul and Barnabas appointed elders for them in each church and, with prayer and fasting, committed them to the Lord in whom they had put their trust.**   **(verse 23)**

The journey lasted about three years. From Jerusalem and through Syria the gospel had already reached and entered several Asian provinces of the Roman Empire. They travelled hundreds of kilometres on foot, on donkeys, by boat. Faith has to take root in a land, in cultures, in human communities. It is not a physical treasure which can be received one day and remain as it is. It is a life which can become stronger or weaker, grow or die out. Paul knows this, so he goes back to the new converts to strengthen them in their faith, because, he says, 'We must go through many hardships to enter the kingdom of God' (*verse 22*). This is one of Paul's great themes. Faith does not get rid of trials – Paul continues to suffer like any other man or woman. But for the Christian suffering can have meaning, it can be a painful moment which leads to the kingdom. Paul dared to speak in these words to the new converts and prepared them for the crossing of new boundaries by appointing elders in every church. You cannot live the life of faith on your own, you must be in the Church with others. Do I live my faith with others or alone? What is my sense of the Church? How do I share in the life of the local community?

✝ *Lord, open our hearts to the riches of your grace. Amen*

For group discussion and personal thought

- What was the turning point in the life of the Early Church? Why was that event so important?
- What have been the turning points in your life with Christ and with others?

110

NEW ROADS AHEAD 3
Come over and help us

Notes by Borlabi Bortey

based on the New Revised Standard Version

Borlabi Bortey is a minister of the Methodist Church of Ghana; he serves the publishing house of the Council of Churches in Ghana (Asempa Publishers) in the field of Christian literature development.

When the Early Church accepted the challenge of spreading the Good News among non-Jews, it had to come to terms with the conditions under which this assignment could successfully be carried out. This week's readings reveal the difficult circumstances in which the apostles had to work. Just as Paul, the central figure in this drama, and his colleagues persevered, so we need to press on to 'make disciples of all nations'. However, if we are to succeed, we must also learn to rely on the Holy Spirit for the courage and guidance we need.

Text for the week: Acts 17.30 – 31

Sunday May 13   Acts 15.1 – 21

NO DISCRIMINATION   The Early Church had to confront the problem of how to deal with non-Jewish believers. Peter's experience in the house of Cornelius (*Acts 10.44 – 48*) provided an insight for the guidance of the Church.

> **Peter stood up and said to them, 'My brothers, you know that in the early days God made a choice among you, that I should be the one through whom the Gentiles would hear the message of the good news and become believers. And God, who knows the human heart, testified to them by giving them the Holy Spirit, just as he did to us; and in cleansing their hearts by faith he has made no distinction between us and us.'**   **(verses 7 – 9)**

The difficulty with which the early Jewish Christians had to struggle was how to relate to non-Jewish Christians. This is a problem that recurs in all societies in all generations. The eruption of ethnic clashes ('ethnic cleansing') in many parts of the world in recent years has provided convincing evidence of how deep-seated the problem of discrimination is among human beings everywhere. All over the world, today, we need to appreciate the truth in the insight that God granted Peter: all people everywhere have equal standing before God. This means that other people (blacks, whites, racial minorities etc.) have the same dignity as ourselves and we must accept this and relate to each other in this way.

† *Heavenly Father, grant us grace to give equal dignity to all people everywhere, whatever their colour, race or creed, so that we may live in peace with one another.*

Monday May 14 Acts 16.1 – 10

DISCOVERING GOD'S LEADING AND GUIDANCE The decision of the leaders of the early Church (*Acts 15*) to admit Gentiles into the Church without insisting that they must observe Jewish ceremonial and ritual laws such as circumcision, encouraged Paul to expand on his work among the Gentiles. However, Paul submitted himself to God's guidance in deciding which regions or towns he could or could not visit to preach the good news.

> **When they had come opposite Mysia, they attempted to go into Bithynia, but the Spirit of Jesus did not allow them; so, passing by Mysia, they went down to Troas. During the night Paul had a vision: there stood a man of Macedonia pleading with him and saying, 'Come over to Macedonia and help us.' When he had seen the vision, we immediately tried to cross over to Macedonia, being convinced that God had called us to proclaim the good news to them.**
>
> **(verses 7 – 10)**

It is not clear how Paul was able to decide that his 'dream' was a real message or direction from God, or how the Holy Spirit gave his directions to Paul and his team. Although it would be nice to be told what God wants us to do in very clear terms, God's guidance in a particular situation does not always seem to come in simple or clear terms. Perhaps the silence of Scripture on how the Holy Spirit spoke to the early missionaries, or exactly how Paul received his vision, should teach us that there are no strict rules on how to know God's guidance. It may vary from person to person, and we should be cautious about accepting someone else's experience as the only way to discover God's will. If we learn to depend on God, he will grant us his guidance whenever the need arises.

† *Dear God, grant us the fellowship of your Holy Spirit which we need to keep us in tune with you in our everyday lives.*

Tuesday May 15   Acts 16.11 – 24

RECEPTION AND OPPOSITION We often seem to think that if we encounter difficulties in life, it is because we have deviated from God's plan for us. St Paul's experience in Philippi reveals a different picture: we can encounter both success and difficulties precisely where God wants us to serve.

> **A certain woman named Lydia, a worshipper of God, was listening to us; she was from the city of Thyatira and a dealer in purple cloth. The Lord opened her heart to listen eagerly to what was said by Paul. When she and her household were baptized, she urged us, saying, 'If you have judged me to be faithful to the Lord, come and stay at my home.' And she prevailed upon us.**   **(verses 14 – 15)**

After the wonderful conversion of Lydia's household, disaster struck when Paul cast out the spirit of divination in a slave girl. Paul and Silas were dragged to the magistrates.

> **The crowd joined in attacking them, and the magistrates had them stripped of their clothing and ordered them to be beaten with rods. After they had given them a severe flogging, they threw them into prison and ordered the jailer to keep them securely.**   **(verses 22 – 23)**

Like Paul, we should expect that we may sometimes have to endure suffering precisely for doing what God requires of us and not necessarily because we have deviated from doing God's will.

† *When we experience mixed fortunes or difficulties in life, grant us grace to endure and not to doubt your guidance or leading in our lives.*

Wednesday May 16   Acts 16.25 – 40

GOD OPENS DOORS THROUGH DIFFICULT TIMES Paul and Silas maintained their confidence in God in spite of the misfortune they suffered. They prayed and praised God and their faith was rewarded: an earthquake opened the prison gates. The jailer, fearing that the prisoners had escaped, was about to kill himself.

113

> But Paul shouted in a loud voice, 'Do not harm yourself, for we are all here.' The jailer called for lights, and rushing in, he fell down trembling before Paul and Silas. Then he brought them outside and said, 'Sirs, what must I do to be saved?' They answered, 'Believe on the Lord Jesus, and you will be saved, you and your household.'
>
> (verses 28 – 31)

God had a purpose in allowing Paul and Silas to be thrown into jail: it opened a door for the salvation of yet another household in Philippi. The jailer's household benefited from their jail experience and, in spite of opposition, the invitation to Macedonia was fulfilling God's purposes. We also need to hold on firmly to our confidence in the saving grace of our Lord Jesus even when we experience hard times. Paul's advice to 'Give thanks in all circumstances' (1 Thessalonians 5.18) comes from his own experience of how God rewards such faith and trust in him.

† Lord, give us grace to continue trusting you even when the going becomes tough.

Thursday May 17   Acts 17.1 – 15

DILIGENT STUDY PRODUCES AN INFORMED FAITH
The mission in Macedonia continued to be a mixed blessing. In Thessalonica, some Jews (and a few Greeks) accepted the message but other Jews opposed Paul and Silas so violently that they were compelled to leave during the night for Beroea, where they received a different reception.

> These Jews were more receptive than those in Thessalonica, for they welcomed the message very eagerly and examined the scriptures every day to see whether these things were so. Many of them therefore believed, including not a few Greek women and men of high standing.   (verses 11 – 12)

The Jews in Beroea checked the truth of Paul's message from the scriptures. Their search paid off: they discovered the truth for themselves and so believed the message Paul preached, that Jesus indeed was the Messiah. It is not enough to believe what we are told. We need to deepen our faith by searching the scriptures for ourselves. We shall be amazed at what we can discover from a diligent study of the scriptures.

† Lord, may your Holy Spirit light up the pages of the scriptures so that as we read your word each day, our lives will testify to your saving grace at work in us and lead others to believe in you.

REACHING OUT TO PEOPLE OF OTHER FAITHS   Paul had to move on from the district of Macedonia because of continued opposition from the Jews of Thessalonica, who pursued him to Beroea. Finally, he crossed from Macedonia to Athens, where he engaged in a vigorous debate with a larger audience of philosophers.

> **Then Paul stood in front of the Areopagus and said: 'Athenians, I see how extremely religious you are in every way. For as I went through the city and looked carefully at the objects of your worship, I found among them an altar with the inscription, "To an unknown god". What therefore you worship as unknown, this I proclaim to you.'**
> **(verses 22 – 23)**

Paul could not be satisfied with the fact that religion was an important factor in the lives of the people of Athens. Their beliefs provided him with an opportunity to lead them on to what he believed was a greater truth: the need to know God and his self-revelation in Jesus. Talking to people of other faiths about Jesus can be difficult. But if we depend on the insight which the Holy Spirit provides, other belief systems can provide a point of contact for the gospel of Jesus Christ.

† *Grant us wisdom, dear Lord, to know how to relate to people of other faiths.*

THE GOSPEL CALLS ALL PEOPLE TO REPENTANCE Paul argued from the Athenians' belief in the existence of many gods to the affirmation that there is one God who is the creator of the universe. From there, Paul went on to declare what this Creator-God requires from his creatures, human beings:

> **'While God has overlooked the times of human ignorance, now he commands all people everywhere to repent, because has fixed a day on which he will have the world judged in righteousness by a man whom he has appointed, and of this he has given assurance to all by raising him from the dead.'**
> **(verses 30 – 31)**

For Paul, the resurrection of Jesus from the dead points to the authority that God has given to Jesus as the final judge of all humanity. In order to receive a verdict of 'not guilty', the essential requirement is *repentance*. This one word sums up all that Paul has been trying to tell people everywhere on this journey – no matter what it cost him.

† *Lord, grant us grace to reach out to people wherever you lead us, and wisdom to share the gospel and bring people into your saving grace by turning their hearts away from sin. Amen*

For group discussion and personal thought

- Discuss some of the causes of conflict in our modern world. In what ways can we, as Christians, contribute to the search for peace and reconciliation?
- How far is it true to say that we could face difficulties or suffer hardships even though we may be doing precisely what God requires of us? What can we learn from this week's readings about how to react to hardships and suffering?

Introduce a friend to

LIGHT for our PATH or **WORDS FOR TODAY**

For this year's books, send us just **£2.00** per book (including postage), together with your friend's name and address, and we will do the rest.

(This offer is only available in the UK, after 1 June 2001. Subject to availability.)

IBRA

Order through your IBRA representative, or from the UK address on page 285.

NEW ROADS AHEAD 4
Do not be afraid

Notes by John Carden

based on the Revised English Bible

An Anglican priest who has worked with the Church Mission Society in Asia and the Middle East, John Carden compiled the WCC Ecumenical Prayer Cycle, *With All God's People.*

'I once saw the track of a bleeding animal across the snow. That was Paul's track across Europe.' This was how one theologian described the hardships and incredible sufferings endured by Paul on his long and arduous journeys with the gospel. It was not a straight track. There were times when Paul changed course, took risks, or sought refuge; times when he was encouraged; times when he needed the company and support of others. As we follow his track this week, we shall meet some of the people who accompanied him on different stages of his journey.

> This day also must my blood flow
> following in that same blood-stained pattern.
> (Toyohiko Kagawa, a Japanese Christian)

Text for the week: Acts 20.24

Sunday May 20   **Acts 18.1 – 17**

OPEN THE DOORS TO CHRIST   In October 1978, a little-known Polish cardinal stepped into St Peter's Square in Rome as Pope and proclaimed the stirring message, 'Be not afraid. Open the doors to Christ!' Nineteen centuries earlier the apostle Paul, newly arrived in Corinth and also at a turning point in his mission, received a message from God very much along the same lines.

> **One night in a vision the Lord said to Paul, 'Have no fear: go on with your preaching and do not be silenced. I am with you, and no attack shall harm you, for I have many in this city who are my people.'**   **(verses 9 -10)**

Paul faced opposition from the Jews, and most of the doors and hearts that opened to Christ belonged to Gentiles. To support him in this mission, God had given him two new companions, exiles from Rome, who were to play a leading role in the life of the Church. In today's mission their places are often taken by African and Asian Christians who, like Aquila and Priscilla, can be found helping struggling Christian communities far from home.

† *Look with compassion, O God, upon the little companies of your faithful people who, in difficult places in the world, are seeking to uphold the banner of the cross, and if the comfort of human sympathy and support seems far from them, be their companion and their source of hope, courage and perseverance. (Prayer of a Ugandan Christian)*

Monday May 21 Acts 18.18 – 28

TIME OUT FOR A HAIRCUT! The stops and starts and frequent changes of direction in the apostolic activity described here seem to indicate that these early servants of the gospel had no clear mission strategy. With a glorious freedom, they simply grasped the opportunities presented to them by the Spirit. And sometimes even Paul went off course.

Paul stayed on at Corinth for some time, and then took leave of the congregation. Accompanied by Priscilla and Aquila, he sailed for Syria, having had his hair cut off at Cenchreae in fulfilment of a vow. (verse 18)

Paul's ritual haircut in Cenchreae was perhaps intended to appease the Jewish Christians, but it seems to have been a false move. Paul usually stood firm against those who wanted all Christians to be Jews first. We all take such false steps from time to time and then have to get back to the right route, which the German theologian Dietrich Bonhoeffer described as 'God's crooked yet straight path'. In Ephesus another character enters the scene – Apollos. In growing churches, then and now, strangers with a calling to preach or heal do suddenly appear. It needs great wisdom and courage to decide whether such a call is genuine and to welcome unusual visitors in the service of the Body of Christ. Aquila and Priscilla seemed to possess these gifts, and gave Apollos their full support.

† *In all the claims made upon our time and energy, help us to discern the leading of your Holy Spirit, and to follow it through.*

Tuesday May 22   **Acts 19.1 – 20**

TAKING RISKS   When Paul returned to Ephesus he found a small group of disciples who had received a form of baptism which was similar to the baptism offered by John the Baptist. We do not know why this baptism was different; perhaps it put too much stress on sin and the need for repentance and failed to convey the sense of release and the assurance of the Holy Spirit promised by Jesus. Paul remains in Ephesus to remedy this:

> **During the next three months he attended the synagogue and with persuasive argument spoke boldly about the kingdom of God.**   **(verse 8)**

Other incidents reported in today's reading point to the risks involved in sharing the gospel across cultural and religious divides, especially in places where popular religion, which is sometimes almost superstitious, plays an important part in the lives of ordinary people. The Christian faith, then and now, is all about taking risks. Can we be the Church without taking risks?

† *Help us, good Lord, to take on in your name the risks involved in being Christians. (Adapted from a prayer used by a group of French women involved in peace and justice issues)*

Wednesday May 23   **Acts 19.21 – 41**

CONFLICT AND DELIVERANCE   The Sri Lankan evangelist D T Niles points out that in the Gospels the mission of Jesus proceeds in three stages. At first he goes to the house of Israel; just before the crucifixion it becomes a mission to the nations; and after the resurrection it is a mission to the world. After the Ascension Paul adds a fourth stage, a mission to the cosmic powers. The cult of the pagan fertility goddess Artemis was in effect the local cosmic power of the time. Her temple played a central role in the life and trade of Ephesus; any threat to her supremacy, and to the pilgrimage trade, was vehemently resisted by those who had most to lose. She had a great and vicious influence on the emotional and popular religious life of the city, so that it was easy to whip up support in defence of her shrine. Paul's preaching was not specifically directed against Artemis, but it brought him into conflict with her power and resulted in ugly violence.

> **The whole city was in an uproar; they made a concerted rush into the theatre, hustling along with them Paul's**

travelling companions ... Paul wanted to appear before the assembly but the other Christians would not let him. Even some of the dignitaries ... who were friendly towards him, sent a message urging him not to venture into the theatre.

(verses 29 – 31)

In Britain recently the same reaction to the conflict with cosmic powers has been seen in the violent opposition to the use of advertising hoardings by the Salvation Army to display horrifying pictures of the universal evils of child poverty, homelessness, drug abuse and prostitution. The prayer featured with them must also have often been on the lips of the Christians in Ephesus:

✝ *Deliver us from evil.*

Thursday May 24, Ascension Day   Acts 20.17 – 24

PAUL'S PERSONAL EVALUATION   'Do you never cry?' a close friend asked Pope John Paul. 'Never outside,' he replied. 'We can be sure, however,' adds the friend, 'that every morning when he brings the world's suffering before the Lord, there are abundant tears "inside".' Having left the Christians in Ephesus in a difficult situation, Paul doubtless thought much about them during his subsequent travels. And so, on his way from Corinth to Jerusalem, he urges the elders from Ephesus to meet him in Miletus. Here Paul delivers his personal evaluation. He is very self-disciplined in the way he describes his activities. He does not focus on his own sufferings; instead, he concentrates on what is essential for building up the Church. His own disappointments and personal danger are unimportant compared with the task assigned to him.

'For myself, I set no store by life; all I want is to finish the race, and complete the task which the Lord Jesus assigned to me, that of bearing my testimony to the gospel of God's grace.'

(verse 24)

Today, Pope John Paul is a notable example of those many people in many lands who, in spite of the demands made upon their physical and spiritual resources, continue to bear 'testimony to the gospel of God's grace'.

✝ *Help us, Lord, to 'run with resolution the race which lies ahead of us, our eyes fixed on Jesus' (Hebrews 12.1 – 2).*

TAKING LEAVE   A Christian minister told how, as a child in a remote rural area of the USA, he frequently took a short cut through a thistle field in his haste to get home from school, and then spent much time removing the burrs from his feet. In later life *Running through the Thistles* became the title of a collection of essays in which ministers of many denominations shared their experiences of leaving congregations for which they had had pastoral responsibility. They often spent time preparing for their arrival in the new place, but gave little thought to how they departed from the old place. As a result, they carried unfinished business (thistle burrs) with them, which made the next phase of their ministry difficult. Paul obviously felt that he had not done enough to prepare the Christians in Ephesus for his departure and he wanted to clear up a number of points regarding his relationship with them, so that he left no unfinished business. After his wonderful instructions to them in verses 28 – 31, with their ominous warning of troubles to come, Paul and the Ephesian elders have a very emotional leave-taking.

> **There were loud cries of sorrow from them all, as they folded Paul in their arms and kissed him; what distressed them most was his saying that they would never see his face again.   (verses 37 – 38)**

The leave-taking was undoubtedly difficult; but both for the Ephesians and for those Paul would meet on the next stages of his journey, it was an incalculable blessing.

✝ *God be in our arriving, and in our departing.*

CHRISTIANS NEVER START FROM SCRATCH   The promise of Jesus in Mark 10.29 – 30, that those who leave behind their natural family for the sake of the gospel will be given even more family members, has been most wonderfully realized in the welcome and caring offered to strangers in the New Testament Church. Today's reading confirms this, with its account of hospitality given and received, shared joys and sorrows, and examples of mutual caring and support against a background of persecution and hardship.

> **At the end of our stay we packed our baggage and took the road up to Jerusalem. Some of the disciples from Caesarea**

came along with us, to direct us to a Cypriot called Mnason, a Christian from the early days, with whom we were to spend the night. (verses 15 – 16)

Present-day believers – especially those who do a great deal of travelling, or those who take the trouble to make contact with the local Christian community when they travel – often say that as Christians they never 'start from scratch', right at the beginning of a relationship. Wherever they are, they can draw on the rich resources of the whole Body of Christ.

† *Walk carefully as you go from here,*
God is there before you.
Walk humbly as you go from here,
the churches await your coming.
Walk softly as you go from here,
for the Spirit is abroad in all the earth,
and the voice of the Spirit speaks in every place.
(Words of an unknown Chinese Christian)

For group discussion and personal thought

- What role does taking risks have in the practice of the Christian faith?
- Share some of your experiences of saying 'goodbye'. Were these good experiences or could they have been handled better?

NEW ROADS AHEAD 5
The Spirit leads us on 1

Notes by Peter Cotterell

based on the Good News Bible

Peter Cotterell is a Uniting Church parish minister in Wynyard, on the north west coast of the beautiful island of Tasmania, Australia. Ordained in 1977, he has ministered in a number of rural parishes. He has also served the Uniting Church on local, regional, state and national committees. He was Moderator of the Synod of Tasmania for 1993-95. Married to Sally, they have four young children.

Jesus knew he was approaching the time of his death. He was concerned that his followers should understand the role of the Holy Spirit and the importance of their future ministry after his resurrection and ascension. The task may have been daunting but they were not alone.

Text for the week: John 14.16 – 17

Sunday May 27   **John 14.15 – 24**

ANOTHER HELPER When I was 16 years old I was introduced to Jesus and he became my closest friend. I began to attend a Bible study group with members of the church where I became a Christian and I read stories I had never seen before. The Bible came alive to me. The Holy Spirit was clearly at work in my life, but there was more that Jesus wanted me to have.

> 'I will ask the Father, and he will give you another Helper, who will stay with you for ever. He is the Spirit who reveals the truth about God. The world cannot receive him, because it cannot see him or know him. But you know him, because he remains with you and is in you.'
>
> **(verses 16 – 17)**

But this was scary stuff! The Holy Spirit in me? It was ten years before I submitted to Jesus' promise and asked him to fill me with the Holy Spirit. I did not feel anything happen as a result of the prayer but was challenged to accept by faith that the prayer had been answered. The next day the change was obvious. I walked around with a permanent smile on my face. I was flooded with an aching longing for people everywhere to come to know Jesus. I also felt something of the deep pain of rejection that God must feel when we turn away from him.

✝ *Lord, continue to fill us each day with the exhilarating power of your Holy Spirit.*

Monday May 28   **John 14.25 – 31**

. **PEACE, ABIDING PEACE** The opening verses of this chapter of John's Gospel are often read at funeral services because of the comfort the words of Jesus can bring to the grieving heart. The Holy Spirit is referred to as the Advocate, the Friend, the Helper, the Comforter. It is the work of the Spirit to minister the things of Jesus to us. Just as the presence of the Spirit may bring great joy and exhilaration, so the Spirit can minister a deep and abiding peace.

> **'Peace is what I leave with you; it is my own peace that I give you. I do not give it as the world does. Do not be worried and upset; do not be afraid.'**   **(verse 27)**

As Jesus approached his own death his thoughts were for his friends and the trials they were about to endure. He reassured them that he loved them and commanded them to love him. It was in this relationship that they would find a secure anchor in the storm about to descend on them. Christians throughout the ages have discovered that in the darkest hour Christ, the light of the world, is with them, and in the presence of the Holy Spirit they find a deep and abiding peace.

✝ *You know our every circumstance, Lord Jesus, our exhilarating joy and our deep despair and through it all you remain in us. Thank you.*

Tuesday May 29   **John 15.18 – 27**

IF IT IS GOOD ENOUGH FOR JESUS...!   Christians are one with Christ. Earlier in this chapter of John's Gospel Jesus used the image of a vine and its branches, reminding us that he is the vine and we are the branches. Only by remaining in the vine can we ever hope to bear fruit for the kingdom. But the response of the world will be mixed. Some will ignore us, pretending not to see; some will welcome the Good News that we bring; others will be openly hostile and persecute us. This is nothing peculiar – it was the same for Jesus.

'Remember what I told you: "Slaves are not greater than their master." If people persecuted me, they will persecute you too; if they obeyed my teaching, they will obey yours too.' (verse 20)

Christians in some parts of the world suffer more open hostility than we do in Australia; we are more likely to be greeted with apathy than hostility. However, the key issue is not one of greater or lesser persecution, it is one of relationship with Jesus. Whether in Australia or in Africa, Christians identify with Jesus, we are made one with him through the power of the Holy Spirit. This is our great privilege and the source of our power to share the Good News.

✝ *Lord, we come to you; hold us close and renew us in the power of your Holy Spirit.*

Wednesday May 30 John 16.1 – 15

A TRINITY OF LOVE Jesus never acts on his own authority; he acts only according to the will of the Father. Similarly the Holy Spirit takes the things of Jesus and ministers them to us.

'When, however, the Spirit comes, who reveals the truth about God, he will lead you into all the truth. He will not speak on his own authority, but he will speak of what he hears, and will tell you of things to come. He will give me glory, because he will take what I say and tell it to you.' (verses 13 – 14)

There is fantastic unity in the things of God. Similarly, when God makes his home with us we do not get just a bit of God but the whole Trinity comes to dwell (*John 14.23*). In some wonderful, mysterious way the whole of creation is caught up in this unity through the saving death and resurrection of Jesus. This is why the Church is constantly called to live in unity, to be servants of one another, to love one another as Christ has loved us. It is so that we may reflect the reality of the perfect unity of God in the mirror of our relationships within the congregation.

✝ *Lord, forgive our foolish ways which fail to reflect your love and unity.*

Thursday May 31 Luke 24.44 – 53

ONLY THROUGH THE SPIRIT Our high calling in Christ Jesus is a daunting prospect if we are left to our own resources.

But thanks be to God, the Holy Spirit comes to empower us to be witnesses to the unity and love of God.

> **'You are witnesses of these things. And I myself will send upon you what my Father has promised. But you must wait in the city until the power from above comes down upon you.'**
> **(verses 48 – 49)**

Just as a torch cannot shine without the power of the battery, so we are powerless without the Spirit. We may pretend, we may even convince some people that we are walking in the power of God, but there is no mistaking the genuine article. When the 'power from above' is present it is like the sap which flows through the tree, carrying life to every branch, or the oil which lubricates each moving part of an engine and stops it seizing up. We may be Christians who love the Lord dearly, we may know the witness of the Spirit that we are children of God, and yet Jesus may still have more to give. Without the Holy Spirit, the power of God, our ministry is less productive. We need the power from above.

✝ *O Lord, do not let us begin this day without the knowledge that we have power from above for the ministry to which you call us.*

Friday June 1   **Isaiah 44.1 – 8**

ONE BRICK AT A TIME   In the stage show *Barnum*, the date for the opening of the legendary American showman P. T. Barnum's American Museum has nearly come. He is sure that the building will never be ready in time, but his wife, Charity, pulls him out of his depression by announcing, in a wonderful song, that the museum will be ready if it is built 'one brick at a time'. God values each individual so much that he has adopted this same strategy, one person at a time.

> **'One by one, people will say, "I am the LORD's."**
> **They will come to join the people of Israel.**
> **They will each mark the name of the LORD on their arms and call themselves members of God's people.'**
> **(verse 5)**

Our mission, empowered by the Spirit, is first and foremost to individuals. We bear witness to the kingdom of God which has already come in the person of Christ, but it is the Holy Spirit who converts by removing the blindness from the eyes so that each person can see. One by one people will say, 'I am the Lord's'. This may seem a slow strategy, but it is the only way that each individual can be treated with the respect due to one created in the image of God.

† *Thank you that you love us so much that you will leave the ninety-nine and individually seek after each one of us.*

Saturday June 2 — Ephesians 4.7 – 16

PEOPLE ARE GIFTS TOO   Jesus is very generous. He gives himself to us in his ministry, death and resurrection; he gives us the Spirit so that we can know who we are and whose we are and be empowered for ministry. But it doesn't end there! He also gives us people as gifts – apostles, prophets, evangelists, pastors and teachers. He wants his Church to be well equipped and strong to fulfil its purpose.

He did this to prepare all God's people for the work of Christian service, in order to build up the body of Christ. And so we shall all come together to that oneness in our faith and in our knowledge of the Son of God; we shall become mature people, reaching to the very height of Christ's full stature. **(verses 12 – 13)**

The Church provides the opportunity to practise living in harmony, living in unity. The image is of a body in which we are all interconnected and the body grows as each part does its assigned task. Our commission is to go into all the world bearing witness to the presence and power of Christ. God has not abandoned his world, he has saved it in Christ.

† *Thank you, Lord, for those in the body of Christ who help to equip us for the task to which we are called. May we be open to their ministry and to the leading of the Spirit so that the world may know that Christ has come.*

For group discussion and personal thought

- In what ways do you see the Spirit at work in your life, in your church and in your community?
- Who are the 'gifts of Christ' to you? How do you show your appreciation and encourage them in their ministry?

NEW ROADS AHEAD 6
The Spirit leads us on 2

Notes by Miriam Lopes

based on the New English Bible

Miriam Lopes is a minister of the Portuguese Methodist Church, in charge of the missionary region of Lisbon which includes two mainly African congregations. She is a member of the theological commission of the European Methodist Council, and has two children.

As its title suggests, this week's theme is about the opening up of new beginnings, new roads, a new way of life, by the Spirit. At Pentecost the disciples passed through a baptism of fire, a new birth into this new life. This new life is described in our readings from the letter to the Romans and the week ends with the great vision from the book of Revelation of the Son of Man in all his glory as the source and fulfilment of the mission of the Kingdom of God.

Text for the week: Romans 8.18 – 25

Sunday June 3   Acts 2.1 – 21

THEY WERE ALL FILLED WITH THE HOLY SPIRIT God created human beings by blowing the fire of his spirit into the body he had made from the dust of the ground (*Genesis 2.7*). Now, in a spectacular way on the day of Pentecost, the same Spirit that was in Jesus re-creates his disciples through a new birth by fire. The Spirit awakens and opens their consciousness and capacities to the universal dimension of the gospel.

> **They were all together in one place, when suddenly there came from the sky a noise like that of a strong driving wind ... And there appeared to them tongues like flames of fire, dispersed among them and resting on each one. And they were all filled with the Holy Spirit and began to talk in other tongues, as the Spirit gave them power of utterance.** (verses 1b – 4)

This same Spirit is always at work, in every age, moving and enabling people to reach out to others across barriers of language or any other difficulty. The love of God is stronger than anything else and when we feel in ourselves the wonderful joy of his love for other people, we too can do incredible things. The Spirit opens out our understanding and our abilities in a way we have never known before. God always provides the skills that we need for our mission.

† *O Lord, we often try to bring people into our own religious group through pride in getting results, and trust too much in our own abilities, instead of breaking out of ourselves, truly loving others and bringing your powerful transforming love to them as instruments of your peace. Please come and change us into loving hearts, open to trust in the power of your Spirit.*

Monday June 4   **Romans 8.1 – 8**

WE ARE FREE FROM OLD CONDEMNATIONS   Can you remember a moment when your people, or people from another nation or group, were liberated from war or oppression and old imprisonments were abolished by a new order? Paul describes the liberation brought by Jesus Christ, who conquers our separation from God, abolishes the old Law and the deadly oppression of our lower nature and opens up a new and different way of life for those who trust him.

There is no condemnation for those who are united with Christ Jesus, because in Christ Jesus the life-giving law of the Spirit has set you free from the law of sin and death.
(verses 1 – 2)

The Spirit cuts through the soil of our old life like the strong roots of a plant – both are filled with the principle of life. There will always be those who prefer to stay in the old, corrupt system; blinded by their own guilt and ambition, they do not notice that they are being dragged towards death. God is a threat to their position because he reminds them that there is another way, a way which they see as too risky to take.

† *O Lord, you are like the woman at the well: you bring your jar to the spring and draw up water so that it can come into the light and be used. Like those many drops of water, you free us from the darkness of death, unite us to you and give us purpose in life. Fill your jar from the water of my life and use it to do your will. Amen*

Tuesday June 5   **Romans 8.9 – 13**

THE SPIRIT WILL GIVE NEW LIFE TO YOUR MORTAL BODIES   Whether you live or die, whether you are good or bad, whether you are ruled by the Spirit or by your sinful nature, does not depend on your family ties, tradition or religious group. What you say you are does not matter. The only true proof that you belong to the Spirit is how you choose to live and make decisions: according to the way of Christ, or according to your lower nature. This battle takes place within ourselves right to the end.

If Christ is dwelling within you, then although the body is a dead thing because you sinned, yet the spirit is life itself because you have been justified. (verse 10)

Once we are free from sin, we shall also be free from death. If Christ is not in us, our own selfishness overpowers us and leads us towards death. But if we choose to be in Christ, our selfishness is killed off. This is the sign that the Spirit is in us and he will raise us as he raised Jesus and we shall live for ever.

✝ *Lord Jesus, help us always to remember the work your Spirit has done in us already, so that we may fight our selfishness with renewed commitment and always choose your way.*

Wednesday June 6   **Romans 8.14 – 17**

BY THE SPIRIT WE ARE GOD'S CHILDREN   As we detach ourselves from our false way of life in order to live the life of Christ, we may find that we lose part of our old identity. Now it no longer matters that we were born into this family, that we live on this side of town, or belong to this group. It is more important that we belong to the largest family of all, which is older than all blood relationships: the universal family which has God himself as its father.

The Spirit you have received is not a spirit of slavery leading you back into a life of fear, but a Spirit that makes us sons, enabling us to cry 'Abba! Father!' (verse 15)

If we remain united to Jesus through suffering and trust him as we die to our old ways and are reborn into God's new world, we shall share in his joy and his sonship.

✝ *God our Father, like a good parent you teach us step by step to walk in your new way and to learn a new kind of loving family relationship in your kingdom. Keep us always in this unity with you and our brother Jesus Christ.*

Thursday June 7   **Romans 8.18 – 25**

HOPE OVERCOMES SUFFERING   Like the pains of childbirth, pain and suffering are part of the process of being born into new life in Christ. But the suffering is small compared to the joy of birth.

> **The created universe waits with eager expectation ... to be freed from the shackles of mortality and enter upon the liberty and splendour of the children of God ... the whole created universe groans in all its parts as if in the pangs of childbirth.   (part of verses 19, 21 and 22)**

We are not separate from the rest of the world. Soon, all creation will experience this new birth. It is hope that enables us to continue suffering without despair, waiting quietly and confidently. And the hoping and suffering, the waiting and trusting will make the joyful end even more precious. It will have greater value because we have longed for it and because, on the way, we have left behind some painful parts of ourselves. It will be a great moment because it has come about in us and through us.

✝ *Thank you, Lord, for the Day we long for, which we feel already in our hearts and our hopes.*

Friday June 8   **Romans 8.26 – 30**

THE SPIRIT PLEADS FOR US   We are weak and need help to get us through the sufferings which come before rebirth. We cannot even pray in the right way. But we are not alone.

> **[The Spirit] co-operates for good with those who love God and are called according to his purpose.   (verse 28)**

The truth is, we are on our way. We have reached a point of no return, even if we do not seem to know how to go on. This is because we have been chosen by God; he has put us where we are because he wants us to be like his Son and to share his glory. So he gives us all the help we need and the best possible company on our road to him – his own Spirit.

✝ *There are moments when our journey is so hard that all we can do is hope, wait and trust you to speak the word or act for our good. Thank you, Lord, that yours is the word of life.*

Saturday June 9   **Revelation 1.9 – 20**

CHRIST IS ALIVE IN GLORY   Christ is both the beginning of our journey and the place where we shall arrive. Through the visions of John he brings hope and confidence to the churches in Asia, the communities of those who belong to him.

> **I am the first and the last, and I am the living one; for I was dead and now I am alive for evermore, and I hold the keys of Death and Death's domain. Write down therefore what you have seen.** (verse 18)

Those who are waiting in suffering and almost in despair, those who do not know how they can continue with the journey, need to know that Christ is the lord of life. Through John's vision and writing, Christ tells us that, by his glory and his angels, he is caring for his churches and that they will enter into that glory. He wants to give them a vision of hope, a vision of the glorious future which will follow their time of pain.

✝ *One day we shall overcome the difficulties of this life and, by the power of your Spirit, fulfil your plan for us. Then, Lord, we shall see as John saw and share your glory. Your will be done, for yours is the glory for ever.*

For group discussion and personal thought

● What are the barriers which stop you proclaiming God's love to other people?
● Do you see faith as a journey along a road? What other pictures could you use to describe our movement towards God?
● What things have you had to leave behind in your journey towards God?

NEW ROADS AHEAD 7
Letting go of the past 1 (Galatians)

Notes by Kate Hughes

based on the New Revised Standard Version

The letter to the Galatians seems to have been written to new Christians who came from a Jewish background. They had turned to the new way with enthusiasm, but then started to question what they had done. Would God really take care of them if they did not earn his love by keeping the Jewish law? Release from the slavery of sin can feel scary – can they cope with freedom, or will they feel safer if they go back to doing things the Jewish way? Paul's letter is a mixture of reassurance, encouragement, scolding and firmness. Underneath it all is a love which cannot bear to see his Galatian children fall back into the prison of the law.

Text for the week: Galatians 3.27

Sunday June 10   **Galatians 1.1 – 10**

NO TURNING BACK In all his letters, Paul is careful to make clear to his converts that the gospel, the good news, he brings them is not his gospel. He did not invent it.

> **Paul an apostle – sent neither by human commission nor from human authorities, but through Jesus Christ and God the Father, who raised him from the dead...**   **(verse 1)**

The gospel that Paul preaches is simply the truth. If something is true, then nothing that human beings can do can change it. Human beings may choose to ignore the truth, or refuse to believe it, but their actions cannot make the truth any less true. So truth is above human feelings. It is there, it will not go away simply because we do not like it, it challenges us to make a decision – choose to believe it or choose not to believe it. Then make a decision to act on the consequences of that first choice.

† *Lord, strengthen me to renew every day my decision to believe the truth of your gospel.*

MAKING OUR OWN DECISION   The decision to accept or reject the truth of the gospel has to be our own decision. Even if we are brought up in a Christian family, at some point we have to make our own decision – do we believe that what we have been taught is the truth? If it is, what are we going to do about it? Other people can tell us about the content of this truth; they can persuade us that agreeing with it is the best thing to do; they can attract us to it by their behaviour and their faith. But they cannot make the decision for us. At some point, we have to look straight at God and say, 'Yes, I think your gospel is true, and I will learn to live according to your teaching' or say, 'No, I do not want to accept your truth; I am going to walk away from it and from you.' In this passage, Paul shares with his readers, and with us, his moment of decision about the truth.

> But when God, who had set me apart before I was born and called me through his grace, was pleased to reveal his Son to me, so that I might proclaim him among the Gentiles, I did not confer with any human being.   **(verses 15 – 16)**

Only after Paul had spent time in the desert country of Arabia, thinking through what it meant for him to accept the truth about Christ, did he make contact again with the Christians in Damascus and, later, with the apostles in Jerusalem.

† *Lord, you send us many people to help us on our way to you; but in the end, the decision is between you and me. Give me the courage to say 'Yes' to you every day of my life.*

RECOGNIZING GRACE IN OTHERS   It is natural, if something has worked for us, to want to share it with other people. But this natural wish to share good ideas can all too easily turn into an insistence that other people must do things our way. Because our experience of God is right for us, we are tempted to criticize others whose experience of God is different. Paul met this problem in his day. Some Jews who became Christians tried to insist that everyone who became a Christian must become a Jew first, be circumcised and keep the Jewish law. Peter, the leader of the apostles, had had a special vision from God before he was prepared to extend the mission of the Church to non-Jews, the uncircumcised Gentiles (*Acts 10 and*

15). Paul refused to be turned aside from his calling from God, which was to bring the good news to the Gentiles.

When James and Cephas and John, who were acknowledged pillars, recognized the grace that had been given to me, they gave to Barnabas and me the right hand of fellowship, agreeing that we should go to the Gentiles and they to the circumcised. (verse 9)

✝ *Grant us, O Lord, the tolerance to accept that not everyone will share our personal experience of you; help us not to criticize them or insist on our way but to rejoice in the variety of your children.*

Wednesday June 13   **Galatians 2.11 – 21**

OUTGROWING THE LAW In yesterday's reading, Paul explained clearly to his readers that even the leaders of the Church in Jerusalem did not insist that any Christians who had never been Jews should be circumcised and keep the Jewish law. Here, he tells how he rebuked Peter to his face for going back on the decision made in Jerusalem. The attitude of the Jewish Christians was understandable. If you have kept strict rules all your life about what you can eat and drink, how you dress and behave, who you can talk to and how you relate to God, it is hard to accept that none of this is necessary. God loves us anyway – and proves it in the life, death and resurrection of Jesus. Living by rules can be secure and comfortable; living by faith can be frightening because there are no boundaries and no clear paths – only our trust in the unfailing love of God.

No one will be justified by the works of the law ... the life I now live in the flesh I live by faith in the Son of God, who loved me and gave himself for me ... if justification comes through the law, then Christ died for nothing.
(part of verses 16, 20 and 21)

✝ *Help me, Lord, to leave the security of having rules about everything and to discover the exhilaration of living in freedom with you.*

Thursday June 14   **Galatians 3.1 – 5**

BELIEVING THE TRUTH The Jewish law had begun as a response to God's choice of Israel as his chosen people. It was what set the Jews apart as special, different from other nations and in a special relationship with God. But the trouble with rules is that they finish up as ends in themselves – it is keeping the rule which becomes important, not the reason for having the rule in the first place. And for the Jews, keeping the law became a way of making sure that God stayed on their side and gave them prosperity and victory over their enemies. When they were defeated and taken into exile by the Babylonians, they had to learn the hard lesson that God wanted a conversion of the heart, not rules about how to fast and how to offer the correct sacrifices in the Temple (*Isaiah 58.5 – 7; Jeremiah 7.3 – 7*). So Paul was appalled when his Galatian converts slipped back into thinking that they had to keep the law in order to earn God's love. They were trying to pretend that the truth they had been told about Jesus did not exist.

> **Does God supply you with the Spirit and work miracles among you by your doing the works of the law, or by your believing what you heard?** (verse 5)

✝ *O Lord, help me to cling to your truth however hard it may be sometimes to believe that it is true.*

Friday June 15   Galatians 3.6 – 18

THE IMPORTANCE OF FAITH This passage is quite difficult to understand, because it is based on a very Jewish way of interpreting Scripture (and Jesus was, of course, a Jew) which seems strange to many people today. But one of the points which Paul is making is that the idea of relating to God through faith in his promises, and not by keeping rules in order to earn his favour, was present right from the beginning of Jewish history. The law got in the way of this faith relationship, but Christ has brought us back to that first promise of blessing.

> **The law does not rest on faith; on the contrary, 'Whoever does the works of the law will live by them.'** (verse 12)

Reliance on the law is not only useless; it actually destroys faith by insisting that faith is not necessary. But we know that using the law to earn God's love is second best; in Christ, we shall be satisfied with nothing less than the full inheritance which God has promised us (*verse 18*).

✝ *O Lord, increase my faith, so that I may inherit all your promises.*

Saturday June 16   Galatians 3.19 – 29

CLOTHED WITH CHRIST Paul stresses that to go back to keeping the law is to take the easier way and to be satisfied with second best. But what does it mean to have faith in God and through faith become his children?

In Christ Jesus you are all children of God through faith. As many of you as were baptized into Christ have clothed yourselves with Christ. (verses 26 – 27)

To be clothed with Christ is not an easy option. It means building up the sort of relationship with God that Jesus had on earth. It means living the kind of life that Jesus lived, so that we reflect his outlook and personality. It means living without rigid rules, because we are always listening to God and finding out what he wants us to do from moment to moment. It means being flexible, so that we use every available opportunity to share God's love with other people of every kind.

✝ *O Lord, help me to live in such a way that people who see me will also see your love and care.*

For group discussion and personal thought

● How important are rules in your relationship with God? Which of your rules are not really necessary?
● What do you think it means to be 'clothed with Christ'?

NEW ROADS AHEAD 8
Letting go of the past 2 (Galatians)

Notes by Patricia Batstone

based on the New Revised Standard Version

Patricia Batstone, a graduate of Hull and Exeter universities, became a Methodist Local Preacher in 1964. She is a freelance writer and publisher, her major title in recent years being *In Debt to C. S. Lewis*, a study of readers' responses to Lewis's fictional writings. She is a member of the Society of Women Writers and Journalists and the Association of Christian Writers. She is married with two sons, one of whom is a Methodist minister.

At the heart of Paul's exchanges with the Galatians is a tension between the demands of the old law and new life in the Spirit. Keeping the Jewish law was a matter of ritual pride, not faith. To Paul, however, the only thing that mattered was what Jesus had accomplished on the cross. The cross was a symbol of freedom from the past and hope for the future life. Against that, all laws paled into insignificance.

Text for the week: Galatians 6.14

Sunday June 17   **Galatians 4.1 – 11**

MINORITIES   Today there is a great emphasis on the rights of children. However, if Paul wrote to the Galatians today he would probably still insist that even children who are heirs to royal thrones need to be treated like slaves, for their own well-being – though in Paul's day it would not have been seen as slavery. Nor is it slavery for today's children. Their understanding of their rights tells them that they can assert themselves: 'I can do what I want' rather than 'I may do what is right'. This attitude means that they are living under law, with no concept of grace, and so they miss out on the privileges of childhood.

> **And because you are children, God has sent the Spirit of his Son into our hearts, crying, 'Abba! Father!' So you are no longer a slave but a child, and if a child then also an heir, through God.**   **(verses 6 – 7)**

Even adults stray. Like 'before and after' advertisements, Paul contrasts enslavement to the elemental spirits with freedom in the Spirit of Christ. Today people all over the world are going back to the 'elemental spirits', trying to find themselves through New Age philosophy rather than seeking Christ who offers freedom and hope.

† *Lord, as I am faced with decisions between what society expects and what I believe to be your will, help me to choose what is right.*

Monday June 18   **Galatians 4.12 – 20**

REMINISCENCES Paul always discouraged people from living in the past, yet here he is, indulging in a fit of nostalgia about the time when he arrived among the Galatians in a poor state of health and shared the gospel with them. No one is quite sure what his illness was but he must have looked terrible. He admits that it was all the more surprising that they were prepared to accept him as he was – and accept the Christ he spoke about. Their goodwill towards him had been exemplary, but they were easily undermined and now they were back where they started. Paul is disappointed with them.

> **It is good to be made much of for a good purpose at all times, and not only when I am present with you ... I wish I were present with you now ... for I am perplexed about you.**   **(verse 18 and part of 20)**

Paul seems to be saying, 'Don't just be Christians when you're in church or in the right company'. We must be prepared to stand out at any time, and sometimes, like a Salvation Army officer in a bar, we may earn respect rather than ridicule.

† *Lord, if I am known for anything at the end of my life, may it be that I chose your way and not my own.*

Tuesday June 19   **Galatians 4.21 – 31**

LISTENING It is much easier to live by a book of rules than by conscience or common sense, even when the rules begin to turn into a strait-jacket. But Paul poses a question:

> **Tell me, you who desire to be subject to the law, will you not listen to the law? ... we are children, not of the slave but of the free woman.**   **(verse 21 and part of 31)**

In other words, they *are not listening*. Blind lip-service will not do. The Galatians are not asking why the rules are there (why, indeed, are any rules in place?). They have failed to see the distinction between slavery and freedom: it is not a matter of ritual observance but of the inheritance that comes with their 'Yes' to Christ – a Yes that put the past in its place and promised a future. We may find Paul's use of the account of Abraham's two sons – one born into slavery, the other the legitimate heir – morally offensive, but it provides a stark illustration of the difference between having no prospects and having a sure and certain hope.

† *Lord, grant me that inner perception that is able to interpret all my experiences in the light of your truth.*

Wednesday June 20   Galatians 5.1 – 12

'RUNNING WELL' A preacher told the story of what happened when yeast got out of hand. The baker's apprentice thought he would be clever, but he did not quite get it right – too much yeast and the risen dough overflowed the bowl.

> **You were running well; who prevented you from obeying the truth? Such persuasion does not come from the one who calls you. A little yeast leavens the whole batch of dough.**
> **(verses 7 – 9)**

They had been 'running well', as Paul put it, but they were not quite mature enough yet to take sole responsibility for their Christian lives. They did not have enough experience from the past to equip them for the future. It is a parable of our lives. What we need is not rules and regulations but the enabling power and guidance to see the task through – a very carefully measured quota of divine yeast. 'Running well' spiritually involves surmounting obstacles, meeting temptation and not succumbing to it, and facing any form of persecution with faith and courage – the divine yeast in the dough of humanity.

† *Lord, I am lifeless until you energize me. Help me to keep 'running well' in the marathon of faith.*

Thursday June 21   Galatians 5.13 – 26

LOVING There is some strong language in this passage, and anyone who thinks it is aimed at them may feel indignant. All this talk of 'biting and devouring'. But consider a rather uncommon old pussy-cat called Magnificat. Magnificat thinks he owns all the houses in our street. In fact, he knows he does and he keeps his eye even on dogs. Woe betide the strange dog or cat who puts a paw over his boundary: he gives a warning growl, puts his claws out, and within seconds the fur is flying. The warrior cat then marches home and demands that we love him enough to pay the veterinary surgeon's bill for his wounds. Because he is an old cat, there is usually a lot of damage and even well-kept cats can infect each other with lethal diseases through their claws. Human beings inflict disease and death on one another in other ways – sometimes physically, at other times mentally, even spiritually. Any unloving action is an assault on the other person. The stranger is to be made welcome, not chased off the territory. That is the forward-looking way of love, the way to live in the Spirit, since

those who belong to Christ Jesus have crucified the flesh with its passions and desires. If we live by the Spirit, let us also be guided by the Spirit. (verses 24 – 25)

† *Help me, Lord, to live in your way, not mine; to put you first, not me; to love others, not hurt them.*

Friday June 22 Galatians 6.1 – 10

HARVESTING The contrast between life under the law and life in the Spirit has dominated this week. The sub-plot is about how each individual works out this conflict in his or her own life. It is not easy, because it involves letting go of too many things that get in the way of progress. But is it *always* wrong to look back? When I see today's date I remember my late father-in-law, because this would have been his birthday; that kind of looking back cannot be wrong. Some memories, like weeds, do get out of hand; not all of them are good. Some of them become distorted and are remembered as better or worse than they actually were. Some are unhealthy. The French theologian Teilhard de Chardin wrote a nostalgic essay about his wartime experiences, but most people prefer to forget their time in the trenches.

You reap whatever you sow. If you sow to your own flesh, you will reap corruption from the flesh; but if you sow to the Spirit, you will reap eternal life from the Spirit.
(part of verse 7 and verse 8)

Living on the past guarantees a poor harvest. Only fresh seed will produce results.

✝ *Lord God, giver of life, you have given me a memory which is often overloaded. Help me to ensure that what is remembered is the fresh seed of peace, not the stale seed of hurt and enmity.*

Saturday June 23   **Galatians 6.11 – 18**

THE CROSS   The preacher stepped forward, opened his Bible and read the text in the old King James version ...

God forbid that I should glory, save in the cross of our Lord Jesus Christ, by whom the world is crucified unto me, and I unto the world.   **(verse 14)**

Miles away a teenager in front of a television watched the preacher and listened avidly to all that the Bible said about Jesus and the cross and why Paul had made his boast – and that night she knelt in her room and told God that she wanted to be a servant, too. In those early days I had huge ideas about how I was going to be of service. The passing years have rubbed off more than the corners and the grand plans seem more inadequate than ever, but the cross remains. The symbol of the cross is crucial to our faith – not the occupied cross of Good Friday but the empty cross of Easter Day, the cross that says that he who was dead is alive and that God is with us as we go forward into all our tomorrows.

✝ *Lord, years may have passed, but I still want to be your servant. Show me new paths, new fields for harvesting, new gifts to be used.*

For group discussion and personal thought

- How can we, as churches and individuals, assess whether we are 'running well' in our Christian service?
- Individual witness can be marred by lifestyle. How can we practise both personal 'freedom in Jesus' and corporate responsibility to our neighbours?

SUFFERING AND A GOD OF LOVE 1
Why have you abandoned me?

Notes by Ngozi Okeke

based on the New American Standard Bible and the New King James Version

---

In recent years, there have been many serious disasters around the world, both natural and man-made. These have caused untold suffering to millions of innocent people. Why doesn't a God of love, if he truly exists, prevent some of these things? As Christians we know that God is alive, all-loving and all-powerful and can intervene. We too get exasperated that he doesn't do so more often and we complain. However, our readings this week show that God does intervene to deliver, heal and bless. May we be encouraged to trust so that we can bring our suffering and pain to him too.

Text for the week: Job 23: 8 – 10

Sunday June 24   **1 Kings 19.1 – 15**

THE STILL SMALL VOICE   In today's reading, we encounter Elijah, a spiritual giant who had just accomplished a mighty miracle in Israel. Following the showdown at Mount Carmel, the rains returned after years of drought. He should have been on a spiritual high, but for some inexplicable reason, he became depressed and ran for his life when threatened by the queen. He dismissed his servant and sat under a broom tree.

> **He requested for himself that he might die, and said, 'It is enough; now, O LORD, take my life, for I am not better than my fathers.'**   **(verse 4, NASB)**

Christians very often place too much emphasis on signs, wonders and miracles, and not enough on their source, God. Elijah's experience of God's greatness and power did not stop him from becoming discouraged. Moreover, at Mount Horeb, when he was at his lowest ebb, it wasn't a show of God's power in wind, earthquake and fire that reassured him, but the still small voice, the gentle soothing of God's presence. Our faith must never be based on our experiences of God's power, but on

God himself because, in our darkest moments, only an awareness of his presence and love can comfort, bless and encourage us.

✝ *Father, thank you that your love and presence reassure us in our times of greatest need.*

Monday June 25   **Luke 8.26 – 39**

HOPELESS CASES?   In spite of major scientific advances in medicine, there are still many diseases without any known cure. There are also addictions to drugs and disturbed patterns of behaviour which have no permanent solutions. We tend to regard these as hopeless cases. The man Jesus met in this story fits easily into this category, for Luke tells us that

> **[he] was possessed with demons ... and was not living in a house, but in the tombs ... He was bound with chains and shackles and kept under guard; and yet he would burst his fetters and be driven by the demon into the desert.**
> **(parts of verses 27 and 29, NASB)**

Jesus' response was to heal and clothe the man, and send him back to his people to witness to what God had done. With God there are no hopeless cases or people or, indeed, situations. Everyone is precious in his sight and within the boundaries of his will he intervenes to bring freedom, wholeness and hope. His infinite power will meet every need and transform any sinner willing to be changed. Whatever your need or problem, do not believe Satan's lie that it is beyond hope. God's power can make impossibilities possible in your life and situations. Trust him!

✝ *Father, give us the faith to believe that you can bring hope and freedom even in the most desperate situations in our lives.*

Tuesday June 26   **1 Samuel 1.1 – 18**

HANG IN THERE!   One example of modern technology I can happily do without is the call hold in offices. 'Please hold', it says, then you have to listen to usually awful music and hold for so long that you begin to wonder whether they have forgotten you. Sometimes, when we pray 'for ever' for something, we begin to wonder whether God too has put us on hold on the heavenly telephone and forgotten we are waiting! Hannah may have felt the same about her barrenness. Taunted by her fellow wife, rebuked by her husband for sulking, wrongly maligned by the priest for drunkenness and seemingly abandoned by God, she,

greatly distressed, prayed to the Lord and wept bitterly.
(verse 10, NASB)

Each of us suffers our own times of 'barrenness' in our work, lives and relationships and we have problems praying with faith to a God who seems to have put us on hold. However, as Hannah discovered, prayer opens the door for God to work in our lives and situations. Our answer may not come as quickly as Hannah's; therefore, while we wait, we must continue to pray passionately, be open to what God may want to teach us and be thankful for the blessings we already have. When it seems God has put you on hold, whatever you do, *don't hang up!*

† *Dear Lord, your timing may be different, but thank you that you always answer our prayers according to your will for our lives.*

Wednesday June 27   **Job 23.1 – 17**

IT'S NOT FAIR, GOD!   Years ago, as a Pastoral Worker, I visited a fringe member who vowed never to pray or step into a church again because God had refused to heal her baby and she had died. People react to tragedy or suffering in different ways. Tragedy drove this woman *away* from God; it drew Job *to* God. He was convinced his suffering was undeserved and that God had been unfair, yet he searched for God.

Oh that I knew where I might find Him,
That I might come to His seat!
I would present my case before Him ...
I would learn the words which He would answer,
And perceive what He would say to me.
(verses 3 – 5, NASB)

Going to God for answers clarified Job's thinking. He knew that God never intimidates us but exercises his authority over our lives with love and care. Though he was confused about God's intentions, he was reassured that things would turn out right in the end. Therefore, he was determined to pass the test of his faith. Like Job we need to learn that the best response to trials is to draw closer to God. In him we shall find comfort and reassurance, as Job did.

† *Lord, thank you that we can trust you even when we can't understand you.*

145

PARADISE LOST   So far this week, we have encountered four people who had to grapple with suffering and seen how God met them within it. Today, we read the story of the Fall, generally regarded as the source of all the suffering in our world. Much has been said and written about why Adam and Eve surrendered to Satan and lost paradise. However, we tend to overlook the greatest miracle in that story:

> **And the Lord God made garments of skin for Adam and his wife, and clothed them.**   **(verse 21, NASB)**

Adam and Eve's attempts to clothe themselves were never going to be good enough because, as Isaiah tells us, our efforts at righteousness are like filthy rags before God (*Isaiah 64.6*). God had to clothe Adam and Eve and to do so, he shed blood by killing animals for their skins. At the moment that paradise was lost, God's grace began to restore the fellowship which had been destroyed, leading in the end to the shedding of the blood of Christ on Calvary. That amazing grace has continued to reach out across time to each of us. Have you responded to it?

† *Father, thank you for your grace which is always reaching out to us. Help us to respond to you so that we can begin to experience true fellowship with you.*

THE ULTIMATE SACRIFICE   Adam and Eve's disobedience cost them paradise and their fellowship with God. God created them primarily for this fellowship, which their sin destroyed. Throughout history, humanity has tried unsuccessfully to restore that fellowship. What we could not do, Jesus achieved at great personal cost. The horror of crucifixion has been dulled by the passage of time. Physically, it was a terrible way to die and Jesus prayed to avoid it if possible. However, the spiritual cost was even greater, for on the cross he cried,

> **My God, My God, why have You forsaken Me?**
> **(verse 1, NKJV)**

All his life, Jesus had lived in unbroken fellowship with his Father. But on the cross, when he died in our place and took the punishment for our sin, that fellowship was temporarily broken. Jesus felt forsaken by God as he took the judgement that we deserved. As a result, he is now the bridge across which we can return to God. The fellowship that was broken when Adam and Eve sinned is now restored. No one need live in spiritual separation from God any longer.

† *Thank you, Jesus, that you endured the darkness that we may enjoy the light.*

Saturday June 30   Isaiah 9.2 – 7

PARADISE RESTORED   Yesterday we saw how Jesus gave his life to restore the fellowship between us and God, broken in the Garden of Eden. This ensured that human beings in every age can live life to the full (*John 10.10*). However, wherever we look in our world today we find pain, suffering, grief and loss; it seems that our capacity for evil is unlimited. The physical paradise is yet to be restored. In today's reading Isaiah gave some wonderful promises about Jesus. He will be called

> **Wonderful Counsellor, Mighty God, Eternal Father, Prince of Peace. There will be no end to the increase of His government or of peace.**   **(part of verses 6 and 7, NASB)**

Jesus' first appearance in the world dealt with our individual need. When he returns he will rule with justice and righteousness and fully restore the physical paradise. There will be complete harmony between all creation (*Isaiah 11*) and his reign will be characterized by peace, a Hebrew word that implies prosperity as well as tranquillity. Never again will our fellowship with God be broken or the peaceful order of God's rule be disrupted. And there will be no more pain ... no more suffering.

† *Thank you, Jesus, for your death which reconciles us to God, so that we too can live in unbroken relationship with him.*

For group discussion and personal thought

- Have you ever felt guilty about feeling depressed? Do you draw any encouragement from Elijah's experience?
- When did you last believe that God would answer your prayer exactly as you prayed it? Does Hannah's experience encourage you?
- The Church has been accused of being ineffective in its witness. Do you believe this is justified? What can the Church do to be more relevant to today's world?

SUFFERING AND A GOD OF LOVE 2
Weep with those who weep

Notes by Estela Pinto Ribeiro Lamas

based on the New Revised Standard Version

Born in Mozambique on a Swiss Presbyterian mission, Estela Pinto Ribeiro Lamas is deeply involved with women's issues: she is a member of the executive of the Federation of Portuguese Methodist Women and editor of *Arvore da Vida* (*Tree of Life*); a member of the Co-ordinating Committee of the Ecumenical Forum of European Christian Women and editor of the *Forum Newsflash*.

This week's readings all deal with situations of weakness: bereavement and grief, physical weakness, moments of despair. But they also remind us that God is with us in our weakness, comforting us, helping us to go on, giving us new hope. And this is a service that we can also give to others: simply being with them, not necessarily saying anything, but sharing their tears and their laughter.

Text for the week: Ezekiel 3.14b

Sunday July 1   2 Kings 2.1 – 14

LET GOD ENTER OUR LIVES   If we allow God to enter our lives, we shall find that he will talk to those around us through our own attitudes and behaviour. That is what happened with Elijah.

> **When they had crossed, Elijah said to Elisha, 'Tell me what I may do for you, before I am taken from you.' Elisha said, 'Please let me inherit a double share of your spirit.'**
>
> **(verse 9)**

Elijah opened his life to God's action in such a way that Elisha could feel God's presence in his life through his contact with the older man. And the influence Elijah had on the young Elisha was so strong that the Elisha did not want to be separated from his master. Elisha never accepted the idea of staying behind; he went with Elijah wherever he was sent by God. He was persistent in his faithfulness to his master and to his God. And after Elijah's death, if Elisha did inherit a double share of his spirit, he in his turn would be used by God to speak to those around him, through Elisha's attitudes and behaviour.

† *O Lord, help us to understand your will and to open our life to your action. Use us to influence the lives of others and to lead them into your kingdom.*

Monday July 2   Mark 10.32 – 34

FOLLOWING The Spirit of God was upon Jesus. The disciples followed him although they did not understand what was going on. Jesus' influence on them was so profound that they did not question what was happening.

They were on the road, going up to Jerusalem, and Jesus was walking ahead of them; they were amazed, and those who followed were afraid.   **(verse 32a)**

We too sometimes walk along with Jesus but do not know where we are going. And like the disciples, this can make us afraid. Where is God leading me? What does he want from me? But we trust him and follow him. This is why prayer is so important. As we open our minds and our hearts to God and learn more about his actions, we shall understand more, grow in trust and be able to live according to his will.

† *Dear Lord, help us always to be willing to follow you and allow you to act upon our lives. Enlighten us by your Holy Spirit so that we can understand what you want from us!*

Tuesday July 3   Matthew 26.31 – 46, 56b

STAY AWAKE AND PRAY Being faithful demands a lot from us. Jesus tells his disciples that they are weak: however much their hearts tell them to watch with Jesus, their bodies are tired out and cannot stay awake. He advises them to pray so that God can strengthen their spirits. On our own, we cannot be faithful; though we want to follow Jesus and be faithful to God's love, earthly things have a great influence upon us. We need God's presence in our lives to strengthen our spirit.

'Stay awake and pray that you may not come into the time of trial; the spirit indeed is willing, but the flesh is weak' ... Then all the disciples deserted him and fled.
    (verses 41, 56b)

Let us listen to Jesus' advice and try to keep in touch with God through prayer. Then we shall avoid getting 'sleepy' and closing our eyes to what is really important in life – being with Jesus.

† *O God, make us aware of our weakness. May we open our lives to your action so that we do not desert you.*

Wednesday July 4   John 19.25 – 27

SHARING SUFFERING   Being part of the Christian family of believers goes beyond the idea of the natural human family. Despite his own suffering, Jesus felt his mother's suffering and tried to lighten it by showing her that, although she was losing him, she could find a son's love in his disciple.

He said to his mother, 'Woman, here is your son.' Then he said to the disciple, 'Here is your mother.' And from that hour the disciple took her into his own home.

(verses 26b and 27)

It is good that we should care for our own natural family. But do we stop with that, or do we really listen to our Lord's voice when he asks us to love our friends and neighbours as well and support them when they are suffering?

† *May we listen to your call, Lord, when you ask us to love and support our neighbours when they are suffering. May we discover our sister or brother in our neighbour and love her or him as you, Lord, expect us to do.*

Thursday July 5   John 11.17 – 37

GOD, THE GENEROUS GIVER   God is willing to give us whatever we ask from him if we live according to his will. God knows everything; he knows if we are faithful to him and sincere in our feelings towards him. He will answer our request according to our faithfulness to his love.

'But even now I know that God will give you whatever you ask of him.'   **(verse 22)**

Martha trusted Jesus. She knew Jesus loved her brother and she also knew that Jesus was the son of God and so had all the power needed to give life back to her brother. But the power of Jesus to raise Lazarus from the dead did not prevent him feeling the grief of Mary and Martha and weeping with them. God can do superhuman actions, but he does not expect us to be anything other than truly human.

† *Jesus, help us to trust you so deeply that, even if things do not go as we expect, we may, like Mary, still have faith in God.*

Friday July 6   **Ezekiel 3.10 – 15**

GOD'S STRONG HAND   God's Spirit lifts us up in moments of despair and suffering. Though we feel weak and seem to faint away, God's hand is strong upon us.

The spirit lifted me up and bore me away; I went in bitterness in the heat of my spirit, the hand of the LORD being strong upon me.

(verse 14)

God never deserts us. He is beside us and when we are weak he supports us and his spirit fills us and lifts us up. Notice that, although God has sent Ezekiel to speak to the Jews in exile, his first action is not to speak, but simply to sit with them and share their shock and despair in silence, stunned by the size of the catastrophe which had happened to them.

† *O Lord, keep your hand upon me! Support me in moments of despair and suffering so that I may not faint away.*

Saturday July 7   **Romans 12.9 – 16**

LET LOVE BE GENUINE   Paul appeals to his brothers and sisters in Corinth to show genuine love. This includes moral qualities such as hating evil, practising hope, patience and perseverance, and being ardent in the Lord's service. But it also includes simply looking out for your neighbours and paying attention to their spiritual state. As John says in his first letter: 'We love because he first loved us' (*1 John 4.19*). God's love acts upon our lives and as a result we can open our lives to our neighbours and give them love.

Rejoice with those who rejoice, weep with those who weep.   **(verse 15)**

How can we be at peace with God if we are not at peace with our neighbours? Our relationship with God influences our relationship with our neighbours – and our relationship with our neighbours will affect our relationship with God.

✝ *O Lord, help us to offer our love and support to our brothers and sisters! May we rejoice with them when they rejoice! May we weep with them when they weep!*

For group discussion and personal thought
- How can we open our lives to God's action?
- Share any experiences you have had of being with people in pain and suffering and finding that no words were needed.
- Think of one practical way in which you can be more open to loving your neighbours with the love which God gives to you – then go and do it.

FAITH *in*
THE FUTURE
*meeting the challenges
of being Christian in today's
and tomorrow's world*

- An NCEC project promoting a view of life with faith at the centre, where society can offer its children hope and purpose

- We need financial support for the project, as well as help with sponsoring and organizing events and research

For further information, contact the National Christian Education Council at the address on page 285.

SUFFERING AND A GOD OF LOVE 3
God of healing

Notes by Val Ogden

based on the New Revised Standard Version

Few topics in the Christian Church are as controversial as healing. We encounter it in such different forms with diverse results, that sometimes our capacity to trust in a healing God is stretched to the limit. The selection of readings below, from both Old and New Testaments, offers varied perspectives on the theme, but with one common aim; to affirm that God, through Christ and through human agents, longs to bring healing wherever there is brokenness. From that we may draw hope and take heart.

Text for the week: Luke 8.48

Sunday July 8   **Genesis 8.1 – 22**

OFFERING THE OLIVE BRANCH   Earlier in this story, God had promised Noah and his family, 'I will establish my covenant with you' (*Genesis 6.18*). But then came the rains and floods, death and destruction. How could Noah be sure that God had remembered his promise?

> **He sent out the dove from him, to see if the waters had subsided from the face of the ground; but the dove found no place to set its foot ... He waited another seven days, and again he sent out the dove from the ark; and the dove came back to him in the evening, and there in its beak was a freshly plucked olive leaf.** (part of verses 8 – 11)

I always imagine Noah with tears in his eyes as the dove presents him with that olive leaf; the first sign of healing and hope in a devastated world. It is God's invitation to begin again. God gives us similar chances to give and receive 'olive branches' as signs of healing and hope. A mother in Zambia found out that her son had been stealing from their neighbour's house. Sad and ashamed, she collected some food and household goods, went to her neighbour's house and knelt at the door to offer them. Is God asking you and me to give or receive an olive branch today?

† *Lord, let there be signs of hope, and let them be shown by me.*

Monday July 9   2 Kings 5.1 – 14

AGENTS OF HEALING   You will find it helpful to read the whole of this passage if you can. It has a happy ending because Naaman, an army commander, was cured of his leprosy (*verse 14*). But notice how many people God used to bring him to the point of healing. There were the Arameans, who had captured an Israelite girl now working for Naaman's wife. The servant girl herself, who spoke of the prophet Elisha's powers. Naaman's wife, who conveyed the message. The King of Aram, who wrote to the King of Israel. Then Elisha himself and his messenger. The story shows that Naaman was expecting Elisha alone to heal him and was cross when he did not even appear in person.

> **'I thought that for me he would surely come out, and stand and call on the name of the LORD his God, and would wave his hand over the spot, and cure the leprosy!'**
>
> **(part of verse 11)**

Naaman wanted to be treated by the top man, much as we might want the top surgeon. But we need to value and thank God for more ordinary agents of healing: the nurse who baths and feeds us, the priest who visits and prays, the friend who waits patiently with us in the surgery. God uses them all.

† *Lord, let there be healing, and let it begin with me.*

Tuesday July 10   Luke 5.12 – 16

SICKNESS THAT SEPARATES   Sickness never separates us from God's love, but attitudes to sickness can separate us from our families and communities. In some places people are still afraid to live with and care for those who are physically disabled or have HIV/AIDS. At the time Luke was writing, people with leprosy were cut off from society and regarded as unclean by the Jews. How unbelievable Jesus' action must have seemed when a leprosy patient said to him,

> **'Lord, if you choose, you can make me clean.' Then Jesus stretched out his hand, touched him, and said, 'I do choose. Be made clean.' Immediately the leprosy left him.**
>
> **(part of verse 12 and verse 13)**

By touching the leper, Jesus chose love over law and inclusion over separation. He demonstrated that no one was cut off from the fellowship he offered. And if Jesus chose that way, he expects no less from his followers. Who are the 'untouchables' in your society? Can you be the hands of Jesus for them?

✝ *Lord, let there be acceptance, and let it begin with me.*

Wednesday July 11   **Luke 5.27 – 32**

SICKNESS OF THE SOUL   Levi the tax collector did not have leprosy, but he too was cut off from society. Jews hated tax collectors, and so did the poor who suffered at their hands. Jesus challenged Levi to change his ways (*verses 27 – 28*) and Luke records that he did. But when the Pharisees asked Jesus why he concerned himself with a corrupt and sinful tax collector, his reply picks up the theme of sickness.

> 'Those who are well have no need of a physician, but those who are sick; I have come to call not the righteous but sinners to repentance.'   **(verses 31 – 32)**

In what way was Levi sick? He apparently had no physical or medical illness. But Jesus finds in him sickness of the soul. A man in love with money. A man with no friends – except, perhaps, other tax collectors. A man with no heart for the poor. A man living daily with the hatred of his community. This is sickness! Just as we may know people who become ill through worrying about money, or depressed because their neighbours never speak to them. These Gospel stories remind us that Jesus recognized sickness in many forms, and came to restore both bodies and souls.

✝ *Lord, let there be the healing of souls, and let it begin with me.*

Thursday July 12   **Luke 8.40 – 56**

NEW LIFE FOR WOMEN   Healing and touch continue to feature in these two linked stories. An adult woman with heavy bleeding braves the crowds and touches the hem of Jesus' cloak. Jesus touches the hand of Jairus's daughter and restores her to life. In both stories, Jesus is discouraged from 'going the second mile' in his care for the women. He is keen to find out exactly who touched him, but Peter (did he see the woman?) plays it down:

'Master, the crowds surround you and press in on you.'
(part of verse 45)

A representative from Jairus's house wants Jesus to turn back:

'Your daughter is dead; do not trouble the teacher any longer.'
(part of verse 49)

It would have been much easier for Jesus to go along with Peter and Jairus's representative – to pretend that the sick woman's touch had never happened, or to avoid contact with a corpse. But no. Jesus' way is to put himself at risk and offer his healing word and touch to his daughters, in a society which largely disregarded them.

✝ *Lord, let there be respect for women worldwide, and let it begin with me.*

Friday July 13   Isaiah 57.14 – 21

GOD'S LONGING FOR HEALING AND PEACE So often in the Old Testament, God offers his people forgiveness and restoration and then finds that they throw the offer back in his face and return to their sinful ways. It is as though God longs to live in peace and harmony with his children, but despairs of it ever happening. These verses from Isaiah express God's dilemma beautifully.

I have seen their ways, but I will heal them;
  I will lead them and repay them with comfort ...
Peace, peace, to the far and the near, says the LORD;
  and I will heal them.
But the wicked are like the tossing sea
  that cannot keep still;
  its waters toss up mire and mud.
There is no peace, says my God, for the wicked.
(verses 18 – 21)

A woman who had been very cruel to her sister's family found that she couldn't sleep at night. She tossed and turned endlessly and had horrible nightmares. The memory of the things she had said and done kept coming back to her until she could no longer stand it. She wrote a long letter of apology, which her sister accepted. Only after that did she sleep peacefully again.

✝ *Lord, let stormy waters be stilled, and let it begin with me.*

HEALTH AND FITNESS Luke records a complete and powerful healing for the lame man at the beautiful gate. From a life of being carried everywhere to a life of energy and activity.

> **Immediately his feet and ankles were made strong. Jumping up, he stood and began to walk, and he entered the temple with them, walking and leaping and praising God.** (verses 7 – 8)

A woman in my congregation had waited a long time for an operation to replace her hip. During the long wait she was in pain and sometimes had to be pushed in a wheelchair. Only weeks after the operation she was walking really well. Now she is swimming and climbing hills! She cannot understand why people who have fit and healthy bodies are too lazy to use them. 'When you can't walk,' she says, 'it's awful. When you can, make the most of it.' Many of our readings this week have focused on healing. How much do we really appreciate the God-given health which is already ours?

✝ *Lord, let there be health and strength, and let me give thanks for mine.*

For group discussion and personal thought

● Discuss 'sickness of the body' and 'sickness of the soul'. In your experience, what are the causes and the cures?

SUFFERING AND A GOD OF LOVE 4
The healing Church

Notes by Tom Arthur

based on the New Revised Standard Version

What kind of healing would you have? The world offers us a healing that enables us to compete and win, to rise above suffering to become 'no-limit' people. But our crucified Lord offers us healing through a redemptive community called 'Church' which celebrates who we really are in the real world as members together of his body. When we are vulnerable to one another and the world, we find our strength.

Text for the week: James 5.13 – 20

Sunday July 15   Luke 10.1 – 11, 16 – 20

TRUE HEALING   Jesus said it wasn't going to be easy. But when seventy of his apprentices came back from their first real plunge into practical ministry, they were intoxicated with success. 'Even the demons are subject to us in your name,' they said (*verse 17*), and they boasted of seeing Satan himself fall from heaven. I remember from the early years of my own ministry praying with two of our church's elders at the bedside of Mrs Bailey. She was in the hospital's intensive care ward. A pillar of the church in her nineties, she wasn't expected to live more than a few hours. But she did, and she always testified that it was that moment of prayer that pulled her through. Wow! My prayer really worked! But as the new days of her life grew to months and then years, her life became increasingly uncomfortable and weary. Was this the fruit of healing? But then I began to learn from her about a new depth of faith, a faith that receives the grace to accept suffering that will not go away and to accept a new kind of strength, stronger than strength of body. She learned to celebrate the gift of a life in which death had a very real part. This, to me, was a more excellent healing. Perhaps we are most well when we can let go and let God be the centre of our lives. That goes for healers, too. I realized that, earlier, I had simply been present in that company of saints when something bigger than all of us happened.

'Do not rejoice at this, that the spirits submit to you, but rejoice that your names are written in heaven.'

(verse 20)

✝ *Thank you, Lord, for claiming me in life and in death, in pain and in rejoicing, in my whole being.*

Monday July 16   **Luke 10.25 – 37**

TRUE LEARNING   Too much Christian education is like the situation which almost happens here, until Jesus steers it in a different direction. The lawyer loves theological puzzles. He is full of curiosity that leads him down one intellectual side road after another.

'Teacher,' he said, 'what must I do to inherit eternal life?'

(verse 25)

How many Bible study sessions have you attended (or attempted to lead!) at which the conversation never moved away from trying to solve such puzzles? In the story of the Compassionate Samaritan, Jesus exposes such playing with words as ecclesiastical games – a luxury that blinds us to the reality of suffering all around us. Too much of what we do as a Church is like this: it convinces us that we are saved from the world only because it effectively shuts out the world's concerns and the wholeness of our own humanity. 'Who is my neighbour?' the lawyer asks. The story shows that a neighbour is not something you can look up in a dictionary or a commentary. It is a way of being in the world that does not 'walk on by' those who are hurting. Such a way of being is eternal life itself. How can the weekly Bible study find its joy in touching the deep pain of the world around us?

✝ *Lord, teach my heart to care.*

Tuesday July 17   **2 Corinthians 1.3 – 11**

NO PAIN, NO GAIN   I am notorious for always dieting, but I threw off all my anxiety about gaining weight when we celebrated a friend's graduation from his course at the Centre for Black and White Christian Partnership in Birmingham. We took him to an Indian restaurant in Coventry where you can eat as much as you like. Of course, I ate all I could and came down for breakfast the next morning suffering, still feeling overstuffed with curry. My 14-year-old daughter Rachel did not miss a beat. 'No pain, no gain,' she joked. But her joke made me think of the reason for our feasting the night before: the Centre's programmes exist to heal the suffering caused by the failure of our British Church to welcome Asian, Afro-Caribbean and African Christians when they arrived here following the break-up of the British Empire. The Centre's hospitality, as famous as my dieting is notorious, is at bottom a fellowship cemented by the experience of suffering, and by the work of comforting others which emerges from such experience. Paul says:

> **Our hope for you is unshaken; for we know that as you share in our sufferings, so also you share in our consolation.** (verse 7)

Those whose faith has been strengthened by sharing the pain of Christ have a precious gift of consolation to share with the rest of us. No pain, no gain. It is a wonderful thing to be included in such a fellowship, and certainly worth cancelling the diet for an evening.

✝ *Lord, gather me into the fellowship of your cross, so that in suffering I may also know the fellowship of your resurrection.*

Wednesday July 18   James 5.13 – 20

A ROLE FOR EVERYONE   Three years ago when I had a stroke and lost much of my sight, I realized how 'British' I had become since I moved here from the US ten years before. I wanted to keep the experience to myself. You know how we British like our privacy. But I was upbraided by a church member who suffers from multiple sclerosis. The church needs you more than ever, she said. We have a ministry to perform. After all, she said, what is the church for?

> **Are any among you sick? They should call for the elders of the church and have them pray over them, anointing them with oil in the name of the Lord.** (verse 14)

To teach us how to pray, those in our midst who long for healing must pray. To teach us how to visit one another, they must ask for our visits and encourage our intercessions, just as those who are cheerful among us must not hesitate to praise in order to teach the rest of us how to praise. Suffering can be part of the glue that holds the church together. Everyone has an important role to play in building up the body of Christ.

Are any among you suffering? They should pray.

(verse 13)

Do it now.

† *Lord, use my pain for your glory.*

Thursday July 19   **1 Corinthians 11.23 – 32**

GOOD MANNERS We did know our manners and were perfectly capable of using them when there was company, but when the family dined as a family my brothers and I were good at stretching for what we wanted with what my mother called the 'boarding house reach'. My Dad had a story from his childhood about table manners. The minister came for Sunday dinner and my grandparents were terribly embarrassed when my uncle Bob kept pestering them for the chicken leg as they sat down at table. We are not always polite when company comes. The minister then asked everyone to bow their heads for prayer, and when they did, and while he prayed, he quietly put the chicken leg on Bob's plate. The minister's gracious attention to the youngest in that company, Dad said, was what manners were all about. Table manners mean being sensitive to the company we keep; bad manners isolate us from others.

For all who eat and drink without discerning the body, eat and drink judgement against themselves.   **(verse 29)**

This has nothing to do with obscure theological questions. It is simply a matter of being gracious. If we grab for ourselves, we cannot see that body which was made whole by the suffering of our Lord Jesus Christ; and if we are unwilling to experience it without suffering in some real way for ourselves, then we make a mockery of it.

† *Lord, show me your broken body made whole in the company that breaks bread together.*

Friday July 20   **1 Corinthians 12.12 – 31a**

POSITIVE AFFIRMATION I had been recommended to serve a new church, but when I rang the provincial moderator I discovered that all he had been told about me was that I couldn't drive, which didn't matter for that particular pastorate. I said I would rather be known for my abilities than my disabilities, so we switched attention to discussing what the call actually required, and how that fitted in with what I actually had to offer. A few days later, discussing 'spiritual gifts' in our house group, a woman confessed that whenever this topic of gifts and abilities came up she remembered that, in spite of raising four of them, she was no good at working with children. Yet she was regularly asked to teach Junior Church. Another member of the house group then shared that he knew nothing about property or finances, so had never found his particular place of service in the church. They were defining themselves by their disabilities, the things they could not do. They were part of the body of Christ, but felt that they were on its fringe. But Paul says,

> If the foot would say, 'Because I am not a hand, I do not belong to the body', that would not make it any less a part of the body. (verse 15)

How can we as a Church affirm others for who they are, instead of labelling them for what they are not and so pushing them to the margins?

✝ *Lord, teach me who I am and to rejoice in that.*

Saturday July 21   2 Corinthians 12.1 – 10

'I CAN'T GIVE YOU ANYTHING BUT LOVE' I once served as pastor for a small urban church in Chicago – not just a small church but, by American standards, an incredibly small church. It was a small boat sailing rough seas. It had a crew of good, fiercely loyal people, but they felt defeated, ignored, overwhelmed by the big ships, the large suburban juggernauts bulging with hundreds and even thousands of members. In a world that finds glory and success in bigness, we were failures. We needed encouragement. Paul says that he has lots he could brag about. He is a spiritual giant. But how would his bragging contribute to building up the Church? The gift that builds up the Church is the gift of weakness, the experience of vulnerability, the pain of defeat.

> I will boast all the more gladly of my weaknesses, so that the power of Christ may dwell in me. (verse 9b)

The weakness that opens up our dependence on one another proves the power of Christ. In the same way, the weakness of small churches forms the backbone of their denominations – in a way that can be statistically verified. There are no back pews in small churches, members know one another as members of a family, and their involvement is high. Per capita giving, both to local programmes and to mission, tends to be higher. There are no 'experts' to carry the load for them. They know what it means to be members together in the body of Christ. In a time when success seems to be worshipped as much in the Church as it is in the world, small churches need to be reminded of the meaning of the cross – that the power of God is made perfect in our weakness.

† *I rejoice in your cross, Lord, for when I am weak, I am strong.*

For group discussion and personal thought

● How can we as a Church affirm others for who they are, instead of labelling them for what they are not and so pushing them to the margins?

SUFFERING AND A GOD OF LOVE 5
Trial and trust

Notes by Emmanuel Asante

based on the New International Version

Emmanuel Asante is an ordained minister of the Methodist Church of Ghana and President of Trinity Theological Seminary, Legon.

If we have to wait a long time for God's promise to be fulfilled in our lives, we are tempted to doubt God's ability to deliver what he has promised, to begin 'helping' God get his plan into action, or to lose our self worth and doubt whether God can act with and through us. This week's readings remind us of God's eternal faithfulness.

Text for the week: Genesis 18.14a

Sunday July 22   **Genesis 18.1 – 15**

LAUGHTER   Sarah, the elderly wife of Abraham, is childless in spite of God's promise to her husband that his own son would be his heir (*Genesis 15.4*). One day, after Sarah has given up hope of ever becoming a mother, the Lord appears to her husband Abraham and affirms his previous promise:

> **'I will surely return to you about this time next year, and Sarah your wife will have a son' ... Sarah was listening at the entrance to the tent, which was behind him ... Sarah was past the age of childbearing. So Sarah laughed to herself as she thought, 'After I am worn out and my master is old, will I now have this pleasure?'**
>
> **(part of verses 10 – 12)**

Waiting patiently for God to fulfil his promise in our lives can be very hard. To cope with a long wait, we may try to force God into action – as Sarah and Abraham did when they agreed to raise children through Hagar, Sarah's maid. Even though this was an acceptable practice in their day, it resulted in painful experiences for them. We may also cope with waiting by deciding that what we are waiting for will never happen; God cannot deliver what he has promised. Sarah's reaction was to *laugh* at God's affirmation of his promise of a baby. She did not laugh because she doubted God's ability to deliver what he had promised, but because she doubted whether God could do it with and through her; her situation seemed hopeless. God's reaction to Sarah's laughter (*verse 14*) indicates that his ability is not limited by our disability. Indeed, our impossibility is God's possibility.

† *Omnipotent God, give us the grace to look beyond our limitations and to experience you in your limitlessness. Surely, with you all things are possible.*

Monday July 23   Ecclesiastes 3.1 – 8, 7.3 – 4

TIME FOR EVERYTHING   Timing is important in human life. There is a proper time, a right moment, to perform certain actions, because the fitting reason and the opportunity will not always be available.

There is a time for everything, and a season for every activity under heaven. (verse 1)

A good steward of time knows that there are two important aspects to every authentic human action: *when* it is done and *how* it is done. Good stewards of time are on the look-out for opportunities to serve God. They know how to use the right moment for doing the right thing – that is, they know how to redeem the time. They try not to waste time because they know that time is short. So they make the most of their opportunities.

† *'Show me, O Lord, my life's end and the number of my days; let me know how fleeting is my life' (Psalm 39.4), that I may apply my heart to wisdom and live as you would have me live.*

Tuesday July 24   John 12.20 – 26

DYING TO LIVE   Jesus defined his ministry in terms of serving and giving his life as a ransom for many (*Mark 10.45*). He believed that his sacrificial death on the cross would bring salvation to all – Jews and Gentiles. When Jesus heard that some God-fearing Greeks wanted to have an interview with him, he saw their request to see him as significant for his approaching crucifixion, which was to bring salvation to many. So when Philip told him that the Greeks had arrived, he said:

> **The hour has come for the Son of Man to be glorified. I tell you the truth, unless an ear of wheat falls to the ground and dies, it remains only a single seed. But if it dies, it produces many seeds.** (verses 23 – 24)

With these words, Jesus points to the principle of life through death. If we want to live we must first die to the self. Any true commitment to Christ involves an experience of death to the old self and resurrection to the new life which comes from the risen Lord. The committed Christian experiences newness of life through death in Christ.

† *Lord Jesus, help us die to the old self so that we may enjoy newness of life in you. Amen*

Wednesday July 25   2 Corinthians 4.7 – 15

JARS OF CLAY   God has entrusted the precious message of salvation in Jesus Christ to frail and fallible human beings. Out of our nothingness flows what is supremely valuable and powerful for the salvation of humanity. But why does it happen like this?

> **We have this treasure in jars of clay to show that this all-surpassing power is from God and not from us. We are hard pressed on every side, but not crushed; perplexed, but not in despair; persecuted, but not abandoned; struck down, but not destroyed.** (verses 7 – 9)

We may be at our wits' end but not at the end of hope and of our possibilities. We are frail and fallible, our bodies are perishable and subject to pain, sin and suffering, but God never abandons us. Our human weakness and suffering provide God with the opportunity to demonstrate the triumph of his power and presence in us.

† *Lord, help us to see beyond our frailty, weakness and fallibility and experience your power and presence in us as we bear witness to your saving grace.*

Thursday July 26   2 Corinthians 4.16 – 5.5

BEYOND THE VISIBLE   We have all had moments in our lives when we were ready to quit. In the moments when he confronted his own frailty and fallibility, his moments of despair, Paul looked beyond the visible and the outward and concentrated on developing his inner strength.

Though outwardly we are wasting away, yet inwardly we are being renewed day by day. For our light and momentary troubles are achieving for us an eternal glory that far outweighs them all. **(verses 16 – 17)**

What are visible to us are the painful and perplexing – but temporary and fleeting – experiences of this present life. Focusing on these visible but temporary experiences can cause us to quit and lose heart. But the unseen presence of the power of God in our lives is our strength, our enabling factor which keeps us strong in weakness, happy in moments of sadness and hopeful in the face of hopelessness. Accordingly we look up and away from the visible appearances of the present, from the troubles we see around us, to the invisible strength, power and hope that are ours in Christ.

† *Lord, our hope in hopeless situations, our strength in weakness, our light in darkness, give us grace to look up and away from the hopelessness, weakness and darkness of this impermanent world to your invisible world of strength, hope and light.*

Friday July 27   **2 Corinthians 5.6 – 15**

DEATH   One of the frightening inevitabilities of life is death. We do all we can to avoid death and use euphemisms ('passed away', 'gone before') when we talk about it. Yet death is inevitable and tells us that we are mortal, that our life on earth is transient. We owe the breath in us to the immortal God in whom we have our being. Paul was not afraid to die because he was confident that death was only a passage to a life of eternity with Christ.

Therefore we are always confident and know that as long as we are at home in the body we are away from the Lord. We live by faith, not by sight. We are confident, I say, and would prefer to be away from the body and at home with the Lord. **(verses 6 – 8)**

The secret of Paul's confidence was his conviction that, because Christ died for all people, all are involved in his death. While the death of Christ confirmed the inevitability of physical death for everyone, for those who by faith are united with him in his death and resurrection, death is also the sign of their death to sin and self. Such people no longer live for themselves but 'for him who died for them and was raised again' (*verse 15*). God has reserved brand-new eternal bodies for those who through faith are committed to his Son Jesus, the Christ. This hope gives us courage and patience to endure the pain of this life.

✝ *Lord, give us the wings of faith to rise within the veil and see the saints above, how great their joys, how bright their glories be. And as you give us this heavenly and glorious vision, make us bold to face this short life and the inevitability of death with courage and hope.*

Saturday July 28   Romans 8.31 – 39

MORE THAN CONQUERORS   Some people think that they are beyond the saving grace of God, they are not good enough for God to save them. What does the Bible say in response to such people?

If God is for us, who can be against us? He who did not spare his own Son, but gave him up for us all – how will he not also, along with him, graciously give us all things?

(verses 31 – 32)

The certainty of God's love assures us that we are never beyond the reach of God's saving love. The God who has given us the supreme gift of his Son will certainly complete his work of salvation in us. The one who, in his love, gave his life for our salvation is not going to turn around and condemn us. The Lord will remain constant in his love towards us. We in turn are expected to remain steadfast in faith and unshaken in our commitment to him. As believers we face many different kinds of hardship, which sometimes make us think that God has abandoned us. Today's passage tells us that we shall never be separated from God's love shown in the work of Christ our saviour.

✝ *Lord, thank you for the assurance that your love for us is constant and that we can count on your saving grace in all life's hardships.*

For group discussion and personal thought

● How can reflection on God's omnipotence help us to overcome our frailty and fallibility?
● The Lord keeps us in perfect peace when we focus on him and not on our weakness. In what sense is this true?
● How can we be hopeful in a hopeless situation?

GOD OF LOVE AND ANGER 1
(Hosea)

Notes by Isaiah Gaddala

based on the New International Version

The topic for this week may sound like a paradox, but the love and anger of God are two sides of the same coin. Today, we try not to emphasize the angry side of God, but to be consistent with the biblical revelation we need to recognize that this is a true portrait of God in both the Old and New Testaments. Some people try to separate the God of the Old Testament (seen as the God of wrath) and the God of the New Testament (seen as the God of love). But this also is not true to the teaching of the scriptures as a whole. What is true of human parental love is even more true of the God who loves us and yet punishes us when we go wrong. Do not think about others when you read the book of Hosea: read it for yourself and gain insights from it for your own daily living.

Text for the week: Hosea 2.13, 16, 19 – 20

Sunday July 29   **Hosea 1.1 – 11**

TRAGIC BUT TRUE!   The book of Hosea is one of the most tragic books in the Bible. Hosea lived and prophesied in the 8th century BC, when many of the Israelites shamefully deserted the living God Yahweh and worshipped Baal. God used his servant and prophet Hosea to act out this 'harlotry' by Israel by asking him to marry a harlot and beget children of unfaithfulness. And Hosea unquestioningly obeyed the Lord and married Gomer and had three children by her. We might wonder, how could Hosea, the prophet of the Lord, do such a thing? But he did! He did it as an act of implicit obedience, in contrast to the whole nation of Israel which had disobeyed the Lord. He also did it to show the faithful love (in Hebrew, *chesed*) of the Lord for the unfaithful (adulterous) Israel. The whole book is intended as an object lesson. However, we must not conclude that the only picture of God we find in Hosea is that of an angry God. There are also numerous examples of his love, such as his promise that the Israelites will be like the sand on the seashore, which cannot be measured or counted. **(verse 10)**

The brightness of God's promises shines through in the last three verses of this dark chapter. In the end, it is God's love that will triumph, not people's wickedness! How do you see God – angry or loving?

✝ *God, I bow down in worship for your innumerable mercies in my life. I have often gone astray from you, but you have brought me back to yourself. Thank you, Lord.*

Monday July 30   **Hosea 2.1 – 15**

THE SOURCE OF OUR BLESSINGS   All too often, we forget the real source of our daily blessings. Are we doing better because of our own efforts? Or do we give someone else the credit for the successes of our daily existence? The Israelites were doing very well at this time, both politically and materially. But they gave the credit for this to the wrong source. They thought that their blessings came through Baal, the prominent Canaanite god. They deserted Yahweh just as Gomer left Hosea and went after other lovers, hoping to do better there.

> **She has not acknowledged that I was the one**
> **who gave her the grain, the new wine and oil,**
> **who lavished on her the silver and gold –**
> **which they used for Baal.**   **(verse 8)**

The results of this painful desertion are spelled out in verses 9 – 13: she '"went after her lovers, but me she forgot," declares the LORD' (*verse 13*). The Lord's punishment is, as always, clear. But his grace is again at work in verses 14 – 15. He will lead Israel away from distractions to the desert so that he can speak intimately to her, restore her lost estate and make the Valley of Trouble (Achor) a valley of hope (*verse 15*), a place of singing. He may be a God of anger, but he is much more a God of love!

✝ *Thank you for being the same yesterday, today and forever. I live because of your grace each moment of the day!*

Tuesday July 31   **Hosea 2.16 – 23**

THE GOD WHO RESTORES   This passage glows with the brightness of God's sunshine. It is God's invocation of his promises for the future. It begins with a restored relationship *(verse 16)*. As it was then, so it is now: forgiveness means restored relationships! If we are rightly related to people, barriers will vanish and misunderstandings will be cleared up. If God is the only husband, there will no longer be any other contenders *(verse 17)*. There will also be an ecological balance in the relationship between the creation and the creatures *(verse 18)*.

> 'I will betroth you to me for ever;
> I will betroth you in righteousness and justice,
> in love and compassion.' **(verse 19)**

The final act of restoration is that of mutual belonging: God and the people belong together. How do we respond to God today in the light of this record of his promises and his great and wonderful acts of compassion? Do we take his goodness for granted? How do we walk with him today? If God is faithful today, have we been faithful to him? He loved us so much that he gave his only son to die for us and by believing in him we can have life eternal and an eternal companion on our daily walk through life.

† *God of restoration, help me to walk in step with your Spirit so that I might remain faithful to you as long as I live!*

Wednesday August 1   Hosea 3.1 – 5

THE COST OF RESTORATION   Gomer returns to her old profession, but God commands Hosea to bring her back. Humanly speaking, it must have been very hard for Hosea to love someone who had deliberately deserted him once more. His 'self-respect' must have been tested to breaking point. But he was a prophet of God under divine orders. In a very real sense he had to represent God and his attitude to the nation of Israel. Later in the book Hosea expresses God's anguish: 'How can I give you up, Ephraim?' *(11.8)*. The Lord is bound by his covenant to the Israelites and though the people have deserted him, he will not abandon them. But the time would soon come when the Israelites would be captured by the Assyrians. After paying redemption money, Hosea told his erring wife,

> 'You are to live with me for many days; you must not be a prostitute or be intimate with any man, and I will live with you.' **(verse 3)**

We feel the pathos in the voice of Hosea – in the voice of God speaking through his prophet. After this Gomer is no longer mentioned; the rest of the book focuses entirely on the Israelites. Like Gomer, they will have to pay a heavy price for their desertion: captivity in a foreign land (*verse 4*). But the eternally gracious God will win them back in the end.

✝ *In you alone, O Lord, I put my trust. Help me to respond to the trust that you put in me by never departing from you!*

Thursday August 2   **Hosea 4.1 – 10**

LIKE PEOPLE, LIKE PRIESTS   How very tragic if those who are supposed to lead people to God end up leading them astray from God! From chapter 4 onwards the Lord rebukes the disobedient Israelites for their sins against him and against each other. And those who are condemned first are the religious leaders – the priests. But before we can agree with God's condemnation of them, we need to understand the background. They had obviously been appointed by Jeroboam, who had ignored the law of the Lord and set up his own religious system and appointed priests (*see 1 Kings 12.25 – 33*) who were not the descendants of Aaron. They were the culprits in this confused and miserable religious situation. The people became victims of this corrupt religious system. The priests fed on the ignorance of the people (*verse 8*) and in turn the people perished because of their lack of knowledge (*verse 6*). The Lord will spare neither of them:

> 'And it will be: Like people, like priests.
> I will punish both of them for their ways
> and repay them for their deeds.'   **(verse 9)**

The people should have been wiser, but in the prevailing climate of rampant religious corruption, they failed to discern the difference between the secular and the sacred. Are we any different today? Do we fail because our leaders fail? Each of us individually is accountable to God, who cannot tolerate any irreligious indulgence.

✝ *Dear Lord, I confess that I am often confused and frustrated by today's leaders of your Church. Help me to look to you and find guidance.*

Friday August 3   **Hosea 4.10 – 19**

IMMORALITY IS INFECTIOUS   This is one of the most tragic passages of Scripture. Hosea is honest enough to give a realistic picture of the sinful life of the people of Israel. It is a sordid portrayal of a nation which has become completely immoral. Oh yes, they had all the trappings of religion. But it was a religion empty of any relationship with a holy and righteous God.

> 'A spirit of prostitution leads them astray;
> they are unfaithful to their God. **(part of verse 12)**

Sin never appears in isolation. It grows out of previous sin and unleashes a chain of actions and reactions. If the priests set a bad example by indulging in temple prostitution, the people copy them, quickly followed by their daughters and daughters-in-law. What does the Lord say to this kind of people? Stop behaving like hypocrites, worshipping in religious places and swearing by the Lord while continuing to sin (*verse 15*). Like a stubborn heifer, the Israelites have become totally indifferent to the ways of the Lord. And so 'a whirlwind will sweep them away, and their sacrifices will bring them shame' (*verse 19*). If immorality spreads like an infection, judgement is sure to follow!

† *Help me to treasure your word in my heart today, O Lord, so that I do not sin against you in word, deed, and action.*

Saturday August 4   **Hosea 5.1 – 7**

FURTHER DIAGNOSIS LEADS TO A FEARFUL DOOM
The Bible declares, 'it is a dreadful thing to fall into the hands of the living God' (*Hebrews 10.31*). The covenant had established a holy alliance between God and the people. But the people broke the covenant by aligning themselves with pagan gods and, ever since, their lives had been lived in moral darkness. The first verse of this chapter includes everyone: priests, people and princes together had sinned against God. God warns them because he knows all about them (*verse 3*). Why did they go wrong? Three answers are given: 'Their deeds do not permit them to return to their God' (*verse 4*); 'Israel's arrogance testifies against them' (*verse 5*); 'They are unfaithful to the LORD' (*verse 7*). They were unfaithful in their personal lives, arrogant towards other people and, more importantly, unfaithful to God. And so the fearful judgement:

> 'When they go with their flocks and herds
> to seek the LORD,
> they will not find him;
> he has withdrawn himself from them.' **(verse 6)**

This divine diagnosis of Israel's sin eventually led God to prescribe a dreadful sentence of judgement: go into captivity. Israel, the northern kingdom, was taken captive by the Assyrians in 722 BC and some of its tribes can still not be traced. It is indeed a dreadful thing to fall into the hands of a holy God.

† *I come to you today, dear Lord, not because of my own righteousness but leaning on your abundant love and mercy. Help me to walk this day in loyalty to you.*

For group discussion and personal thought

● If you know of a family which is experiencing difficulties and in danger of breaking up, how could you minister to them in the spirit of Hosea? If possible, put your thinking into practice.

● What practical steps could you and other members of your local church take as a group to minister to those who are divorced? What can you learn from the book of Hosea to help you in this ministry?

GOD OF LOVE AND ANGER
Hosea 2

Notes by John Holder

based on the Revised Standard Version

John Holder is an Anglican priest who was born in Barbados and is now deputy principal of Codrington College, the Anglican theological college for the province of the West Indies. He also ministers in a small parish and is married with one son.

The prophet Hosea told his people that God was a God of love and compassion – but he also kept before them the harsh fact that they would suffer as a consequence of their wrongdoing. The picture of God as a mother reaching out to embrace her wayward children is one of Hosea's most powerful images, indeed, one of the most powerful images of God in the Old Testament. The community is challenged to respond to God or face the consequences; but even after this, God is still willing and able to heal and restore.

Text for the week: Hosea 6.1

Sunday August 5   **Hosea 6.1 – 11**

A SECOND CHANCE   The prophet Hosea lived in a time of political instability and religious uncertainty. Assyria, the most powerful nation of that time, was sweeping across the Ancient Near East, conquering many countries. It must have been a frightening and confusing time for many in Israel, but Hosea proclaims that Yahweh, the God of Israel, continues to reach out to his people. On behalf of Yahweh he issues an invitation to his community:

> 'Come, let us return to the LORD;
>   for he has torn, that he may heal us;
>   he has stricken, and he will bind us up.'   **(verse 1)**

This invitation implies that many in Israel were turning away from Yahweh. But for Hosea, all was not lost. There was a second chance, or maybe even a third or a fourth. However difficult life was, God was still there inviting his people to return to his way, giving them another chance. Here is a message of great hope. As Christians, we need to share Hosea's conviction that God in his compassion gives us a second chance. Then we can use this as a basis for a solid Christian pastoral and evangelistic outreach to those burdened with guilt who are longing for a second chance.

† *O God, who in your compassion has given us a second chance in Jesus our Lord, help us to do the same for others.*

Monday August 6   Hosea 8.1 – 10

REAPING THE WHIRLWIND   This passage reflects one of the dominant convictions of the prophets of Israel – that a community experiences the consequences of its evil actions. On an individual level, this means that we always pay the price for what we have done wrong. Hosea paints a gloomy picture of the price that his people must pay for their wrongdoing. They have lost sight of the way of God.

> To me they cry,
> My God, we Israel know thee.   **(verse 2)**

But this is a hollow cry, because their actions reflect the very opposite. The weakness of their rulers, suggested in verse 4, points to a leadership crisis. According to Hosea, the role of leadership is to ensure that things go right, by having a strong allegiance to the covenant with Yahweh and obeying his laws of righteousness and justice. This was not being done (*verse 1*), and the Israelites were experiencing the consequences. By sowing the wind the community was reaping the whirlwind. Leadership has to include responsibility. Poor leadership can create many problems for those who are being led; strong leadership can achieve the opposite. This passage of Hosea is a challenge to reflect on leadership and pray for the leaders within the Church, our community and in the wider world.

† *Give us the strength, O Lord, to follow your way with courage and to speak your truth with conviction.*

Tuesday August 7   Hosea 9.10 – 17

SPOILT GRAPES   These verses sound like a death sentence for the condemned. Full of compassion in other places, Hosea here paints a dismal picture of death and destruction. The God of anger is at work. The prophet(s) recalls the early good times that are no more (*verse 10*). Israel in the distant past could be compared to grapes in the wilderness, that is, refreshment and hope in a barren and hopeless environment. She is now detestable, no longer a source of hope. There were two levels to the crisis that Hosea's people were facing. At one level there were the conquering Assyrians, sweeping every nation before them. Israel was in their path and could not escape. At the other level there was the religious condition of Israel. Religion had become a convenient mixture of several religious strands that were alien to Israel and which damaged its identity. This mixture was, for the prophet, a rejection of Yahweh. At this second level, Hosea angrily threatens what will happen:

> **My God will cast them off,**
> **because they have not hearkened to him;**
> **they shall be wanderers among the nations.**   **(verse 17)**

Israel will pay the ultimate price: rejection by Yahweh and loss of his precious gift of the land. In the midst of the national crisis, Hosea does not allow his people to pretend that all is well. He challenges them to face the reality of their own shortcomings and the coming destruction and conquest. Hosea provides the realism that Israel needs.

✝ *Give us the vision, O Lord, to avoid the conditions of life that can lead us and those close to us to disaster.*

Wednesday August 8   **Hosea 10.1 – 12**

THE DANGER OF A DOUBLE ALLEGIANCE   Here Hosea deals with one of his central concerns: the way in which Israel had accepted Canaanite culture. Cultures naturally borrow from each other, but Hosea and other prophets treat the Israelite and Canaanite cultures as completely incompatible. The 'pillars' of verses 1 and 2 and the building of altars refer to the aspects of Canaanite religion which were probably very attractive to the people of Israel. The Israelites probably saw nothing wrong with mixing elements of the Canaanite religion with their own, but Hosea, with his strong belief in Yahweh, would have none of it. For Israel, it must be Yahweh only. There is no room for compromise. The other way, Hosea proclaims, is a road to sure destruction.

> **I will come against the wayward people to chastise them;**
> **and nations shall be gathered against them**
> **when they are chastised for their double iniquity.**
>
> **(verse 10)**

Today we may find it difficult to understand the passion of Hosea. We live in multi-cultural communities and accept a multi-cultural world where truth can be found in many places and, some people would argue, in many religions. But Hosea was concerned with allegiance and commitment. He was addressing a community which had once clung to the belief that Yahweh was its only God, who had entered into a covenant relationship with this community, Israel. The allegiance and commitment were not only to Yahweh but to everything that made Israel what it was. There are many things which threaten our own belief in God and in the person we have become over the years. We often need the passion and conviction of Hosea to deal with these threats. We often need his passion to remain committed.

✝ *Lord, give us the courage to live by all we claim to believe about you.*

Thursday August 9   **Hosea 11.1 – 11**

LOVE THAT WILL NOT GROW COLD This is one of the most moving passages in the entire Old Testament – indeed, in the entire Bible. In verses 1 – 4 and 8 – 9, God is presented to us as a loving, devoted parent who finds it very difficult to punish a wayward child. Yahweh the God of Israel is shown as a mother who fusses over her self-willed young child (*verses 3 – 4*). These verses bring hope after the judgement and destruction of chapters 8 – 10. Yahweh recalls his past relationship with Israel. He was a devoted parent, doing everything that a loving, caring, compassionate mother would do for her young child. His love stands firm, in spite of the way that Israel has tested and tried it. His love and compassion will not disappear. The anger will fade, the destruction will be stopped:

> **I will not execute my fierce anger,**
> **I will not again destroy Ephraim.**   **(verse 9)**

Yahweh's love and compassion will bring about a return to the land from exile (*verses 10 – 11*) – the two things which everyone needs in order to survive: freedom, and a country we can call our own. Verses 5 – 7 remind us that God has compassion even when we offend him. In all our own relationships with family, friends and others, let us work to ensure that there is a large measure of compassion.

† *O God of compassion, who forgives us when we sin and welcomes us back when we stray, help us to share your compassion with others.*

Friday August 10   **Hosea 12.2 – 9**

ISRAEL THE OPPRESSOR The theme of Israel's sin returns. The breath of hope that we experienced in chapter 11 has evaporated and we once more face the harsh reality of a country that is plunging into destruction. Verse 2 shows Yahweh as a judge, sitting in judgement over the accused, Israel. He is fair in his judgements and Israel (Jacob) will be punished only for what he has done wrong. In verses 3 and 4 we are taken back to the well-known stories of Jacob, who became Israel's hero ancestor through his tricks and activity. It is the God whom the ancestor Jacob encountered and embraced who now brings judgement upon the hero's descendants. Like the commander of an army, he is God of hosts (*Yahweh sabaoth*) and has the power to punish his enemies. He remains in absolute control, in spite of the power of the Assyrians with their invincible army. There are times when our own world seems to be falling apart, times when we too need the faith of the prophet Hosea. We can find some comfort and encouragement in his words:

> **Hold fast to love and justice,**
> **and wait continually for your God.**   **(part of verse 6)**

In conditions of chaos and destruction, corruption and a lack of commitment, Hosea still speaks of Yahweh who provides experiences of salvation. For him, no experience can rob Yahweh of this saving power. Although this saving power of Yahweh will not cancel out the consequences of Israel's actions, it will work to move Israel away from the very conditions which produced those actions and return the people to the earlier days of their closer relationship with Yahweh. Our relationship with God can also be threatened, and sometimes, like Hosea, we need to recall the times when we were closer to God and then work to get back there.

† *O God, help us to follow you, our God of hope who leads us to experiences of salvation.*

Saturday August 11   **Hosea 14.1 – 9**

YAHWEH IS WAITING AND READY TO FORGIVE This last chapter of the book of Hosea is a desperate plea to Israel to return to Yahweh their God. The image of the caring parent of chapter 11 returns. To help them to return, the people are given a prayer of repentance and confession (*verses 2 – 3*). Here Yahweh is not a God of judgement and anger but a God of love and compassion. The book of Hosea ends on a very warm, compassionate and caring note.

> I will heal their faithlessness;
> I will love them freely,
> for my anger has turned from them. (verse 4)

At the very end of Hosea's book, a brand-new page opens in the Yahweh-Israel relationship. In the Old Testament prophets Yahweh's last word to Israel is never a word of judgement, but a word of hope. As Christians, we can relate to this profound understanding of the Israel-Yahweh relationship, because our faith is also based on this understanding of God. The movement from Good Friday to Easter is also a statement about the God who is never content with chaos and destruction. He wants resurrection, not crucifixion. This week's readings from the book of Hosea can provide us with a balanced and realistic understanding of our relationship with God. This relationship does not shield us from the consequences of our own actions, but offers us hope of restoration beyond the consequences. The unpleasant experiences of this life can never destroy God's love and care for us. This is the hope upon which we stand.

† *O Lord of compassion, keep hope alive in us.*

For group discussion and personal thought

- When last did you give anyone a second chance? How about today?
- Are repentance and forgiveness still treated as important Christian qualities today?
- Do we need to emphasize far more a God of compassion?
- For Hosea, no one in his community was beyond the point of return in their relationship with God. What effect could this message have on your community?

THE POWER OF DREAMING 1
Dreams, fantasies or nightmares?

Notes by Peter Tongeman

based on the New International Version

Peter Tongeman is a retired Baptist minister who has worked in town and country churches, national youth leadership, and as an Area Superintendent. He was President of the Baptist Union of Great Britain for a year and is now a freelance writer and poet.

Most dreams result from the mind's strange wanderings in sleep and are forgotten soon after waking. But dreams can also express inner yearnings and hope for the future. Martin Luther King's famous speech incorporated his longing for freedom from oppression. 'I have a dream that my four little children one day will live in a nation where they will not be judged by the colour of their skin, but by the content of their character.' Day-dreams are not related to reality and usually drift into fantasy. Nightmares, which are often frightening, usually arise from extreme anxiety or indigestion! As we explore some of the dreams of the Bible, we shall try to discover their significance both for the dreamer and for ourselves.

Text for the week: Hebrews 11.1

Sunday August 12   **Hebrews 11.1 – 3, 8 – 16**

VISUALIZING THE FUTURE   No one has achieved anything worthwhile without a vision. A politician visualizes a radical change in society and works for it. An architect visualizes a building and draws up a plan. A Christian leader, confronted by the suffering brought about by human greed and selfishness, sees the possibility of a new and better world through the spread of the gospel. Vision, accompanied by faith and action, achieves lasting results. Abraham, living in Haran, dreamed of a future far away and in circumstances yet to be revealed. A future that would be shaped with God's help and sustained by his presence.

He was looking forward to the city with foundations, whose architect and builder is God.   **(verse 10)**

He set out in faith ready for whatever the future might bring, sure of what he hoped for and certain of what he did not see (*verse 1*). The character of Abraham and all the people listed in Hebrews 11 is marked by determination and obedience. They were people whose vision for life and the future was God-given:

> **they were longing for a better country – a heavenly one. Therefore God is not ashamed to be called their God, for he has prepared a city for them.** (verse 16)

† *Grant me, O Lord, a vision of what is possible, earnest desire to work for it, and strength to achieve it.*

Monday August 13   Genesis 32.22 – 32

DREAM OR REALITY? An anxiety dream, or nightmare, confronts the dreamer with a desperate situation that cannot be resolved, until you wake up perspiring! Jacob's 'nightmare' experience involved a wrestling match with a stranger who turned out to be God himself. It lasted all night and left him exhausted.

> **When the man saw that he could not overpower him, he touched the socket of Jacob's hip so that his hip was wrenched as he wrestled with the man. Then the man said, 'Let me go, for it is daybreak.' But Jacob replied, 'I will not let you go unless you bless me.' ... Then the man said, 'Your name will no longer be Jacob, but Israel, because you have struggled with God and with men and have overcome.'**
> **(verses 25 – 26 and 28)**

This incident probably represents Jacob's inner struggle. He had cunningly snatched their father's blessing from his older brother and fled. Now his conscience pricked him. He was terrified that Esau would seek revenge. The inner struggle through that night left him humbled and broken as he recognized his sin and longed to be free. By morning his outlook was changed. Jacob ('deceiver') had become Israel ('overcomer').

† *Lord, like Jacob, my shortcomings are all too apparent. As I wrestle with them, grant me inner strength to overcome what is evil and pursue what is good.*

A DREAM OF SUPERIORITY

> Joseph had a dream, and when he told it to his brothers,
> they hated him all the more. He said to them, 'Listen to this
> dream I had: We were binding sheaves of corn out in the
> field when suddenly my sheaf rose and stood upright,
> while your sheaves gathered round mine and bowed down
> to it.'   (verses 5 – 7)

Seventeen-year-old Joseph's dreams were as much the result of
his father's foolishness in spoiling him as his own sense of
superiority over his brothers. Naturally, they resented him.
How frequently relationships are damaged by a false sense of
superiority! A newly promoted manager drops his former
friends for new ones with supposed higher status. A young
person, fresh from exam success, dismisses others who did less
well. A newly appointed minister foolishly *demands* respect
instead of working patiently to earn it. Paul advised, 'Do not
think of yourself more highly than you ought' (*Romans 12.3*).
Peter tells us to look up to God rather than down on others.
'Humble yourselves ... under God's mighty hand, that he may
lift you up in due time' (*1 Peter 5.6*).

† *Loving God, forbid that a spirit of superiority should damage my
relationship with others. Teach me humility so that I may value
others as much as myself.*

DREAMS EXPLAINED

> [Joseph] asked Pharaoh's officials who were in custody
> with him in his master's house, 'Why are your faces so sad
> today?' 'We both had dreams,' they answered, 'but there is
> no-one to interpret them.' Then Joseph said to them, 'Do
> not interpretations belong to God? Tell me your dreams.'
>   (verses 7 – 9)

Joseph attributed to God his ability to interpret his fellow-
prisoners' dreams. For Pharaoh's former butler it meant life and
hope; for the baker, execution. Helping others interpret life's
problems and mysteries is a role that alert Christians can
sometimes exercise. The problem of suffering, experience of
life's uncertainty, the meaning of life itself, are matters that
puzzle and perplex many people. Drawing alongside them in
friendship, listening as burdens are shared and offering

sympathy in trouble are ways of letting others know that someone cares. Then, when bitter questions are asked – 'Why? Why me?' – or doubts expressed concerning the purpose and direction of life, a Christian can point gently to a heavenly Father who knows and loves; to Jesus whose life and teaching help to make sense of living; and to a hope that extends beyond the grave into eternity.

† *Father God, keep me alert to the pain and insecurity that others may bear and grant me wisdom to offer comfort, insight and hope.*

Thursday August 16   Genesis 41.14 – 32

A CHANGE OF DIRECTION Two years after the butler was restored to office, he overheard Pharaoh recounting a dream. He remembered Joseph and spoke up for him.

So Pharaoh sent for Joseph, and he was quickly brought from the dungeon. When he had shaved and changed his clothes, he came before Pharaoh. Pharaoh said to Joseph, 'I had a dream, and no one can interpret it. But I have heard it said of you that when you hear a dream you can interpret it.' 'I cannot do it,' Joseph replied to Pharaoh, 'but God will give Pharaoh the answer he desires.' **(verses 14 – 16)**

'God moves in a mysterious way his wonders to perform' (William Cowper). Through an unexpected event, Joseph's long wait was rewarded. He was given honour and responsibility beyond imagination. God's time had come. The years of suffering had prepared him for such a time as this. 'It was not you who sent me here, but God', he later told his brothers (*Genesis 45.8*). Nelson Mandela also endured long years of imprisonment until, in his country's hour of need and opportunity, he was released and elected President of South Africa. We may be assured that 'in all things God works for the good of those ... who have been called according to his purpose' (*Romans 8.28*).

† *Lord, help me to trust you when I am perplexed and cannot see the way ahead. Remind me that your purpose is still to be revealed.*

Friday August 17   Jeremiah 23.21 – 32
BOGUS DREAMS

I have heard what the prophets say who prophesy lies in my name. They say, 'I had a dream! I had a dream!' 'Yes,'

> declares the LORD, 'I am against the prophets who wag
> their own tongues and yet declare, "The LORD declares."
> Indeed, I am against those who prophesy false dreams',
> declares the LORD. 'They tell them and lead my people
> astray ... They do not benefit these people in the least.'
> (verses 25, 31 – 32)

Some dreams seem to offer attractive possibilities but
eventually fail to satisfy. Dreaming of material prosperity,
important as this is, does not of itself bring happiness or lasting
benefit. Handled unwisely, it quickly gives way to greed and
selfishness, displacing Christian values like love, service and
sacrifice. Those who claimed to be prophets in Jeremiah's day
delighted in offering what people wanted rather than what
God, in his righteousness, desired for them. Without reference
to God, human aspirations alone lead people astray. Every
believer's aim must be to hear and obey God's word of truth
rather than human desires. By listening, they are turning 'from
their evil ways and from their evil deeds' (*verse 22*).

† *Help me to recognize and resist all false promises and bogus ideals*
that lead astray. Attune my ears to your voice, O Lord, that I may
discern what is true and right and live by it.

Saturday August 18   Matthew 27.15 – 26

WARNING IGNORED

> When the crowd had gathered, Pilate asked them, 'Which
> one do you want me to release to you: Barabbas, or Jesus
> who is called Christ?' For he knew it was out of envy that
> they had handed Jesus over to him. While Pilate was
> sitting on the judge's seat, his wife sent him this message:
> 'Don't have anything to do with that innocent man, for I
> have suffered a great deal today in a dream because of
> him.'   (verses 17 – 19)

Pilate, governor of Judea, found himself in an impossible
position when Jesus was brought to him for judgement.
Believing that Jesus was innocent, in justice he should have
released him. But he was afraid of the Jewish leaders who
threatened a riot if Jesus was set free. Either way, Pilate was in
trouble. His wife recognized Jesus' innocence and warned him.
But Pilate yielded to pressure. Warnings of conscience and
plain justice were ignored. A rail crash in England in which
many died occurred because warnings of equipment failure

were ignored. A swimmer, despising warnings of strong currents, was swept away to his death. We cannot avoid responsibility for our own actions and the consequences.

✝ *From weak and cowardly decisions, from foolish disregard of what is right, from deafness to the voice of conscience, refusing truth, eyes blinded to the light – Lord Jesus Christ deliver me, lest I prolong your Calvary.*

For group discussion and personal thought

● What dreams do you have for the future? Are they consistent with Christian values? How can you best seek to achieve them?

Online to God

● An exciting collection of original prayers, written by young people from many parts of the world and complemented by lively illustrations and activities

● An ideal present for 7–12-year-olds

● Also valuable for teachers, group leaders and parents

UK price £4.50

IBRA

Order through your IBRA representative, or from the appropriate address on page 285.

THE POWER OF DREAMING 2
Discerning the message

Notes by Alec Gilmore

based on the Revised English Bible

Alec Gilmore is a Baptist minister with 20 years' pastoral experience in England followed by a literature ministry for the benefit of the Third World and Eastern Europe as Director of Feed the Minds. He lives in Sussex and is a freelance writer and lecturer, mostly on biblical topics. He has published a number of books.

What matters is not the dream but the perception. Not what we see, but how we see, interpret and understand, and what we do as a result. Through the stresses and strains of an ancient Babylonian king and the personal experience of Jesus we learn how to see beneath the surface, to hear outside our normal range, and to get a new grasp of what is happening to us and around us.

Text for the week: Matthew 13.16

Sunday August 19   **Daniel 2.1 – 16**

EXPECTING THE IMPOSSIBLE   Nebuchadnezzar has had a dream. His problem is not what it means. It is that he cannot remember what the dream was and demands that his wise men tell him. They cannot. If he does not know, how can they? The request is crazy. The expectation is totally unreasonable. So they tell him.

> **What your majesty asks is too hard; none but the gods can tell you, and they dwell remote from mortals.**   **(verse 11)**

Yet we all do it. Sometimes we suffer from others who do it. We imagine that whatever the problem is, something can always be done about it. Something can surely be done to take away my pain, cure my illness, bring back my loved one, find me a job, prevent street accidents, reduce violence, etc, etc. Daniel comes at it differently. He sees that the first step is not what happened, but why such an unreasonable request is being made (*verse 15*). After all, if Nebuchadnezzar cannot even remember it, why is he worrying about it? Perhaps he is unable to handle the situation but expects somebody else to do so. Perhaps he is angry and has to shout at somebody. Perhaps he is under stress. But surely somebody can do something!

† *Lord, when I find myself expecting the impossible, help me to take a look at myself. Why am I doing it?*

Monday August 20   **Daniel 2.17 – 35**

RECOGNIZING THE TRUTH God's solutions do not always come in visions, or indeed in ways that we expect. That is often why we miss them. Sometimes we have to work at them for ourselves. And that is what Daniel did. He worked out what sort of things were worrying the king and then fed back to him an image of his problem. He does not actually tell Nebuchadnezzar anything that he does not know already, but he does help him to recognize it and face up to it. Recognizing truth is not always about learning something we did not know, getting more information or even meaning. It may be simply coming at the problem in a different way, or actually facing up to something we have been trying to avoid. When that happens Daniel is careful to point out that this insight is a gift from God.

There is in heaven a God who reveals secrets ... This is the dream and these are the visions that came into your head.
(verse 28)

† *Father, when I find myself facing an impasse, please help me to look for a solution in a different place. When it helps, thank you. When it requires something from me, give me a push.*

Tuesday August 21   **Daniel 2.36 – 47**

UNDERSTANDING THE TRUTH Daniel interprets the dream and Nebuchadnezzar is duly humbled. But actually knowing the dream (or even the interpretation) does not really help very much. It certainly does not change anything, and there is no suggestion that Nebuchadnezzar did (or even could do) anything about it. He may now know what it was all about. He sees. He hears. He finds it all very worrying and shattering, but he still does not understand. So Daniel does not leave it there. He suggests that Nebuchadnezzar may have been looking in the wrong place and points him to a kingdom of a different sort:

the God of heaven will establish a kingdom which will never be destroyed, nor will it ever pass to another people ... it will itself endure for ever.   **(verse 44)**

Having 'seen' in a different way himself, Daniel now invites the king to do the same. The sort of 'kingdoms' that have been worrying the king are not the ones that really matter – he needs to look beyond and above. Jesus was saying much the same thing when he talked about the kingdom of God in so many of his parables.

† *Lord Jesus, forgive me when I get so obsessed with a few things very close to me and lose touch with the wider picture. Teach me how to look above and beyond.*

Wednesday August 22   **Matthew 2.19 – 23**

JOSEPH'S ANXIETIES Joseph seems to be the victim of competing messages or 'hunches'. One says it's OK to go back. The other says no, perhaps it isn't. It was not possible for both dreams to have been 'the voice of God'. Not all dreams are. Like Joseph, we have to use common sense. Most of us know the experience: the nightmare has passed and we feel a wonderful sense of relief. The worry was unwarranted or, if it was warranted, it is no longer. No need ever to worry again. We 'feel' better. But then the old anxieties come back.

> **But when he heard that Archelaus had succeeded his father Herod ... he withdrew to the region of Galilee, where he settled in a town called Nazareth.**   **(verse 22)**

Caution is called for. Such caution may not be necessary. It may not be right. It may not be what God wants. We may even be thwarting his purposes. But he can still use us – by working now through our caution just as much as he would have worked through our obedience. Jesus will be brought up in Nazareth.

† *Father, help me to walk obediently in your way, but thank you for reassuring me that when my own wisdom leads me by a different route you can still fulfil your purposes through me.*

Thursday August 23   **Matthew 13.10 – 17**

SPEAKING IN PARABLES Parables are about things you cannot be *told*. You can only discover them for yourself. They have to be true for you! And, like the best drama, theatre and children's stories, they can be taken at many levels: the superficial and the literal, the deeper or hidden (that is, for you personally), or as a basis for discussion (that is, the result of sharing ideas with others, where working out the meaning may even be more important than the meaning itself). Two and two may be four. But some people see it as twenty-two. And if one member of a group says, 'two and two what?' you could be in for a long debate! Parables are like that. To some they are just stories. To some they have a lesson or point a moral. But to those who are prepared to put them in a different setting, in the New Testament or in contemporary life, they have an infinite capacity to touch new depths. Try it with one or two of your favourites. The rewards of discovering new meanings and interpretations can be very satisfying.

> **Happy are your eyes because they see, and your ears because they hear.** (verse 16)

† *Lord, open my eyes, that I may see.*

Friday August 24 **Luke 4.16 – 30**

FAILED DISCERNMENT Jesus goes home and is given a warm welcome. They are proud of him. They invite him to 'preach' and he makes a fair impression (*verse 22*), but Jesus knows what they are saying:

> **'We have heard of all your doings at Capernaum; do the same here in your own home town.'** (verse 23)

But it is not like it was in Capernaum. And Jesus thinks he knows why:

> **'no prophet is recognized in his own country.'** (verse 24)

They are not really 'hearing' him. *He* may be doing the same as he did in Capernaum, but *they* are not in a mood to recognize him. Why? Are they really so impressed by him that they cannot hear what he says? Is he too close to them, so that familiarity dulls insight? Or too remote, tackling issues that they do not consider all that interesting or important? Or perhaps they *do* hear, only too well, and do not like it! Certainly what makes the situation explode is the suggestion that other people understand Jesus' meaning, even if they don't!

† *Father, when I find myself taking things for granted and getting bored, or being angry because changes and new ideas are forced upon me, help me to take myself in hand. It could be you trying to get through.*

NEW SATISFACTIONS   The usual interpretation of verses 7 – 11 is the very obvious one that here we have a lesson in humility: take the lower place. And Proverbs underlines this:

> **Do not push yourself forward at court**
> **or take your stand where the great assemble;**
> **for it is better to be told, 'Come up here',**
> **than to be moved down to make room for a nobleman.**
>
> (verses 6 – 7)

But two other notes ought not to be missed. One, try to avoid being humiliated or made to look silly. Two, take the lower place so that you can have the satisfaction of being noticed (*verse 10*). Better to get a reputation for 'being honoured' than for grabbing. Verses 12 – 14 are similar and equally obvious. Choose the poor and humble rather than the rich and mighty. Be Magnificat! But again, avoid any suggestion of looking for anything in return. Let your satisfaction be in your generosity. Both stories suggest something positive in recognition and honour, and in happiness, joy and satisfaction. There is no need to feel guilty about that, but learn to find it in different places and in different ways.

† *Father, make me always recognize all those places where I normally get my thrills, but help me to discover joy and satisfaction in other places too, and perhaps occasionally where I never thought of looking.*

For group discussion and personal thought

- Identify one thing you have learned this week about 'seeing' or discernment and reflect on how it could make a difference to your daily life.
- Make a short list of some of the characteristics you might expect to find in a kingdom that will 'endure for ever' (*Daniel 2.44*). What are the chances of it happening and what prevents it?
- Can you recall any moments in your own experience when, looking back, you think you misinterpreted what God was saying, but it turned out for good all the same?

THE POWER OF DREAMING 3
God's dreams

Notes by Philip Wetherell

based on the New English Bible

Philip Wetherell is the Director of Christians Abroad, an ecumenical advice and consultancy agency. In the past he has been a missionary teacher in Namibia, directed a religious education centre in England, worked for the United Society for the Propagation of the Gospel and been the UK administrator of an NGO working in Zambia.

When we dream, we discover some of our deepest feelings and fears. We may find it hard to discover or come to terms with what they mean. God's dreams are about his hopes and promises for us, and we come across them in the songs and stories of his faithful followers. The week's readings begin and end with the same dream – God's promise for all creation, not earned but given through his grace – God's ultimate gift and dream for all creation.

Text for the week: Isaiah 25.8

Sunday August 26   **Genesis 1.1 – 5, 20 – 31**

A DREAM OF HOW IT MIGHT BE We cannot think of a loving God who is not a creator and, from what we know of God, what he creates must be good. That is the refrain at the end of every day of the creation dream. God creates from nothing – the greatest vision and dream that there can be. He sees a world in which there is light rather than darkness, order rather than chaos, and in which creatures live in harmony under the care and protection of human beings. His representatives on earth, the humans made in his own image, are there to carry forward that vision:

> **God created man in his own image ... male and female he created them. God blessed them and said to them, 'Be fruitful and increase, fill the earth and subdue it.'**
>
> **(verses 27 – 28)**

Many of our dreams are shattered, and it seems as if God's dream will suffer the same fate. But, as we shall see, he never gives up.

✝ *Lord, when I am tempted to give up, help me to persevere in the things I know are right, so that I may be your representative in this world.*

Monday August 27   Isaiah 5.1 – 7

A DREAM OF JUSTICE   Through his prophet, God sings his dream of justice. Israel is God's beloved, his special people, and they have let him down – badly. They are like a vineyard which has had care and attention lavished on it but which has failed to bear fruit. Instead, it has yielded wild grapes and as a result it will not be pruned or hoed and will grow thorns. God will command the clouds to send no more rain – only God can do that! This is a passionate denunciation of the oppression of the poor and powerless; Israel risks losing its special place in God's heart.

> **The vineyard of the LORD of Hosts is Israel,**
> **and the men of Judah are the plant he cherished.**
> **He looked for justice and found it denied,**
> **for righteousness but heard cries of distress.**   **(verse 7)**

Yet, as we shall see, God's dream that one day there will be a community living in justice and peace remains part of his hope for Israel.

✝ *Lord, may I work for your kingdom of justice and peace, to make your dream a reality in my community.*

Tuesday August 28   Isaiah 11.1 – 9

A DREAM OF A NEW BEGINNING   This familiar prophecy, known to us from Christmas readings, is a vision of the ideal king with supernatural qualities. It tells of a man on whom God's Spirit of wisdom, understanding, counsel, power, knowledge and fear of the Lord will rest. He will rule over a land of justice in which the paradise of the Garden of Eden will be restored. Children will play safely with wild animals, who all seem to have become vegetarian! The king cares for all that has been created, rather than rules over it, and favours the poor and the humble. True peace will come to Israel – not just victory over opponents or even the end of war, but the return of paradise under a just judge. But while the results will be felt and seen by all, the origin of all this is spiritual. There is a religious basis for this social justice.

> **They shall not hurt or destroy in all my holy mountain;**
> **for as the waters fill the sea,**
> **so shall the land be filled with the knowledge of the LORD.**
> **(verse 9)**

Justice comes through God's Spirit and is seen in a new heaven and earth which are both full of the knowledge of the Lord. The real dream is that we should have that knowledge and see it as the foundation and beginning of a just life.

✝ *Lord, may I come to know you more deeply and make my own new beginning in a just and spiritual life.*

Wednesday August 29   **Isaiah 25.6 – 8**

A DREAM FOR THE WHOLE EARTH   The dream starts where the last one finished – on the mountain of the Lord. Rather than a vision of peace and harmony, this is a party! There will be a rich banquet, the best food and the finest wines. It is a heavenly banquet, the party which celebrates being with God. But that is just the dream. It is a symbol of a happy future.

> **On this mountain the LORD will swallow up**
> **that veil that shrouds all the peoples ...**
> **he will swallow up death for ever.**   **(parts of verses 7 – 8)**

This is the clearest statement about death in the whole of the prophetic writings. Tears will be wiped away, immortality is possible. Our disobedience has meant that God's intentions have been temporarily thwarted. Death was not intended at the beginning; paradise was meant to be everlasting. Now, in God's dream as understood by the prophet, it will be possible for the original promise to be fulfilled – for the whole earth, all peoples, all the nations.

> **Then the Lord GOD will wipe away the tears from every face and remove the reproach of his people from the whole earth.**
> **The LORD has spoken.**   **(verse 8b)**

✝ *Lord, let me live my life as if I truly believe that your promise of life after earthly death is for me.*

Thursday August 30   **Isaiah 35.1 – 10**

A DREAM OF A PERFECT PLACE   We all have our dreams of the perfect place or future situation. For the homeless person it may be a home – any home will do; for someone unemployed it may be a job – any job. For others the perfect place may be a favourite holiday destination or perhaps an ideal place for retirement. In this passage, it is a place for those who are returning from physical and spiritual exile – and it is perfect. The wilderness will burst into flower, disabled people will lose their disabilities, wild beasts will be banished, the anxious will become strong. Every human uncertainty, weakness or illness will be done away with. Although this passage is not as poetic as some of the other verses we are looking at this week, it gives us a wonderful picture. But if these are the physical changes which the dream says will accompany a return from exile, what spiritual changes may happen in us if we turn again to God? We will go along a 'Way of Holiness':

> By it those he has ransomed shall return
>   and the LORD's redeemed come home;
> they shall enter Zion with shouts of triumph,
> crowned with everlasting gladness.   (verses 9b – 10)

✝ *Lord, help me to prepare myself to walk in the way of holiness, to come to the perfect place which is the home of the redeemed.*

Friday August 31   Isaiah 33.13 – 24

A DREAM OF SECURITY Like yesterday's passage, this dream is again of a glorious future, but this time it is seen in terms of safety and security. Barbarous people will no longer be seen; in the rivers that flow in what was previously desert, there will be no threat from enemy ships; and Israel's holy city of Jerusalem, often threatened, will be secure like a tent whose pegs will never be moved (*verse 20*). Like yesterday, the dreamer's expectations of those who hear his words are set out very clearly. Yesterday, we were told that no unclean person could pass along the Way of Holiness; today we are given a list of sins which will disqualify people. They are social sins, the kind which weaken communities: extortion, taking bribes, pretending we know nothing about evil in the world around us. But the person who is upright and truthful,

> that is the man who shall dwell on the heights,
>   his refuge a fastness in the cliffs,
> his bread secure and his water never failing.   (verse 16)

Such people help to produce a secure society in which everyone takes a full part and has a full share – the sick, the blind and the lame are the examples given in the dream (*verse 23*). In that society, the sins of the people who live there are pardoned.

✝ *Lord, help me to play my part in my society, so that all can have an equal share in its benefits, and all will be pardoned.*

Saturday September 1   **Matthew 20.1 – 16**

A DREAM OF ULTIMATE EQUALITY Like Monday's reading, this is a vineyard scene – but this time we are concerned about the workers, not the crop. Like many of the parables of Jesus, this is a dream of the Kingdom of God. The owner of the vineyard gives everyone the same treatment, although some have laboured far longer than others. He is generous to some, without being unjust to others. Those who are called first have no right to be offended.

> **The owner turned to one of them and said, 'My friend, I am not being unfair to you. You agreed on the usual wage for the day, did you not? ... I choose to pay the last man the same as you ... Why be jealous because I am kind?'**
> **(part of verses 13 – 15)**

This story was probably remembered as a rebuff to Jewish Christians who resented the privilege of salvation being extended to non-Jews. But today we can look to the future instead of the past. The reward is the same for all who have been faithful, who have done what they were asked to do. A loving and gracious God gives no special favours. We are all equal in what we receive from God – and that is so much more than anything we have earned by our own labour. It cannot be measured against our fellow Christians. It is the ultimate gift, the ultimate dream.

✝ *Lord, may I learn not to measure myself against others, but instead be thankful for the value of your ultimate gift of life in your kingdom.*

For group discussion and personal thought

● What, for you, would be your perfect place? What, for you, would be a picture of perfect security in society? What, for you, are the signs of a just and equal society?

THE POWER OF DREAMING 4
Transformation

Notes by David Huggett

based on the Good News Bible

There may be truth in the suggestion that we are all either 'doers' or 'dreamers', but that is an over-simplification. Today the emphasis is on getting things done. Success and accomplishment are frequently the only yardstick used to measure an individual's worth. To balance that we need those who are prepared to dream – poets, artists, prophets. Not that dreaming is a soft option. If it is to be useful it demands hard work and discipline combined with practical application in order to transform life. Those who regard themselves as primarily 'doers' soon discover how important it is to dream as well. Such time out is not wasted: instead, it gives depth and meaning to work. Take time this week to allow the dreams of these ancient writers to transform your doing and dreaming.

Text for the week: Isaiah 61.1 – 3

Sunday September 2   **Isaiah 43.14 – 44.5**

NEW BEGINNINGS   Not only are Christians members of a worldwide family of amazing richness and variety, but we also belong to the people of God, with a history stretching back thousands of years. The story of Israel is quite a mess. We have sympathy for them because our lives show the same pattern of frequent failure. Like them we remember thankfully all that God has done for us, but we also remember how often we have failed to live up to what he wants us to be. Happily for the Israelites, and for us, God does not dwell on our past. Instead he reminds us to

> **Watch for the new thing I am going to do. It is happening already – you can see it now!**   **(part of verse 19)**

God promises to give us the opportunity to make a fresh start. So he offers us forgiveness if we have sinned; renewal if our vision has become dim; refreshment if our zeal is flagging. In other words we can become all that, in our best moments, we dream of being.

✝ *Lord, like the land of Israel we are thirsty for your blessings. Pour them out upon us and all your people today so that our lives may be transformed.*

Monday September 3   **Isaiah 51.1 – 6, 12 – 16**

NO NEED FOR DOUBT   Last Christmas I was given a small book about tracing my ancestors. Following its instructions was not only fun; it also told me quite a lot about myself. The people of Israel were often urged to trace their ancestors.

'Think of your ancestor, Abraham, and of Sarah, from whom you are descended. When I called Abraham, he was childless, but I blessed him and gave him children; I made his descendants numerous.'   **(verse 2)**

In spite of God's promises the people had doubts. Why should God take any account of them – prisoners in a foreign land, one of the smallest and weakest nations? God reminds them of their humble origins and how he brought them to where they are today. If that is not sufficient encouragement, he goes on to explain that he has a much greater purpose. His people are to share in his redeeming plan for the whole creation. Make no mistake. We are a part of a very big thing, and though there may be many occasions when we doubt our worth, each of us has a crucial part to play in the bringing about of God's transforming purposes for the world.

✝ *Enlighten the darkness of our minds, stretch forth your helping hand, confirm and give us strength; that we may arise and confess you and glorify you without ceasing all the days of our life, O Lord of all. (From the Nestorian Liturgy)*

Tuesday September 4   **Habakkuk 2.1 – 3**

IT TAKES TIME   The prophet's problem was a simple one – prayer that appears to be unanswered. Israel was under the oppressive rule of the mighty Babylonians. They were suffering and, what made it worse, it was at the hands of a godless and cruel power. Surely God should step in and do something. Think of similar situations in our modern world. Recently a Baptist church in Azerbaijan was stormed by security police and its pastor was carried off to prison. And like Habakkuk we ask, 'Where was God in all this?' The answer the prophet received was neither very complete nor entirely satisfactory. As the moving words at the end of the prophecy show (3.17 – 19), Habakkuk's own life was transformed as he learned to trust in God's ultimate justice and wisdom even when he did not understand what God was doing. Meanwhile God reminds his servant that dreams can only become reality if we wait patiently for his timing.

> **'What I show you will come true. It may seem slow in coming, but wait for it; it will certainly take place, and it will not be delayed.'** (part of verse 3)

† *Lord, when I am puzzled by your seeming silence, help me to wait quietly for you to speak in your own time and way.*

Wednesday September 5   **Isaiah 61.1 – 11**

SOCIAL JUSTICE   The dream of transforming our society has often been a strong force in the lives of Christians. Think of great social reform movements like the abolition of slavery, the reform of prisons, anti-racism, the dismantling of apartheid, the fight against poverty and disease, and you will immediately think of names like William Wilberforce, Elizabeth Fry, Martin Luther King, Desmond Tutu, and Mother Teresa. All of them emphasized social justice because they believed it was important to God.

> **The Lord says, 'I love justice and I hate oppression and crime.'** (part of verse 8)

Jesus applied the first three verses of this chapter to himself, reminding us that his mission, and therefore our mission, is to the whole person. So Oscar Romero, the Archbishop of El Salvador, who was murdered as he preached, was right when he said, 'A church ... that forgets to protest injustices, would not be the true church of our Redeemer.'

† *Father of the forsaken, strength of the weak and provider of the needy, help me to see injustice when it exists in my community and to play my part in getting rid of it.*

Thursday September 6   **Isaiah 66.10 – 14**

RESTORATION   If you have ever felt the pain of acute homesickness you will know how God's people were feeling. Isaiah was writing to a people in exile who dreamed longingly of their homeland. It was a long 'dark night of the soul' as the years slipped slowly by and it seemed that God did not notice their predicament. Worse still, some of their own people who should have known better jeered at their situation (*verse 5*). But God had not forgotten them:

> The Lord says, 'I will bring you lasting prosperity ... You will be like a child that is nursed by its mother, carried in her arms, and treated with love.' (verse 12)

The idea of prosperity may seem a hopeless dream for those in our modern world who are far from home or perhaps even homeless. But the word should probably be translated 'peace'. In the Old Testament God's blessing was thought of in terms of material prosperity and wellbeing. Christians know that true prosperity is spiritual and that our real wealth is in heaven.

† *Lord, whenever I am depressed, lonely or homesick remind me that my true wealth is in your love for me.*

Friday September 7   **Ezekiel 47.1 – 12**

GOD RESTORES HIS PEOPLE

> On each bank of the stream all kinds of trees will grow to provide food. Their leaves will never wither, and they will never stop bearing fruit. They will have fresh fruit every month, because they are watered by the stream that flows from the Temple. The trees will provide food, and their leaves will be used for healing people. (verse 12)

The dreams we remember when we wake up can often seem bizarre and filled with fantasy. Perhaps we feel like that about Ezekiel's remarkable vision. Although he gives us a picture that is full of beauty, it still seems strange to modern eyes. Probably we are wise not to attempt to interpret all the details: just concentrate on the main symbols and the ideas they convey. The first of these is the picture of the river, a common symbol for the life and refreshment that water brings. Ezekiel promises such new life for God's people. The other major symbol is that of the restored Temple, which has been described in considerable detail in the previous chapters. The Temple is, of course, connected with worship and so the thrust of this vision is that renewed spiritual life is closely associated with a renewed attitude of worship.

† *May my worship of you refresh my spirit and glorify your name, Lord.*

THE CITY OF GOD   At first sight it may appear that this is simply a re-run of yesterday's prophetic vision. Certainly there are many similarities: a life-giving river and trees that provide food and medicine. There are also some significant differences: here is a city, not a temple, and the emphasis is on the glory and light of God's presence that fills the city.

> **The throne of God and of the Lamb will be in the city, and his servants will worship him. They will see his face, and his name will be written on their foreheads.**
> **(part of verse 3 and verse 4)**

This is a glorious dream of a future when sin, injustice, disease and darkness will be ended and when God's kingdom will finally come. But we limit God if we think of it as only a dream of the future. The city of God exists now. What is written here can be experienced here and now. The roots of the picture go back to the first chapters of Genesis, where the beginning of God's plans for humankind begin to be unfolded. But now 'the King is among us'. Life in all its fullness is to be lived. The dream can become a reality because the Lamb of God has taken away the sin of the world.

† *Come with me, Lord, wherever I go, and may the glory and light of your presence in me dispel the darkness of this world.*

For group discussion and personal thought

● What areas of your own life or the life of your community need transforming? Suggest some immediate steps you could take to begin the process.
● Why is water an important symbol in the Bible? What other symbols are important for Christians? How can they enrich our understanding of God's purposes?

THE POWER OF DREAMING 5
Do dreams come true?

Notes by Joy Pegg

based on the New International Version

Joy is a mother of three and grandmother of two who spent several years with her young family as a missionary linguist in Papua New Guinea. She now thoroughly enjoys her work as a library assistant in her home town of Tewkesbury in England. Much of the rest of her time is spent as a distance learning tutor with the Open Theological College, exploring creative and meditative approaches to worship and walking her beloved Welsh mountains.

In the context of this week's readings, dreams seem to include not only actual dreams that occur while the recipient is asleep, but also visions that fill one's heart, based on some hope, promise or prophecy. In our context they are all based on God's intentions for humankind and his ability to fulfil them. The part played by various people in accepting the dream or choosing the appropriate response to a set of circumstances is also important.

Text for the week: Deuteronomy 30.19 – 20

Sunday September 9   **Genesis 45.1 – 15**

TO SAVE LIVES   The background to today's reading is in Genesis 37, where God gives young Joseph dreams in which his family bow down to him. But these were not given to annoy Joseph's family, or to swell his own head. God had a specific purpose in mind, as Joseph explains to his brothers.

> **'And now, do not be distressed and do not be angry with yourselves for selling me here, because it was to save lives that God sent me ahead of you ... to preserve for you a remnant on earth and to save your lives by a great deliverance.'**   **(verse 5 and part of verse 7)**

The passing years seemed to make the fulfilment of Joseph's God-given dreams impossible. Attacked by his brothers, sold by them as a slave, cheated by his master's wife, Joseph was eventually thrown into an Egyptian jail. For many years he did not even see his family. But God was still working. When we find that things seem to be going very differently from how we imagined they would, let us look again at Joseph's comment on his situation.

'So then, it was not you who sent me here, but God.'
(part of verse 8)

At times, God communicates his intentions through dreams – they have a purpose.

† *Lord, thank you that you have a purpose for what is happening in my life right now, even if I don't understand it.*

Monday September 10   **Deuteronomy 30.15 – 20**

NOW CHOOSE LIFE Yesterday we saw that God could communicate his intention through dreams. The immediate context for today's reading is the covenant renewal ceremony at Moab, which is described in chapter 29. The Lord has promised Israel long life in the land they are about to enter. Moses reminds them of the Lord's intentions for them in Deuteronomy 29.29: 'The secret things belong to the LORD our God, but the things revealed belong to us and to our children for ever, that we may follow all the words of this law.' From this we learn that we have a choice and a part in making the dream come true – for good or ill.

See, I set before you today life and prosperity, death and destruction ... For the LORD is your life, and he will give you many years in the land he swore to give to your fathers, Abraham, Isaac and Jacob.
(part of verses 15 and 20)

God's intention is clear – to do his people good – and now it was about to become reality. But to share in the dream they must choose the condition – blessing or cursing – by obedience to the word (that is, the thing revealed) rather than disobedience.

Now choose life, so that you and your children may live and that you may love the LORD your God, listen to his voice, and hold fast to him.
(part of verses 19 and 20)

Dreams coming true involve choice and obedience.

† *Dear Lord, I choose you today, and in so doing I choose life in all its fullness.*

NATURAL OBSERVATION Jeremiah went to watch the potter at work and was told that he would learn from this. A potter has a picture in mind and when a pot does not come out right (is marred) he rolls it into a ball and starts again. God's intention can be altered (marred) by the actions of men. So although the Lord was planning a disaster against Judah, it could be reversed if they reformed their ways and actions.

'Go down to the potter's house, and there I will give you my message.' So I went down to the potter's house, and I saw him working at the wheel. But the pot he was shaping from the clay was marred in his hands; so the potter formed it into another pot, shaping it as seemed best to him.   (verses 2 – 4)

Marred, in this context, means that something is not working out as expected. So, even the intention to destroy a nation because of its evil ways could become 'marred' when they repent and can therefore be formed into another pot and not destroyed.

'O house of Israel, can I not do with you as this potter does?' declares the LORD. 'Like clay in the hand of the potter, so are you in my hand, O house of Israel'... Now therefore say to the people of Judah and those living in Jerusalem, "This is what the Lord says: Look! I am preparing a disaster for you and devising a plan against you. So turn from your evil ways, each one of you, and reform your ways and your actions."'   (verses 5 – 6 and 11)

God is in control and does what he intends, but we can have an influence.

† *Lord, let me respond to your word and then trust that you will shape everything as seems best to you.*

Wednesday September 12   **Matthew 11.2 – 6**

THE ONE WHO WAS TO COME Psalm 118.26 tells us that 'Blessed is he who comes in the Name of the LORD.' This blessed one had been expected for centuries, and so John asked his question:

'Are you the one who was to come, or should we expect someone else?'   (verse 3)

It was important to John that he identified the fulfilment of this long cherished dream and Jesus pointed him to the evidence:

> 'Go back and report to John what you hear and see: The blind receive sight, the lame walk, those who have leprosy are cured, the deaf hear, the dead are raised and the good news is preached to the poor.' (verses 4 – 5)

Because we know that God does make dreams come true, when we see the evidence for ourselves we can believe it.

† *Dear Lord, thank you that you give clear evidence of a dream come true.*

Thursday September 13   Acts 2.1 – 18

THE DREAM COMING TRUE   Peter tells the crowd that what they are seeing and hearing is the dream (the prophecy of Joel, or God's intention) coming true.

> **In the last days, God says,**
>   **I will pour out my Spirit on all people.**
> **Your sons and daughters will prophesy,**
>   **your young men will see visions,**
>   **your old men will dream dreams.** (verse 17)

Here we see another part of God's redemptive purpose to restore his original plan. In Genesis 11.4 we read that the people who built the tower of Babel said that they wanted to make a 'name for ourselves'. This was not God's intention and so he scattered them and they could no longer understand what was being said. Now the disciples are all 'declaring the wonders of God' and we read that 'each ... hears ... in his own language' (*verse 8*). God still has his original plan. Prophecy, vision, dreams – these are all about God's intention. And, when they are God-given, they will come true.

† *Dear Lord, thank you for not giving up on your desires.*

Friday September 14   Romans 15.22 – 33

NOT QUITE AS PLANNED   Here we read of a dream that was more like a longing within Paul's heart. He really wanted to go to Rome and was looking forward to visiting the Christians there on his way to Spain.

> **Since I have been longing for many years to see you, I plan to do so when I go to Spain. I hope to visit you while**

passing through and to have you assist me on my journey there, after I have enjoyed your company for a while.
(part of verse 23 and verse 24)

The dream was fulfilled but not in the way that Paul thought. For him, Rome was not a stopping-off point on his way to Spain; it was probably his final stopping point on this earth. He was arrested in Jerusalem and sent for trial in Rome. It is God's will (intention) that is the deciding factor – not our plans. But he also works in us 'to will and to act according to his good purpose' (*Philippians 2.13*).

† *Dear Lord, as we make our plans for the future, let us be glad that you can overrule everything and happy to be led by you.*

Saturday September 15   Philemon 1 – 21

DOUBLED DREAMS   Philemon, a wealthy Christian, had a dream – that he would have a slave who would be really useful. And he thought his dreams had come true one day when he acquired a new slave; he even named him Onesimus, meaning useful. But, instead of being useful, Onesimus ran away and Philemon could not find him. His dream was at an end. But he had not counted on the amazing workings of God, and now he was to get Onesimus back.

I [Paul] appeal to you for my son Onesimus, who became my son while I was in chains. Formerly he was useless to you, but now he has become useful both to you and to me.
(verses 10 – 11)

Onesimus had a dream of freedom as well, but now through God's providence, two dreams were to become doubly true.

Perhaps the reason he was separated from you for a little while was that you might have him back for good – no longer as a slave, but better than a slave, as a dear brother.
(verses 15 – 16a)

† *Dear Lord, thank you that your plans are beyond our wildest dreams.*

For group discussion and personal thought
- Have you experienced a time when your dream came true?
- How does God communicate his intentions to us today?

INTERNATIONAL BIBLE READING ASSOCIATION
1020 Bristol Road, Selly Oak, Birmingham, Great Britain B29 6LB

ORDER FORM – For 2002 Books

Please send me the following books:

Name: _____

Address: _____

_____

_____ Postcode: _____

*To qualify for 2002 books at these special IBRA readers' prices, this order form must be used (photocopies not accepted). Your order will be dispatched when **all** books are available.*

Code	Title of Book	Quantity	Unit Price	Total
ZYW0991	Words for Today 2002		£5.00	
ZYL0992	Light for Our Path 2002		£5.00	
ZYL0993	Large Print Light for Our Path 2002		£9.00	
ZYF0897	Finding Our Way Together Book 1		£6.50	
ZYF0910	Finding Our Way Together Book 2		£6.50	
ZYF0938	Finding Our Way Together Book 3		£6.50	
ZYF0974	Finding Our Way Together Book 4		£6.50	
ZYF0897-SET	Finding Our Way Together series (4 BOOKS)		£20.00	
ZYS1000	Sharing God's Word 2002		£5.50	
ZYD0989	Discovering Christ *Advent & Christmas*		£6.50	
ZYD0994	Discovering Christ *Ascension & Pentecost*		£6.50	
ZYO0990	Online to God		£4.50	
ZYE0213	Everyday Prayers		£5.50	
ZYM0325	More Everyday Prayers		£5.50	
ZYF0495	Further Everyday Prayers		£5.50	
ZYL0781	Living Prayers For Today		£12.50	
ZYM0902	More Living Prayers For Today		£12.50	

I enclose cheque (Payable to IBRA)	Total cost of books
Please charge my MASTERCARD / VISA / SWITCH Card No:, Issue No (Switch): ☐☐	Post – UK free Overseas – add £3.00 airmail per book
☐☐☐☐☐☐☐☐☐☐☐☐☐☐☐☐	Donation to International Fund
Expiry Date: _____	TOTAL DUE

Signature: _____ *Payments in <u>Pounds Sterling</u>, please*

The INTERNATIONAL BIBLE READING ASSOCIATION is a Registered Charity

International Bible Reading Association

Help us to continue our work of providing Bible study notes for use by Christians in the UK and throughout the world. The need is as great as it was when IBRA was founded in 1882 by Charles Waters as part of the work of the Sunday School Union.

Please leave a legacy to the International Bible Reading Association.

An easy-to-use leaflet has been prepared to help you provide a legacy. Please write to us at the address below and we will send you this leaflet – and answer any questions you might have about a legacy or other donations. Please help us to strengthen this and the next generation of Christians.

Thank you very much.

International Bible Reading Association
Dept 298, 1020 Bristol Road
Selly Oak
Birmingham B29 6LB
Great Britain
Tel. 0121 472 4242
Fax 0121 472 7575

Our solicitors are **Pothecary and Barratt**, Talbot House, Talbot Court, Gracechurch Street, London EC3V 0BS

 Charity No. 211542

THE POWER OF DREAMING 6
God beyond the dreams

Notes by Joy Pegg

based on the New International Version

If we are to have any faith that dreams will come true, then it is vital that we come to know more about God who is beyond them. The dreams will always embody and reflect the character and purpose of God.

Text for the week: 1 Timothy 1.17

Sunday September 16   **Numbers 12.1 – 8**

GOD WHO MAKES HIMSELF KNOWN God has always wanted to make himself known. Man and woman were originally made in his image (*Genesis 1.27*), and although they so soon wanted to hide from the Lord God, he still sought them, calling, 'Where are you?' (*Genesis 3.9*). Through the following centuries he continued to share his heart.

> 'When a prophet of the LORD is among you,
> I reveal myself to him in visions,
> I speak to him in dreams.   **(part of verse 6)**

The prophet would then let other people know what God wanted them to hear. Moses was so special and humble that the Lord spoke to him differently.

> But this is not true of my servant Moses;
> he is faithful in all my house.
> With him I speak face to face,
> clearly and not in riddles.   **(verse 7 and part of verse 8)**

In whatever way God chooses to do it, he clearly desires to communicate with us.

† *Thank you, Lord, for communicating with us. Help us to be open to receive what you say.*

Monday September 17   **1 Kings 3.1 – 15**

THE GREAT GIVER Not only does God want to communicate with us but he also wants to give us things.

Solomon was king and showed his love to the Lord by following his word and doing what was right.

At Gibeon the LORD appeared to Solomon during the night in a dream, and God said, 'Ask for whatever you want me to give you.' (verse 5)

Let us listen to what Solomon goes on to ask.

'Give your servant a discerning heart to govern your people and to distinguish between right and wrong.' (part of verse 9)

God has a heart of concern for his people, that they should be looked after in a just way, but he is also an abundant and generous God who gives us much more than we ask for.

The Lord was pleased that Solomon had asked for this. So God said to him, 'Since you have asked for this and not for long life or wealth for yourself ... I will do what you have asked ... Moreover, I will give you what you have not asked for...' (part of verses 10, 11, 12 and 13)

✝ *Thank you, Lord, for your loving care of me and for all the good things you have so generously given me.*

Tuesday September 18   **Ezekiel 1.22 – 28**

AWESOME   Ezekiel has experienced the trauma of defeat, exile and the loss of most things familiar. He was down by the Kebar river in Babylonia (*verse 1*) with the other exiles. 'The hand of the LORD was upon him' and he saw 'visions of God' for the 'heavens were opened' (*verses 1 – 3*). God was about to communicate with him and commission him to speak to the Israelites. But first God gave Ezekiel a glimpse of his glory.

This was the appearance of the likeness of the glory of the LORD. When I saw it, I fell face down, and I heard the voice of one speaking. (part of verse 28)

When reading a passage like today's reading, it is important to remember that no one has seen God at any time and the following description is only 'the appearance of the likeness' and not a description of God himself. But the majesty, power and glory of it can still fill our hearts and remind us of the One with whom we deal.

Above the expanse over their heads was what looked like a throne of sapphire, and high above on the throne was a figure like that of a man. I saw that from what appeared to be his waist up he looked like glowing metal, as if full of fire, and that from there down he looked like fire; and brilliant light surrounded him. Like the appearance of a rainbow in the clouds on a rainy day, so was the radiance around him. **(verses 26 – 28a)**

✝ *Dear Lord, though we know you as our friend, may we never forget that you are the Lord our God.*

Wednesday September 19   Isaiah 60.1 – 5, 19 – 22

THE EVERLASTING LIGHT   The 'you' in this passage refers to Zion, but it can be further related to the Church and ultimately to the end of time. We are all to be 'for the display of [God's] splendour' (*verse 21*), and this communicating, generous and awesome God is the one who makes this possible.

> **'Arise, shine, for your light has come,**
>   **and the glory of the LORD rises upon you.**
> **See, darkness covers the earth**
>   **and thick darkness is over the peoples,**
> **but the LORD rises upon you**
>   **and his glory appears over you.'**   **(verses 1 – 2)**

Most people have seen a hill, a mountain or even a tree totally transformed as the rays of the rising or setting sun catch it and set it ablaze. But these glories of nature are transitory and we need to be there at the right moment to catch them. The everlasting light of God is different.

> **The sun will no more be your light by day,**
>   **nor will the brightness of the moon shine on you,**
> **for the LORD will be your everlasting light,**
>   **and your God will be your glory.**
> **Your sun will never set again,**
>   **and your moon will wane no more;**
> **The LORD will be your everlasting light,**
>   **and your days of sorrow will end.**   **(verses 19 – 20)**

Let your spirit bathe now in that light.

✝ *Dear Lord, I am amazed that your everlasting light should shine even on me. I delight to reflect your glory to all around me.*

Thursday September 20   **Luke 15.1 – 10**

REJOICING   From the awesome glories of the past two days we turn to something more familiar.

> 'Suppose one of you has a hundred sheep and loses one of them. Does he not leave the ninety-nine in the open country and go after the lost sheep until he finds it? And when he finds it, he joyfully puts it on his shoulders and goes home. Then he calls his friends and neighbours together and says, "Rejoice with me; I have found my lost sheep" ... In the same way, I tell you, there is rejoicing in the presence of the angels of God over one sinner who repents.'
> **(verses 4 – 6 and 10)**

We have all known the anxiety and the relief of losing and finding something. But when it involves real searching, everything is intensified. Pictures of the rescue of a young child who had been buried for days in the devastation caused by the Turkish earthquakes of 1999 are still vivid in my mind's eye, and I can still hear the cheers that went up when he was lifted clear.

† *Dear Lord, thank you that you came and found me and that heaven rejoiced with you at my repentance. I feel so loved.*

Friday September 21   **Acts 26.4 – 23**

A LIGHT FROM HEAVEN   Here Paul is giving his defence before King Agrippa. Again we see how God makes the first move in communicating with Paul.

> 'On one of these journeys I was going to Damascus ... About noon, O King, as I was on the road, I saw a light from heaven, brighter than the sun, blazing around me and my companions. We all fell to the ground, and I heard a voice ... "I am Jesus, whom you are persecuting ... I have appeared to you to appoint you as a servant and as a witness ... to open their eyes and turn them from darkness to light, and from the power of Satan to God."'
> **(part of verses 12 – 16 and 18)**

Jesus says 'I will show you', 'I will rescue you' and 'I am sending you'. He is one who directs, delivers and commissions. Think back on times in your own life when you have experienced the intervention of Jesus in these ways.

† *Dear Lord, thank you for those times in my life when you have come to me in so many different ways.*

GIVER OF GRACE   Paul has received such grace and mercy from God, and has known the Lord's keeping power through so many years and adventures, that he can speak to young Timothy from great experience.

> **The grace of our Lord was poured out on me abundantly, along with the faith and love that are in Christ Jesus.**
>
> (verse 14)

Paul recognized what we discovered earlier this week, that he was to display God's glory, in this instance by witnessing to the Lord's great patience.

> **But for that very reason I was shown mercy so that in me, the worst of sinners, Christ Jesus might display his unlimited patience as an example for those who would believe on him and receive eternal life.**   (verse 16)

As so often happens when Paul is writing, he gets carried away with the wonder of what he is declaring. We can end this week's study with the same hymn of praise:

> **Now to the King eternal, immortal, invisible, the only God, be honour and glory for ever and ever.**   (verse 17)

† *Dear Lord, we become lost for words but still need to multiply them to even begin to express the wonder of your Being. We worship you.*

For group discussion and personal thought

● Does knowing more about 'God beyond the dreams' help in our whole understanding of this area?
● What other aspects of God's being, which we have not discussed, are important to you?
● In what ways can we as individuals and in community display the glory of God?

CHALLENGES FOR CHANGE 1
Why change?

Notes by Rodney Dreyer

based on the New International Version

To grow is to change. To change is to be challenged by every aspect of our lives – in our courage, our convictions, our choices. How do we respond? This week's readings look at some of the ways in which the people of the Bible were challenged.

Text for the week: Isaiah 1.18 – 20

Sunday September 23   **Amos 2.6 – 16**

A CHALLENGE TO COURAGE Amos prophesied in the Kingdom of Samaria under King Jeroboam the Second, who ruled between 784 and 744 BC. The phrase 'The Word of the Lord' or 'Thus says the Lord' is often repeated like a refrain, like a blast of a trumpet to awaken the conscience:

This is what the Lord says...   **(verse 6a)**

The prophets have the courage not only to speak about God but to realize that they are speaking in his name. God speaks through them. John the Baptist is recorded as saying, 'I am the voice of one calling' (*John 1.23*). Amos was a shepherd from a small village south-east of Bethlehem. He is one of the prophets who use vivid images to describe the catastrophe which will come upon the people if they are not converted. We should not quieten our conscience too easily today, pretending that those so-called prophets of doom lived in very different times and used language which was unnecessarily harsh. Jesus also spoke in the same way; he said, 'Unless you repent you too will all perish' (*Luke 13.5*). God will not accept social injustice or corruption. God will not tolerate them for ever. God is a just God.

✝ *Lord, challenge and change us in your service today. Amen.*

Monday September 24   **Amos 6.4 – 7**

COMPLACENCY CHALLENGED The nation was guilty because the people were falsely complacent, full of a confidence which was false.

You lie on beds inlaid with ivory
and lounge on your couches. (verse 4a)

They trusted in the military leaders and not in the Lord. The people were also self-indulgent and very unconcerned about the people of the land who were hurting. After all, they thought the Day of Judgement was far away – but was it? Did God appoint three judgements for them: death, destruction and defeat? Those who ate at banquets, who enjoyed meals at marvellous tables, would become corpses and the great houses would be left in ruins. Syria would bring defeat. And so we ask, in whom do we put our trust? In the Lord or in idols? In whom do we boast?

† *Lord, challenge and change us in your service today. Amen*

Tuesday September 25 Isaiah 14.8 – 17

THE CREATURE CHALLENGED The fall of Babylon was much more than simply the deposing of a proud king.

All your pomp has been brought down to the grave,
along with the noise of your harps. (verse 11a)

Behind the social, political, religious and military system of Babylon was the enemy of God. The enemy rebelled against God and wanted to take to himself the worship which belonged only to God. 'I will make myself like the Most High' (*verse 14*). This is his ambition and it is the temptation that the enemy puts before the creature, the human beings created by God, in the book of Genesis. The world today worships and serves the creature rather than the Creator. Human beings have become their own god and worship only themselves: as it is said, 'I am a self-made man and I worship my creator'. The Christian, however, is called to be like Jesus Christ in all things, to grow up into him who was obedient to God and always sought his will. May we be conformed to the likeness of his Son (*Romans 8.29*).

† *Lord, challenge and change us in your service today. Amen*

Wednesday September 26 Jeremiah 6.9 – 15

CONTEXT CHALLENGED The people of Israel were challenged to change because the prophet Jeremiah saw the coming invasion and warned the people, but they would not listen to him.

> **To whom can I speak and give warning?**
> **Who will listen to me?** (verse 10)

He saw the sicknesses, the wounds and the problems of the nation and he pointed to God as the only source and measure of healing. False prophets always give a superficial diagnosis and a false remedy for their contemporary contexts. This often leads a nation into judgement. As we respond to the challenge to change today, perhaps we can reflect on the need not only to look at the surface but to get to the heart of the contextual issues of our day. Jeremiah saw the people's confusion about which way to go. The new religions confused them, so he called them back to God's way, to seek the old paths; he was not trying to persuade them to repeat the good old days but to go forward to do God's will in their own day. So in our day may God give us the grace to be honest with ourselves in our situations and about our contexts.

† *Lord, challenge and change us in your service today. Amen*

Thursday September 27 **Jeremiah 23.1 – 4**

CONFIDENCE CHALLENGED Out of love, God places expectations on us. God expected the leaders of his people to guide and love and care for them. But these shepherds in Judah were selfish and disloyal to God's covenant with his people.

> **'Woe to the shepherds who are destroying and scattering the sheep of my pasture!'** (verse 1)

The shepherds in today's reading scattered the people and did not protect or provide for them. Jeremiah looks forward to a time when God will gather them and establish his kingdom in righteousness and peace and justice. The prophet challenges the shepherds' confidence to rule in God's name. The more we serve others in the name of Christ, the more we can be like Christ to them today and the more God's kingdom can be established in our lives. Our confidence in God is built up. As we meet challenges to change, we change so that God may be glorified in us and his kingdom may come more fully into our lives and the lives of those around us. We grow in confidence that God will love, guide and care not only for others but also for ourselves.

† *Lord, challenge and change us in your service today. Amen*

Friday September 28   **Luke 16.14 – 18**

CHOICES CHALLENGED   In this particular chapter Luke shows Jesus talking about money and the proper place of money in our lives.

> **The Pharisees, who loved money, heard all this and were sneering at Jesus.**   **(verse 14)**

Jesus talks about three choices that we can make about the role of money in our lives. We can waste money, or we can serve God with money; or, as Jesus suggests here, we can try to serve God *and* money. The Pharisees tried this third alternative, to serve God *and* money, but could not do it. Even trying to do it was a huge mistake! We, too, cannot serve both righteousness and unrighteousness, what is greatest and what is the least, what is honoured by God and what God abhors. The world measures people by how much they get, but God measures people by how much they give. Winston Churchill said, 'We make a living by what we get, we make a life by what we give.' We can use the words of Jesus as an opportunity to change our attitude to money and to the gifts which God gives us. Money can help to make us or it can help to break us. The choice is ours.

✝ *Lord, challenge and change us in your service today. Amen*

Saturday September 29   **Isaiah 1.11 – 20**

CONVICTIONS CHALLENGED   Isaiah lived in a time when there was great concern for the spiritual state of the nation, rather than for the political success of the leaders of the nation. Outwardly it seemed as if the nation was prosperous and even religious, but God saw a different picture. His people were rebellious. He regarded their popular religious meetings as futile and a cause for grief :

> **'The multitude of your sacrifices – what are they to me?' says the LORD.**   **(verse 11a)**

In fact their religious meetings and worship defiled the people instead of making them clean. This is a salutary reminder to us that sin breaks God's heart, it cheapens and denigrates a nation or an individual and invites God's judgement. Yet, God graciously offers his forgiveness if we will repent (*verses 18 – 20*).

✝ *Lord, challenge and change us in your service today. Amen*

For group discussion and personal thought

- How do you approach the need for change in your life?
- How do you go about deciding upon, or choosing from, competing options for change in your life?

Discovering Christ

A new series by IBRA editor Maureen Edwards

- Offers new perspectives on Christ and the Gospel stories
- Challenging questions, addressed by writers of widely differing experience and cultures
- Share the joy and fun of Christian celebrations in different contexts

Book 1: Advent & Christmas

Book 2: Ascension & Pentecost

Book 3: Lent & Easter *in preparation*

UK price £6.50 each

Order through your IBRA representative, or from the appropriate address on page 285.

CHALLENGES FOR CHANGE 2
Hear the cries of the poor

Notes by Carol Mouat

based on the New Jerusalem Bible

The readings this week speak to us of God's plea for us to hear the voice to the poor. The key words are poverty, call, faith and trust.

Text for the week: Exodus 3.7 – 8

Sunday September 30   **Exodus 3.1 – 10**

HEAR THE CRIES OF THE POOR   We must be attentive to the many voices in our midst that are crying out for help.

> **Yahweh then said, 'I have indeed seen the misery of my people in Egypt. I have heard them crying for help on account of their taskmasters. Yes, I am well aware of their sufferings. And I have come down to rescue them.'**
>
> **(verses 7 – 8)**

Some of us may never experience the pain and oppression of poverty; but we cannot detach ourselves from the poverty which surrounds us. We are confronted daily by inhuman tragedies taking place all over the world. We see the horrors of poverty in our streets and on the television, and read about them in our daily newspapers. We cannot close our eyes and ears to the cry of the poor, but the most challenging action for each one of us is: How do we respond to this cry?

✝ *Merciful Father, we call on you to help us hear the cry of the poor, and give us the courage to respond to it in a meaningful way.*

Monday October 1   **Amos 8.4 – 7**

CHANGE   In this reading Amos is warning people not to exploit others and to change from their corrupt behaviour.

> **Listen to this, you who crush the needy and reduce the oppressed to nothing,**
> **you who say, 'When will New Moon be over**

so that we can sell our corn,
and Sabbath, so that we can market our wheat?'

(verses 4 – 5)

We do not have to travel far to see and experience fraud and exploitation. It happens in the workplace and the marketplace, on our streets and sometimes even in our homes. We are called to change this corrupt behaviour in ourselves. We are also challenged not to exploit other people in any way.

† *All powerful Father, we call on you to help us to overcome our weakness when we are tempted to exploit people and to change any corrupt behaviour in ourselves.*

Tuesday October 2   Luke 16.19 – 31

GENEROSITY   This reading reminds us of the importance of being generous to all people, especially those who are more disadvantaged than ourselves.

'My son, remember that during your life you had your fill of good things, just as Lazarus his fill of bad. Now he is being comforted here while you are in agony.'   **(verse 25)**

The man who experienced riches on earth is now in torment, and the man who suffered poverty and hardship on earth is now experiencing bliss. While on earth, the rich man was aware of Lazarus's poverty, pain and isolation, yet he did nothing to alleviate his affliction. He was insensitive to this man's plight, and lacked generosity to go out of his way to be of service to him.

† *Jesus, you came to save the poor, you identified with the poor and suffering. Help us never to become complacent, but always ready to share our riches with others who are needy.*

Wednesday October 3   James 5.1 – 6

SHARING WITH OTHERS   James uses strong words to address those who are not prepared to share their riches with the poor.

Weep for the miseries that are coming to you. Your wealth is rotting, your clothes are all moth-eaten. All your gold and your silver are corroding away, and the same corrosion will be a witness against you and eat into your body. It is like a fire which you have stored up for the final days.

(verses 1 – 3)

We enter our heavenly home empty-handed. We cannot take any of our possessions with us. Unless we learn the art of sharing our treasures with those who are less fortunate than us, we are told by James that we are unlikely to enter the Kingdom of Heaven. Sometimes it is easy to give material goods away, but it is not always easy to be generous in the giving of our precious time to people who make demands on us. We may also be called to work on a particular project for the poor, and this could be a big challenge for us.

† *Jesus, you reached out to the poor and distressed. We ask you to give us generous hearts and prepare us to give at all times without seeking a reward.*

Thursday October 4   **Hebrews 5.1 – 10**

CALL TO LEADERSHIP   The author of Hebrews is clearly pointing out that the call to the royal priesthood is a call from God.

> **No one takes this honour on himself; it needs a call from God, as in Aaron's case. And so it was not Christ who gave himself the glory of becoming high priest, but the one who said to him: 'You are my Son, today I have fathered you', and in another text: 'You are a priest for ever, of the order of Melchizedek'.**   **(verses 4 – 6)**

Power and control are often identified with leadership. We see in our society how people who are in positions of leadership can misuse and abuse their power of authority. This can even happen within the Church. If we are called to serve the Lord in any leadership role within the Church – prayer group, Bible study group etc. – we can never take pride in ourselves. It is a call from God, and he deserves the glory. It is the Lord who gives us the strength and power to perform these duties; these gifts do not belong to us, they are not possessions. True leadership means complete dependence upon God.

† *Lord, when you call us to leadership, help us to come to you empty-handed so that we can be filled by your strength and power.*

Friday October 5   **Luke 18.1 – 8**

JUSTICE   In this parable we experience the God of justice. The widow persists in demanding her rights under the law:

> 'I want justice from you against my enemy!' For a long time
> he refused, but at last he said to himself, 'Even though I
> have neither fear of God nor respect for any human person,
> I must give this widow her just rights.'   (verses 3b – 4)

The widow is a figure of powerlessness standing before a very
powerful person. Sometimes, if we experience being powerless
in the face of power, this can paralyse us into doing nothing.
She gained justice for herself by insisting on her rights and not
giving up.

✝ *Loving Father, help us to be more assertive when struggling for our*
rights, especially when we are faced with abusive and powerful
people in society.

Saturday October 6   Isaiah 65.17 – 25

NEW CREATION   The prophet Isaiah speaks of new life, and
this involves change.

> For look, I am going to create new heavens and a new earth,
> and the past will not be remembered
> and will come no more to mind ...
> be joyful, be glad for ever
> at what I am creating.   (verses 17 – 18a)

The joyful news in this reading is that we can be filled with
hope for the future. We no longer need to dwell on the past and
perhaps some painful memories. The future is filled with joy
and peace. But we cannot do this for ourselves. It is a free gift of
re-creation from God to those who are utterly poor and
powerless.

✝ *Lord, we praise and thank you for the beauty of creation, and we*
pray that we may always be filled with the spirit of hope and joy.

For group discussion and personal thought

● Who are the people in your parish and in your
   neighbourhood who are crying out for help, and how can
   you be of assistance to them?
● What are some of the signs of hope that you experience in
   your church?

CHALLENGES FOR CHANGE 3
Change is possible

Notes by Mike Pennington

based on the Jerusalem Bible

All is not well in the world. Listen to the radio, watch television, read newspapers and that is obvious. Some problems seem impossible to solve – no-one knows what to do about them. There may seem to be a simple solution, but nothing is done because people would be inconvenienced or, more usually, lose some of their profits. Other problems seem to be caused by the awkwardness, arrogance, or evil of human beings. Perhaps if we could get people right, the world's difficulties would disappear, peace would come and the good things of God's creation could be much more evenly distributed. How can we change people? People of faith try to answer this question, but sometimes answers don't come!

Text for the week: Luke 19.10

Sunday October 7   **1 Samuel 2.1 – 10**

GUIDANCE FROM TWO LADIES Arrogance, mighty, sated, many, wicked, strength – these words from the Song of Hannah after the birth of Samuel describe what many people in the world see in the society around them. The Christian message is that life does not have to be like this. God has a particular concern for the poor, the weak, the dispossessed and those with no voice. Hannah's Song is reflected in Mary's Magnificat (*Luke 1.46 – 55*):

> **Yahweh is an all-knowing God and his is the weighing of deeds.** **(part of verse 3)**

The force for change is God himself – he acts through people of faith. The work is never easy; often it seems to fail in the short-term; it is always demanding – and has the power of divine and human love to hold it together!

† *Lord, you call me to be your servant in the world. Give me grace to see with your eyes, to speak with your voice and to act according to your will.*

Monday October 8   **Lamentations 3.19 – 26**

WHAT CAN I DO?   It is easy to become disheartened when changes which we believe are in accordance with the will of God don't seem to happen, . We may think that we have got it wrong, or that we are not clever or strong enough to do the work. We may feel that our personal desires and feelings have got in the way. Here Jeremiah reminds us that we do not decide the time-scale – time is in the hand of God. So there is always hope, one of the great Christian virtues.

> **The favours of Yahweh are not all past, his kindnesses are not exhausted; every morning they are renewed; great is his faithfulness.**   **(verses 22 – 23)**

✝ *Lord, to you a thousand years are a single day. But I have only a few years of my life to do your work. Show me that I cannot do all you want for the whole world. I know you will be satisfied if I just finish the smaller tasks before me.*

Tuesday October 9   **Luke 18.18 – 30**

WHAT AM I ON THE ROAD TO BECOMING?   A journey along a road, whether walking or driving, brings new scenes with every step and bend. We remember what we have come past. We look for signposts to direct us. We need places to get food and drink – possibly to spend the night. At nightfall we need lights – perhaps we carry them with us, or they may be on the road or in a town or village ahead of us. A journey is a process of constant change and development. Early Christians were called 'Followers of the Way' (*Acts 9.2*). Today's passage teaches various people that they are on different stages of their spiritual journey. One of them has not coped with his money. Others have not understood God's power. Saint Peter has not understood the implications of what he and other close followers of Jesus have done. All of them discover this in answer to the first question put to Jesus:

> **'Good Master, what have I to do to inherit eternal life?'**
> **(verse 18)**

We ourselves still need to ask that question today, because, whatever we have done in the past, we still have further progress to make on our journey through the spiritual life. Change is still called for, however long we have lived. We need to find the answers to our questions – and there are some questions that we are too ashamed to ask. Perhaps we need to hear the answers to those questions more clearly than any others.

✝ *Lord, give me the courage to look at my life in your world, the wisdom to see where the two do not fit together, and the determination to change what I am.*

Wednesday October 10   **Luke 19.1 – 10**

WHAT MAKES A MAN A BIG MAN? Zacchaeus, standing in the middle of a crowd, wasn't tall enough to see Jesus. Sometimes he is described as 'a little man' – and the opposite of that must be a big man. Whilst Zacchaeus may not have been big in terms of how far his head was above the ground, he showed himself to be a big man in other respects. Local people had made up their mind about him. They knew his reputation and felt that he had probably made his fortune by keeping some of the taxes he had collected for his own use. Why did Jesus single him out? This was a turning point in his life and in the way he behaved:

> **'I am going to give half my property to the poor, and if I have cheated anybody I will pay him back four times the amount.'**   **(verse 8)**

Four times the amount stolen was the rate of restitution imposed by Roman law on convicted thieves. It was higher than the rate normally demanded by Jewish law, so in his changed attitude to his work, and the people who were involved with it, Zacchaeus was going much further than anyone could have reasonably asked.

✝ *Lord Jesus, you said, 'When you have done all you have been told to do, say, "We are merely servants: we have done no more than our duty"' (Luke 17.10). This reminds us that whatever we do to bring about your Kingdom, there is always more change needed in the world.*

Thursday October 11   **Luke 19.45 – 48**

PEOPLE WHO SHUT THEIR EARS TO THE CALL FOR CHANGE Christians know that Jesus calls them to make changes in their lives. There are parts of our lives which are not as God wants them to be and, being sorry, we try to alter them. That is hard to do, and it is even harder to keep our good intentions. We speak of 'repentance' and this may be connected with wrong relationships with individuals – family, neighbours, customers, colleagues. But in the Temple Jesus found a whole system which was wrong – a place of prayer, teaching and holiness had become dedicated to money-making and exploitation. He acted directly to put things right. People in our own times have, as we say, acted as 'whistle-blowers', reporting wrong things to more senior people. That is not an easy thing to do and it can cause many problems – not just for the people who are misusing their power and responsibility. And clearing out those who are doing wrong does not always change their minds and understandings. So we read:

The chief priests and the scribes, with the support of the leading citizens, tried to do away with him.

(part of verse 47)

† *Lord, give us grace to see our own faults as well as those things which are wrong in the world around us. Then, Lord, make us sensitive to your calling and courageous in word and deed.*

Friday October 12   Luke 20.1 – 8

WHO ARE YOU?   In every part of the world this question is frequently asked – often as a challenge. 'Why do you think you can tell me what to do, where I can go, what I can have?' Some see money, family ties and roots, land, education, being elected or appointed by others and many other things as giving someone authority. Whether or not that is justified, there is another authority – a much deeper authority that has a mystical quality about it. Christians believe that they stand with the authority of God behind them. It is not easy to explain the things of the spirit in human terms. Jesus makes the temple authorities realize this by making them face up to their treatment and understanding of John the Baptist.

'John's baptism: did it come from heaven, or from man?' ... Their reply was that they did not know where it came from.

(verses 4 and 7)

† *Lord Jesus, help me not to put human values on things of the Spirit, so that I can learn that the things of this world can change if only I let you have your way.*

Saturday October 13   James 1.9 – 18

STAND FIRM!   Today's reading starts with the same thoughts as Hannah and Mary voiced (see last Monday's notes). James' words are like those of the Psalmist: 'Man lasts no longer than grass, no longer than a wild flower he lives' (*Psalm 103.15*). Here is the change which is above all other changes! Here are reminders of resurrection.

Happy the man who stands firm ... [he] will win the prize of life, the crown that the Lord has promised to those who love him. (verse 12)

But be warned! James confronts us with what we all know so well: life can be distorted by sin! Rather than becoming the harvest first-fruits of creation, we can appear much more like fruit that has gone rotten on the branch.

† *Lord, the glory of what you promise is revealed in your resurrection. Help me to change so that I share in your risen life, leaving the old life behind in the waters of my baptism.*

For group discussion and personal thought

- What situations are you in now which you believe need to be changed if they are to be in accordance with God's will?
- What needs to be said or done to make that change?
- Who will speak out when there is wrong-doing or injustice?
- What might be the result if what we say is challenged or not believed?

CHALLENGES FOR CHANGE 4
Pray for change
(Week of prayer for world peace)

Notes by Kate Hughes

based on the New Revised Standard Version

We may know that we need to change, that the world around us needs to change. We may know how we and the world need to change. But we cannot bring about change on our own. We need to be in constant touch with God – not only for the strength to change, but to understand exactly how he wants us to change and what we need to do to bring it about. Change which is not in accordance with God's plan for his world will never be successful. Keeping in touch with God is prayer.

Text for the week: Luke 11.9 – 10

Sunday October 14   **Daniel 6.10 – 22**

PRAYER – AN ILLEGAL ACTIVITY Today's reading reminds us that in some parts of the world, Christianity is a persecuted religion. You yourself may live in a country where meeting publicly for worship with other Christians is criticized by the state or by the majority religion and church buildings are attacked. In Daniel's case, even his personal prayer in the privacy of his own house is illegal and as a result he ends up in the lion's den. But it never seems to occur to Daniel that he might stop praying.

> [Daniel] continued to go to his house, which had windows in its upper room open toward Jerusalem, and to get down on his knees three times a day to pray to his God and praise him, just as he had done previously.   (part of verse 10)

Do we take prayer for granted, as an activity we can choose to do or not do, as we feel like it? Or do we remember what a wonderful privilege it is to be able to talk to God and hear what he has to say to us – a privilege we would do anything to safeguard?

✝ *O God, help us never to take for granted the immense privilege of prayer, but to treasure it and guard it even when others persecute us or ridicule us for spending time with you.*

YOUR KINGDOM COME   I lived in South Africa for ten years, at the height of the apartheid era. All my friends were politically aware, several of them spent time in jail, and everyone had their own ideas about what ought to be done. But no one seemed to have much idea about what South African society would be like when apartheid was finally defeated. The laws which kept the races apart and oppressed the black majority could be changed, but how would a new government tackle the huge problems of poverty, unemployment, lack of housing and AIDS?

> **One of his disciples said to him, 'Lord, teach us to pray.'**
> **(part of verse 1)**

We need to learn how to pray for change – not presenting God with a 'shopping list' of things we want him to do to fulfil our ideas, but putting ourselves in line with *his* plans. In other words, we need to pray '*Your* kingdom come'.

† *Your way, not mine, O Lord.*

ASK, SEARCH, KNOCK   Today's reading reminds us that God has a solution to the problem of hunger.

> **'If you then, who are evil, know how to give good gifts to your children, how much more will the heavenly Father give the Holy Spirit to those who ask him!'**   **(verse 13)**

If he is a loving Father, as we believe he is, then he *must* have a plan for ensuring that all his children have enough food. We can guess at some of the things he wants: greater sharing of the world's resources; better farming methods; better management of the environment. But we cannot see the whole picture. We can only go on asking God to show us what to do, go on searching for more ways of helping the hungry, go on knocking at the door of heaven to remind ourselves that without the help of the Holy Spirit we can do nothing. This is true of all the problems we bring to God, not only the problem of hunger.

† *O God, help us to keep asking, searching and knocking for ways to change ourselves and the world, for we know that you are our loving Father.*

NOT TRUSTING IN OURSELVES　True prayer begins with honesty: speaking honestly to God about ourselves and our ideas and admitting to him that we do not have all the answers – or even any answers at all!

> **But the tax collector, standing far off, would not even look up to heaven, but was beating his breast and saying, 'God, be merciful to me, a sinner!'**　　　　　　　　　　**(verse 13)**

Our ideas, our plans, even our desire for change, are influenced by the fact that we are sinners. We have mixed motives, we are patronizing to those we want to help, we settle for small, easy changes when what we need is complete conversion. We are not doing God a favour by talking to him and offering him our help; we have to begin by admitting that without him we can do nothing. We need his mercy, his love which alone can bring about change and which takes us on as partners in spite of our sins.

✝ *O God, in your love be merciful to me, a sinner.*

TURN AGAIN TO GOD　Change usually means a change of direction, turning from following one road to following another. For Christians, therefore, change should always mean turning back to God and getting back on the right road.

> **When your people Israel, having sinned against you, are defeated before an enemy but turn again to you, confess your name, pray and plead with you in this house, then hear in heaven, forgive the sin of your people Israel.**
> 　　　　　　　　　　　　　　　　**(verses 33 – 35a)**

This is the meaning of the Greek word which is translated into English as 'repentance' – turning round, changing direction. And this is an important part of prayer. As we pray, we get back on the right road, we fix our eyes on God so that we can see where we are going and how we are going to get there. Sin can paralyze us or plunge us into despair. Or we can repent and allow God to pick us up and set us back on the right road. God's forgiveness and restoration can transform sin into an opportunity for change and growth.

✝ *O God, help us not to get stuck in sin, but to know that with the help of your grace we can use our sin and our repentance as an opportunity to get back on to the right road.*

WALK IN ALL HIS WAYS   At the dedication of the temple which he has built in Jerusalem, Solomon stresses that it is above all a place for prayer, not only for the people of Israel but for foreigners as well. Jesus reminds the Jews in the temple of this fact when he drives out those who have turned it into a market (*Matthew 21.13*). But prayer alone is not enough.

> 'Therefore devote yourselves completely to the LORD our God, walking in his statutes and keeping his command-ments, as at this day.'   **(verse 61)**

Our physical presence at a time of prayer must be backed up by obedience to God. What we learn about God and from God in prayer needs to be translated into obedient action – action which will often involve change.

✝ *O God, help us to bring to prayer our past efforts to obey you and take from prayer a new determination to do your will.*

Saturday October 20   **1 Timothy 2.1 – 8**

PRAYER – A SUBVERSIVE ACTIVITY   It is easy to criticize the leaders of our society, our nation and other nations. But those who have great power are open to great temptations and they need our help to do what is right. So Paul tells the little communities of Christians to pray

> for kings and all who are in high positions, so that we may lead a quiet and peaceable life in all godliness and dignity.   **(verse 2)**

Prayer can support those who are trying to rule justly. Prayer can also be a subversive activity, undermining those who use power wrongly. Several years ago, I cut down a tree in my garden. The stump was left, but I could not dig it up because its roots were too deep. Instead, I drilled a few holes in the top of the stump and poured paraffin into them. I went on putting paraffin into the holes and it soaked away into the remains of the tree and eventually killed off the stump. The paraffin penetrated into the roots of the tree and destroyed it. Our prayer can do the same for tyrants and oppressors. If we continually soak someone with God through prayer, eventually the power of his love may be able to destroy what is evil in them and change them for the better.

† *O God, where there is no love, put your love so that even those who misuse their power may in the end find love.*

For group discussion and personal thought

- Is prayer one of the most important things in your life? If it is not, what can you do to change this situation?* How can you make your own prayer more honest?
- Share one way in which prayer has helped you to change in the past year.

BIBLE EXPLORATION:
REMEMBERING MARY

- Explore different images of Mary in the Gospels, and the connections with our own stories, memories and experience.
- Remember Mary as a woman of bold, visionary and faithful discipleship from whom we can learn much today.

Workbook for 7–11-year-olds:
- Bible-based activities for groups and individuals
- Art, craft, creative writing, puzzles, discussion

Study Guide for house groups and leaders:
- Ideas and activities for house groups and Bible study
- Guidelines for leaders of children's groups

Contact NCEC for details of price and availability.

NCEC

Order through your IBRA representative, or from the appropriate address on page 285.

CHALLENGES FOR CHANGE 5
A new respect (Ruth)

Notes by Aileen Khoo

based on the New International Version

Aileen Khoo has worked in the Methodist Church in Malaysia for 28 years. Currently she is Director of Christian Education at Trinity Methodist Church, Petaling Jaya. She particularly enjoys leading Bible studies, especially experimenting in participatory Bible study methods.

We hate change. Change interrupts. But everything changes, the stars and planets, the moon and the sun. A seed changes into a plant, a bud into a flower. The story of Ruth, probably written in its present form after the Babylonian Exile although the setting is from the time of the Judges (very early in Israel's history), shows how one woman coped with change. It was a time of controversy over Israel's relationship with foreigners. The prevailing policy of exclusiveness needed to be changed; hence the story of Ruth, a foreigner who married a Jew and became the great-grandmother of David from whom Jesus' ancestry can be traced. As Ruth is a short book, the week begins with Jeremiah, the prophet of the Exile, looking forward to a change for the better.

Text for the week: Jeremiah 29.4 – 5

Sunday October 21   **Jeremiah 29.1, 4 – 7**

CHANGE OF ENVIRONMENT   Jeremiah lived in troubled times. Powerful Assyria had destroyed Samaria and exiled the cream of Israel. Later, the Babylonians destroyed Jerusalem and its temple and the remnants of Israel were enslaved. The glorious days of David and Solomon were only a fading memory. The people lost their political freedom and their cultural and religious identity. When all was lost, Jeremiah proclaimed the message of hope. He challenged them to work for change for a better future.

> **Build houses and settle down; plant gardens and eat what they produce.**   **(verse 5)**

233

We are people with pasts which are permeated and tormented by guilt. We carry our guilt into the future, unable to shake it loose. God promised the Israelites that their past was finished and everything had become fresh and new. Our sins are no longer held against us. Is our future full of anxieties? The new creation guarantees a future of confidence and hope, with God in control. If we bear the guilt of our past and are anxious about the future, we shall feel an awesome emptiness regarding the present. But those who experience a whole new world of change become filled with vitality and purpose. We know where we have been and where we are going. We build and plant and harvest. Each day is new, offering many possibilities.

✝ *Help us, Lord, to see the changes that life imposes on us not as disasters but as opportunities.*

Monday October 22   Ruth 1.1 – 14

CHANGE OF FORTUNE   Severe famine drove Elimelech, a Hebrew, to leave home and emigrate with his wife Naomi and their two sons to a foreign land. The sons married foreign wives. All went well for a time and then Elimelech died, followed by both sons, leaving the three widows with no means of support. The loss of the breadwinner's income can be difficult for the remaining spouse. Today there are various options such as life insurance, social security, pension benefits, employment. Naomi, Orpah and Ruth had none of these options, but one opportunity did open up for them:

> **When she heard in Moab that the Lord had come to the aid of his people by providing food for them, Naomi and her daughters-in-law prepared to return home from there.**
>
> **(verse 6)**

Just when we think we are safest, when all is going well and we have settled down, something happens that changes our lives – a divorce, retrenchment, financial loss, an accident, illness or death. These interruptions irritate us and upset our schedules, our relationships, our energy. We must cope with change or it will distract and disrupt important relationships and drain us of the energy we need to invest in more meaningful activity. Change will not go away, but we need not allow it to play havoc with our lives. We can integrate change into our lives in a positive way. Although self-pity is tempting, resist it. Visualize new possibilities. Coping is often the beginning of a new change in our lives.

† *Help us, Lord, to see the changes that life imposes on us not as disasters but as opportunities.*

Tuesday October 23   **Ruth 1.15 – 22**

CHANGE OF HABITAT

> **So Naomi returned from Moab accompanied by Ruth the Moabitess, her daughter-in-law.**   **(verse 22)**

When Naomi moved to Moab she 'went out full'. She had a husband and two sons. But she returned to her native land empty because all three men had gone. She had only a woman by her side, a liability. Ruth's words, however touching, did not encourage Naomi. She made no attempt to build a new life around her daughter-in-law. She was too old to marry, too old to change. So she resolutely faced widowhood. 'How would the girls live, alone and in a foreign land?' thought Naomi. Naomi, Orpah and Ruth each made a decision. Orpah made a responsible choice with Naomi's encouragement. Ruth's choice was unusual. She chose to take her chances among strangers in a strange land. Elimelech left his country and his God for Moab. In contrast, Ruth was willing to leave her own land out of loyalty to Naomi. In the new land she might face hostility, abuse and discrimination. Ruth's relationship with others was remade, reshaped, remoulded. Hostility, hate and rejection were changed into love and acceptance. She unselfishly left her own home and family to care for her mother-in-law. Ruth, a foreigner, accepted Israel's God.

† *Help us, Lord, to see the changes that life imposes on us not as disasters but as opportunities.*

Wednesday October 24 (United Nations Day)   **Ruth 2.1 – 23**

CHANGE OF DUTY   Everything is going badly for you. Your life is one long series of regrets and nothing seems worthwhile. What will you do? Give up trying? Allow discouragement to paralyze you? Refuse to fight back? Then remember Ruth! Ruth and Boaz made major, life-changing decisions. Ruth chose to risk her own future to care for her widowed mother-in-law. Boaz chose to protect and eventually marry this impoverished foreign woman. Why was Ruth surprised by Boaz's unexpected kindness? Human nature often says: 'If I take care of you I may not have enough for myself. If you need something then work for it yourself. Your misfortune is not my fault. You are responsible for yourself.' But the covenant community had been taught to help the destitute, the widows and the foreigners. They were not isolated individuals. They were family, a community. They cared for one another!

'I've been told all about what you have done for your mother-in-law since the death of your husband – how you left your father and mother and your homeland and came to live with a people you did not know before.' (verse 11)

We, as a global community, have a responsibility for one another. We can no longer say, 'To each their own'. We are one in the family of God.

✝ *Help us, Lord, to see the changes that life imposes on us not as disasters but as opportunities.*

Thursday October 25   Ruth 3.1 – 18

CHANGE OF CONDITION Naomi asked Ruth to take a great risk by going to Boaz in the middle of the night. Why did she suggest this? Naomi believed that a woman's happiness and fulfilment was to have a husband and sons; they were the only sources of a woman's security and worth. Naomi defined 'full' and 'empty' in relation to sons. Naomi urged Ruth to go to Boaz and 'he will tell you what to do' (*verse 4*) but, in actual fact, it was Ruth who told Boaz what to do: 'Spread the corner of your garment over me, since you are a kinsman-redeemer' (*verse 9*). Ruth the widow had become Ruth the future wife. Naomi would no longer be empty handed.

Then she told her everything Boaz had done for her and added, 'He gave me these six measures of barley, saying, 'Don't go back to your mother-in-law empty-handed.'
(verses 16b – 17)

Ruth moved Naomi from emptiness to fullness by her action. She used every opportunity in a patriarchal world to bring about her liberation and create a secure future for herself and her family.

✝ *Help us, Lord, to see the changes that life imposes on us not as disasters but as opportunities.*

Friday October 26   Ruth 4.1 – 12

CHANGE OF STATUS Boaz went through the legal ritual of acquiring Ruth as his new wife. The unnamed relative had first claim to buy Elimelech's land and Ruth with it. He originally said yes but later changed his mind. He probably saw Ruth as a property to be gained, whereas Boaz saw her as a life companion. The witnesses toasted Boaz and congratulated him. This transaction called for a celebration.

May the Lord make the woman who is coming into your home like Rachel and Leah, who together built up the house of Israel. (verse 11)

Celebration projects our dreams into the future, allowing us to invent a satisfactory ending for the unravelling plot of the present. Boaz worked for the liberation of Ruth and Naomi from destitution and towards hope. How will you and I react to the challenges of the future? We can choose to opt out, run away, shut down, sit around or launch out. How far are you willing to carry family responsibilities? Ruth was expected to do what it took two earlier women to do: to build up the house of Israel!

† *Help us, Lord, to see the changes that life imposes on us not as disasters but as opportunities.*

Saturday October 27   **Ruth 4.13 – 22**

CHANGE: A NEW BEGINNING

And the Lord enabled her to conceive, and she gave birth to a son. (verse 13b)

Whenever a baby is born there is change. There is newness, a beginning, a new possibility, a new opportunity. In the words of the Indian poet Rabindranath Tagore, 'Every child comes with the message that God is not yet discouraged of man.' Because Ruth and Boaz chose to live their lives with kindness, loyalty and love, God blessed them greatly and, through them, Israel and the whole world. Ruth, a foreigner who married an Israelite, began a family line which led through the great King David to the Saviour Jesus Christ. In Ruth's day, the Jews had never even thought of having a king. Nobody dreamed that the child they named Obed would be the grandfather of a king. The story of Ruth shows how one woman accommodated change and became part of the salvation story. 'Your daughter-in-law, who loves you and who is better to you than seven sons, has given him birth' (*verse 15b*). Ruth's faithfulness to her mother-in-law had been rewarded. But the happiest person of all was Naomi as she held the grandson on her lap.

✝ *Help us, Lord, to see the changes that life imposes on us not as disasters but as opportunities.*

For group discussion and personal thought

● Look back over the times of great change in your own life and circumstances. Can you see any examples of how what may have seemed at the time to be disasters became opportunities for growth and greater good?

LETTERS TO THE THESSALONIANS 1

Notes by Heather Ward

based on the New International Version

Heather Ward is a Methodist Local Preacher who has worked as a teacher in Zimbabwe and as a residential social worker in a hostel for adults with learning difficulties.

The apostle Paul believed that God had called him to go and preach in Macedonia (*Acts 16.8 – 10*). He obeyed, and when he arrived in Thessalonica he preached first to the Jews, but when they became hostile to his message he also preached to the Gentiles. At times he was imprisoned and his life was threatened. However, people in Thessalonica believed his message.

Text for the week: 1 Thessalonians 5.23 – 24

Sunday October 28   **1 Thessalonians 1.1 – 10**

THANKSGIVING

We always thank God for all of you, mentioning you in our prayers. **(verse 2)**

Paul, Silas and Timothy are sending Christian greetings and the assurance of their prayers to the church in Thessalonica. They are thankful that the faith of these people in the risen Christ has enabled them to turn from idols and receive the Holy Spirit with joy. Because of their faith through persecution, the Christian message has been proclaimed to others. We may pray for other people, and we thank God for his goodness to us, but do we remember to thank God in our prayers for other people – especially for those who are shining examples of faith in difficult circumstances? Do we talk about renowned believers, in the way that others discuss pop stars – or the non-Christians in Macedonia discussed the heroes of the chariot races? To look for faith and goodness in others and admire them will do far more to build up our local church than gossip and criticism.

✝ *Loving Lord, give me the courage to witness to you, even when I may be criticized or persecuted because I believe in your love and power.*

TROUBLED BUT NOT PUT DOWN

> **You know, brothers, that our visit to you was not a failure.
> We had previously suffered and been insulted in Philippi,
> as you know, but with the help of our God we dared to
> tell you his gospel in spite of strong opposition.**
>
> **(verses 1 – 2)**

In these verses there is a different tone from chapter 1, where Paul
was praising and encouraging the Thessalonians. Now he is
examining his motives and those of his fellow workers, who had
had to leave Thessalonica because of the hatred of the Jews. While
they had been there they had tried not to be a burden to their hosts
(in other places Paul had worked as a tent maker, so he may have
earned his keep by doing this in Thessalonica). There seems to
have been a misunderstanding between the apostles and the local
people, hinted at in verse 4 ('We are not trying to please men but
God, who tests our hearts') and verse 1 ('Our visit to you was not a
failure'). Paul and his companions had been careful to be open and
honest with the Thessalonians and not sponge on them – how
often people are put off the Church by the behaviour of
churchgoers!

✝ *'Search me, O God, and know my heart ... and lead me in the way
everlasting' (Psalm 139.23 – 24).*

THE VICTOR'S CROWN

> **For what is our hope, our joy, or the crown in which we
> will glory in the presence of our Lord Jesus Christ when he
> comes? Is it not you? Indeed, you are our glory and joy.**
>
> **(verses 19 – 20)**

Paul speaks of the troubles of the Church in Judea and reminds
the Thessalonians that the Jewish leaders there persecuted the
Christians because the leaders could not accept the
Resurrection and the coming of the Holy Spirit. The
Thessalonians are not alone in their suffering – indeed,
suffering is a sign of an authentic Christian community. Paul
rejoices that they have remained faithful, and their witness
gives him joy and hope. His crown of glory will be from the
victory of their faith in their time of persecution.

✝ *Lord, I pray for people I know who are trying to live out their Christian life but find it hard, because of what other people say or do to discourage them.*

Wednesday October 31   **1 Thessalonians 3.1 – 6**

TIMOTHY'S VISIT

Timothy has just now come to us from you and brought good news about your faith and love. He has told us that you always have pleasant memories of us and that you long to see us, just as we also long to see you.   (verse 6)

Because Paul had not been able to return to Thessalonica to reassure himself that the Christians had remained true to their new-found faith, he had sent Timothy to report on the church there. He found that their faith and love were still strong, in spite of the persecution they had had to face. Although there seem to be suggestions in chapter 2 that relationships had sometimes been difficult between Paul and the Thessalonian church, verse 6 gives no indication that these tensions remain. Both Paul and the Christians in Thessalonica would welcome a return visit, and Paul shows a touching concern for his children in the faith.

✝ *Forgiving Lord, as we examine ourselves, help us to forgive those who have criticized us, and when we have hurt others, show us how we can seek reconciliation and renew our friendships.*

Thursday November 1   **1 Thessalonians 3.7 – 13**

FAITH AND PERSEVERANCE

We were encouraged about you because of your faith ... since you are standing firm in the Lord.
(part of verses 7 – 8)

Paul and Silas had to be smuggled out of Thessalonica at night because of persecution. What an encouragement it must have been to them to hear that the new church was standing firm in spite of their troubles. Paul still hopes to return one day and advise them in any problems they may have. In the meantime, he is praying for them and shows genuine delight at their progress in the Christian life. These verses are full of warmth and generosity – are these the outstanding characteristics of our relations with other Christians?

† *Lord, we pray for Christians in countries where there is persecution; help them to stand firm in their faith.*

Friday November 2   **1 Thessalonians 4.1 – 12**

LIVING TO PLEASE GOD

For God did not call us to be impure but to live a holy life. Therefore, he who rejects this instruction does not reject man but God, who gives you his Holy Spirit. (verses 7 – 8)

Paul calls the newly converted Christians to dedicate themselves to God's way of living, both in sexual matters and by not taking advantage of other people. The words in this passage could easily have been written to people in many parts of the world today. The moral standards of society today are often low. Young people are growing up with the idea that faithfulness in marriage does not matter, and sex before and outside marriage are accepted as normal. Paul was quite sure that this is wrong. We know from our own experience of modern society that sexual immorality can lead to marriage breakdown and the spread of diseases like AIDS. At the same time, Paul praises the Thessalonians for their growth in love – even while saying that, like all of us, they could do more.

† *Father, forgive our failure to live in your way, as individuals, as a Church, and as a nation.*

Saturday November 3   **1 Thessalonians 4.13 – 18**

THE COMING OF THE LORD

We believe that Jesus died and rose again and so we believe that God will bring with Jesus those who have fallen asleep in him ...Therefore encourage each other with these words.   **(verses 14 and 18)**

The early Church believed that Jesus would come again in the very near future. In Acts 1.10 – 11, after Jesus had been taken into heaven, the disciples saw two men who said that Jesus would return. The Holy Spirit came and filled their hearts and changed their lives, but the promise of Jesus' return had not been fulfilled. Now the question for the Early Church was, 'What would happen to those who had already died? Would they be called too?' What do we believe about death? Have those we knew and loved already gone to be with the risen

Jesus? Will they come back with him? We do not know the answer. However, if we already know the power of God's Holy Spirit in our lives, guiding us in the way we live and teaching us to love and care for our neighbours, surely we can face death with the hope that we shall meet with our Lord, even if we have not met him face to face on this earth.

† *Loving heavenly Father, your Holy Spirit has helped us to live this life; help us to trust you for our future when we die.*

For group discussion and personal thought

● Think of the young people in your church and neighbourhood. What problems and discouragements do they have which will influence whether they want to call themselves Christians at school, college or the workplace? How can the church community support and encourage them?

● Does your church look outside itself to support people in need in the local community, and people in other countries who are persecuted by other religious or political groups or suffering from poverty, war, famine and the effects of AIDS? What more could it do?

LIVING PRAYERS series

● Compiled by Maureen Edwards, one of IBRA's editors
● User-friendly for individuals, groups and churches

Living Prayers For Today:

● Prayers for private devotions and public worship
● Modern and well-known older prayers from different parts of the world

More Living Prayers for Today:

● Focuses on the Christian festivals
● Includes some prayers for everyday use

UK price £12.50 each

IBRA *Order through your IBRA representative, or from the appropriate address on page 285.*

LETTERS TO THE THESSALONIANS 2

Notes by Joaquim Armindo Almeida

based on the New International Version

Joaquim Armindo Pinto de Almeida lives in Porto, Portugal. He earns his living as a mechanical engineer but also has a degree in theology and teaches Pastoral Theology at the Portuguese Catholic University. He is a catechist and reader in the Roman Catholic Church.

In today's liberal society, the poor seem to get poorer while the rich get richer; money which should go on economic development is spent on arms; traditional culture is destroyed by technology; and many people seem to be concerned only with their own pleasure. In such a world, it seems an irony to talk about the coming of the Kingdom of God. But although the Christians in Thessalonica are so worried about exactly when the kingdom will come, in many ways it is already here. The kingdom is here when Christians wait gladly and patiently for the coming of the Lord and use the waiting time for prayer and action.

Text for the week: 2 Thessalonians 2.3

Sunday November 4   **1 Thessalonians 5.1 – 11**

THE END OF THE WORLD The Thessalonians seemed to expect the end or *parousia* to come at any moment. The arrival of Christ was imminent and then believers would clearly and visibly be taken up to heaven. But Paul tells them firmly that there is no need to worry about when the end will come. The only people who need to fear the coming of Christ are those who live in the darkness of sin.

> **You are all sons of the light and sons of the day. We do not belong to the night or to the darkness. So then, let us not be like others, who are asleep.**   **(verses 5 – 6a)**

Light is the symbol of life and darkness is the symbol of death. Paul often uses this contrast between life and death, light and darkness. Christians live in the light, because Jesus has been raised from the dead and is already with us every day. So it does not matter if no date has been given for the end of the world. We can continue to share the work of Christ as he transforms the present world and brings an end to war, hunger and exclusion. Because Christ's work of ending the present state of this world goes on, we must stay awake and alert; we have the task of bringing the light of Christ to others.

† *Spirit of God, make us bearers of light each day, in a new world – the world in which we live, which can become the Kingdom of Heaven.*

Monday November 5   **1 Thessalonians 5.12 – 28**

THE CHRISTIAN IN COMMUNITY For Paul, moral behaviour now is influenced by the end or *parousia* to come. Christian behaviour is governed by the fact that Christians belong to a community. Paul's moral teaching is about life in community and the need to help each other; so he tells the Thessalonians how to act towards each other: encourage, admonish, respect, love, live in peace, warn, help, be patient, be kind, be joyful always, pray continually, give thanks, test.

We urge you, brothers, warn those who are idle, encourage the timid, help the weak, be patient with everyone.

(verse 14)

If the Thessalonians behave in this way, then the risen Christ is already present. If they give the whole of themselves, spirit, soul and body (*verse 23*) to the work of God, then the Kingdom of Heaven is already here. Each of them should concentrate on doing God's will now, today, not waste their energies looking for a kingdom in the future.

† *Fill each one of us, Lord, with the courage to be good Christians in our own communities.*

Tuesday, November 6   **2 Thessalonians 1.1 – 12**

THE HOPE Most scholars today agree that this second letter to the Christians in Thessalonica was probably not written by Paul himself, but by one or more of his followers. However, as we have seen from Paul's first letter, the central theme of this second letter – the imminent coming of Christ – was very important in his preaching. Here, however, the question is not about when the end of the world will take place, but how Christians should prepare for it.

Therefore, among God's churches we boast about your perseverance and faith in all the persecutions and trials you are enduring. (verse 4)

2 Thessalonians makes an important point: the Christian faith is expressed in this actual, physical world. Therefore Christians should not run away from the world but work within it, like salt in food. Although verse 4 does not speak directly about hope, it is hope which runs through the letter. Like the community at Thessalonica, we shall experience persecution. It would be nice if the Kingdom of God could come without any effort from us, and if there were not so many problems in the world and within ourselves. But the persecution and the difficulties are the work of human beings, not of God. It is God who gives us the hope to go on.

† *Lord Jesus, in the middle of all our tribulations, help us to be strong enough to open ourselves to your service in true hope.*

Wednesday November 7   **2 Thessalonians 2.1 – 12**

THE COMING OF THE LORD   This section speaks again about the next coming of the Lord. However, the writer explains that this end event will be preceded by persecution, rumours and the appearance of a 'man of lawlessness' who will proclaim himself to be God.

And then the lawless one will be revealed, whom the Lord Jesus will overthrow with the breath of his mouth and destroy by the splendour of his coming. (verse 8)

This follower of Satan will be defeated by the final coming of the Lord, the impious will be destroyed by the power of the gospel. There will be a final battle between love and collective hate. The breath of God's mouth is aimed, not at individuals, but at collective sin. Even now, it destroys false values and principles and impious economics and culture.

† *Lord Jesus, release us from impiety and from false prophets, and free us to proclaim your gospel.*

Thursday November 8   **2 Thessalonians 2.13 -17**

THE CHRISTIAN COMMUNITY SHOULD ADVANCE   In this passage the argument of the letter is taken a step further. If the expected *parousia* is not coming and the lawless man is not to be feared, it is also true that the Lord *does* come and his risen life is strengthened by every step that the Christian community takes in faith, hope and love. This is the gospel of the Lord which brings us to the kingdom prepared for all men and women. To present God as he is, to witness to his kingdom, to denounce the injustices that produce wars, to live in brotherhood and solidarity – this is the way the Christian community must follow, because the only weapon that the gospel gives it to fight evil is the weapon of love.

May our Lord Jesus Christ himself and God our Father ... encourage your hearts and strengthen you in every good deed and word.   (part of verse 16 and verse 17)

The most important task of the Christian community is to travel towards the kingdom, and at the same time to bring that kingdom into existence. This involves loyalty to the faith we have been taught, prophetic witness and following Jesus without fear.

† *Lord Jesus, give comfort to our hearts and strength to fight evil with your weapon of love.*

Friday November 9   **2 Thessalonians 3.1 – 5**

PRAYER   Following a path which started with *parousia* and continued with the word of the gospel, we come now to the need for prayer. The writers of this letter could not leave out what is most precious to Christians: the living force of prayer. Prayer expresses our relationship with God, as we say with Samuel, 'Here I am' (*1 Samuel 3.6, 8, 16*). Prayer unites us in active solidarity with the first disciples; prayer and faithful action together make up our commitment to God. St Teresa of Avila said that 'God has no other hands but yours', and in prayer we put our hands into the hands of God, for the coming of the Kingdom of Heaven and to fight against sin. Prayer expresses our confidence in the Lord and his presence in our lives.

But the Lord is faithful, and he will strengthen and protect you from the evil one.   (verse 3)

The Lord is good and faithful, he will never leave us as orphans. This is why prayer is so important; it is talking to God, because there are things we need to discuss with him, but it is also listening to what God wants to say to us. Even listening is not enough – do we really want to hear and obey?

† *Lord Jesus, teach me how to pray.*

Saturday November 10　　　　　　**2 Thessalonians 3.6 – 18**

FINAL ADVICE　The writers have finished their letter to the church in Thessalonica. They have praised them for their work for God, for the love between them and their enthusiasm and confidence. Now the writers have one final word of advice, about the need to work for a living. On the one hand, those who work for the Church should be supported by the Christian community. On the other hand, Christians should give an example to others, and those who can work should do so. This warning has deep implications.

> **We hear that some among you are idle. They are not busy; they are busybodies.**　　　　　　　　　　　　**(verse 11)**

Living without any purpose is not the same as waiting for the Kingdom of God. Idleness is unfair to others. Those who are idle do not earn what they eat; they are impious and bring the Christian community into disrepute, and they deserve to be excluded and warned in love by the rest of the community. This final advice is very clear, but the tension between the two groups must not be allowed to destroy the love which exists in the church in Thessalonica. The final prayer is for peace 'at all times and in every way' (*verse 16*).

† *Lord Jesus, teach us to work in our community and always to be an example to the world.*

For group discussion and personal thought

- In what ways do we share God's work of creation and with him make the world in which we live?
- How can the Christian community fight the economic factors which produce greater and greater poverty?
- Are we waiting for the Kingdom of God or are we living in the kingdom already? What signs are there of the kingdom in our Christian community?

PROFILE: KING DAVID 1
(Readings from 1 and 2 Samuel)

Notes by Iain Roy

based on the Good News Bible

Iain Roy is a retired minister of the Church of Scotland, still active in preaching and writing.

Even today, it is very difficult for us to separate great men and women from the myths which tend to surround them. Publicity machines and spin doctors present us with the image of them which they want us to have. Both the first and second books of Samuel present us with a similar challenge. They present a particular picture of King David, but both of them leave us in no doubt of his importance.

Text for the week: 1 Samuel 16.11 – 12

Sunday November 11   **1 Samuel 16.1 – 13**

GOD'S CHOICE   As we often do ourselves, Samuel made the mistake of judging others by external appearance.

> **When they arrived, Samuel saw Jesse's son Eliab and said to himself, 'This man standing here in the LORD's presence is surely the one he has chosen.' But the LORD said to him, 'Pay no attention to how tall and handsome he is. I have rejected him, because I do not judge as people judge. They look at the outward appearance, but I look at the heart.'** (verses 6 – 7)

Few of us will admit how the height, appearance, skin colour, or even dress of others influence our perception of them. It can lead us, at least temporarily, to inflate the worth of some people and underestimate the worth of others. But Eliab was not God's choice. Samuel did not need sight, he needed insight to make the choice of youthful David. Insight is an even more precious gift than sight. This is how God sees us – in depth, the soul not the surface. How often have we discovered the real worth of others when we have got beyond how they look to what they are!

✝ *Lord, help us to see others as you see them – as they are, but also with forgiveness and compassion.*

Monday November 12 1 Samuel 16.14 – 23a

HEALING MINISTRY In this one chapter of the first book of Samuel we have two different accounts of how David came to be a member of the royal household of Saul. The first account suggests divine guidance, the second suggests human choice. This latter was based on David's musicianship and the therapy it could provide for a tormented king.

> **His servants said to him, 'We know that an evil spirit sent by God is tormenting you. So give us the order, sir, and we will look for a man who knows how to play the harp. Then when the evil spirit comes on you, the man can play his harp, and you will be all right again.'** **(verses 15 – 16)**

The conflict between God's guiding and human choice is more apparent than real. God's will is most often done through men and women, in particular through those who let God's Spirit educate what they think and do. Thus the prime necessity in the Christian life is a mind open to God and humanity, not blinded by prejudice or filled with hate. We can all sing a better and more healing song to others when we let God's love guide us and fill us.

✝ *Lord Jesus, show us how to relate to others in a fruitful way, so that we may do them good and not evil, and create calm in their lives and in ours.*

Tuesday November 13 1 Samuel 18.6 – 16

FORGIVENESS AND FULFILMENT In the last days of Saul's life it is hard to decide which destroyed his personality more: his own inadequacies as a king or his envy of David.

> **In their celebration the women sang, 'Saul has killed thousands, but David tens of thousands.' Saul did not like this, and he became very angry. He said, ' ... They will be making him king next!' And so he was jealous and suspicious of David from that day on.** **(verses 7 – 9)**

Envy is a deadly sin. We can never realize our own true potential when we worry more about what other people do rather than what we do ourselves. This is why a great deal of Jesus' teaching centres on our awareness of our own inadequacies rather than the failings of others (*see, for example, Matthew 7.3*). It is only when we have come to terms with our own shortcomings that we can appreciate other people's strengths and also develop the particular gifts that God has given us. It is honest self-appraisal and God's forgiveness which unlock our potential.

† *Father, help us to appreciate what others can do which we cannot do, and help us to do the things we can for you and for your kingdom.*

Wednesday November 14 1 Samuel 19.1 – 18

LIVING POSITIVELY There can hardly be a better description of what one person's relationship to another should be than this description of David's relationship to Saul.

> **Jonathan praised David to Saul and said, 'Sir, don't do wrong to your servant David. He has never done you any wrong; on the contrary, everything he has done has been a great help to you.'** (verse 4)

If we can do others no wrong but rather be of some help to them, we stand in a relationship to them which would meet with Jesus' approval. Jesus was always more concerned in his teaching with our attitude to others than their attitude to us. The high standards he sets us are based on what we are prepared to deliver to others: to forgive as we are forgiven (*Matthew 6.12*), to do to others as we would like them to do to us (*Matthew 7.12*). The emphasis in Christian living must always be on the positive, not the negative, qualities of living.

† *Lord, show us how you forgive so that we may see better how to forgive; show us how you love so that we may see better how to love.*

Thursday November 15 1 Samuel 24.1 – 22

A COMPLEX MAN As his story in the Old Testament shows, David's character was complex. He was capable of love and lust, of kindness and cruelty, of forgiveness and hatred. Here we see him at his most forgiving.

> **David crept over and cut off a piece of Saul's robe without Saul's knowing it. But then David's conscience began to trouble him, and he said to his men, 'May the LORD keep me from doing any harm to my master, whom the LORD chose as king!'** (verses 4b – 6a)

We are told that David's conscience was his guide. Conscience is a personal sense of right or wrong which gradually evolves. It is not a popular modern concept. Today, morality more often comes down to what we see as best for us. We need to recover the idea of the Christian conscience, which sees life and others through a mind and heart educated by Christ's compassion and forgiveness. It will help us to be more generous to others in our attitudes and relationships.

† *Lord Jesus, help us not to dwell on the wrong others have done us but to think about the good you have done us, so that we may learn to be as generous in spirit as you are.*

Friday November 16   **2 Samuel 1.1 – 16**

COMMON GRIEF There is personal grief and there is common grief. Personal grief for family or friends is a burden that is often private and all too often it is carried alone. Common or shared grief is a different phenomenon. It is a community's sense of loss. It is this kind of grief which David and his followers show here.

> **David tore his clothes in sorrow, and all his men did the same. They grieved and mourned and fasted until evening for Saul and Jonathan and for Israel, the people of the LORD, because so many had been killed in battle.**
>
> **(verses 11 – 12)**

Natural disasters, tragic accidents, war, premature or violent death can all create common grief. People find themselves drawn together in a grief which embraces everyone rather than just some people. This collective sense of loss often leads to a mutual need to comfort. The more we can see individual grief in this way, as a shared grief, the more we will be able to comfort one another in Christ's name.

† *Remind us, O Lord, that the death of one person diminishes all of us, so that we may learn to share with others their sense of loss and grief in a way which strengthens and comforts them for your sake.*

Saturday November 17   **2 Samuel 1.17 – 27**

KINDLY REMEMBRANCE Whether David wrote all the psalms which bear his name is not really relevant. The Bible essentially presents him as a poet, one who sees life with a sharper image and a deeper insight than most human beings. So David's lament was almost as generous in the way he saw Saul, a king with feet of clay, as it was in the way he saw Jonathan, his friend.

Saul and Jonathan, so wonderful and dear;
   together in life, together in death;
   swifter than eagles, stronger than lions.
Women of Israel, mourn for Saul!
   He clothed you in rich scarlet dresses
   and adorned you with jewels and gold.   (verses 23 – 24)

Too often there is something grudging in our remembrance of others. We remember the wrong they did, the mistakes they made, rather than the good they achieved, the successes they had. It is a good thing that Jesus did not think of others like that. Peter betrayed Jesus as surely as Judas did, yet Peter's faith is the rock on which Christ built his Church. James and John were sometimes a quarrelsome, envious pair but they were also Jesus' dearly loved and faithful servants. The advice of Paul to us, to consider others better than ourselves (*Philippians 2.3*), is sound. If David was a better king than Saul, perhaps it started here with his remembrance of the good that Saul had done rather than the evil.

✝ *Christ, help us to remember the best things in the lives of others, so that we may overcome the worst in ourselves through both this remembering and your grace.*

For group discussion and personal thought

● 'You did not choose me; I chose you' (John 15.16). Does the choice of David as king help us in any way to see how God chooses us for his work and witness?

● How can prayer help us to be honest in the way we show ourselves to other people?

● Have you experienced situations which united you as a community or a church in a shared grief? How did sharing the grief help you all to heal?

PROFILE: KING DAVID 2
(Readings from 1 and 2 Samuel)

Notes by Peter Tongeman

based on the New International Version

The story of David is told in Scripture with surprising frankness. Good qualities and bad are included. There are lessons to be learned both from his example and his failure. Generosity, wise leadership, determination that God should be given central place in the nation, are followed by occasions of self-questioning, kindness, prayer and, sadly, a serious moral lapse. His humanity, combined with strong religious faith, made him a popular and highly successful king of Israel.

Text for the week: 2 Samuel 6.18

Sunday November 18   **2 Samuel 2.1 – 11**

A GENEROUS KING It is common to seek revenge when roles are reversed in such a way that conquerors are themselves conquered, the powerful become weak and the weak powerful. Not so with David. Forced into hiding by King Saul's jealousy and violence, pursued relentlessly by his army almost to the point of death, David refused to retaliate, even sparing Saul's life when it was within his grasp (*1 Samuel 26.6 – 12*). Now Saul had died, by his own hand, and David had been anointed king of Judah. His first act was not revenge but reward for those who had treated Saul with kindness and respect.

> **When David was told that it was the men of Jabesh Gilead who had buried Saul, he sent messengers ... to say to them, 'The LORD bless you for showing this kindness to Saul your master by burying him. May the LORD now show you kindness and faithfulness, and I too will show you the same favour because you have done this.'**   **(verses 4b – 6)**

In some Balkan countries such as Serbia, the culture demands revenge for every act of aggression – insult for insult, hatred for hatred, life for life. Only Christian values can break the cycle and bring kindness for hurt, good for evil (*Romans 12.19 – 21*).

✝ *Set me free, O Lord, from a desire to repay evil for evil. Grant me grace and courage to overcome evil with good.*

A RESPONSIBLE KING There is no privilege without responsibility. David, having reigned over Judah for seven years, was now made king over all Israel, uniting twelve disparate tribes in one nation. His privileges included residence in Jerusalem, called 'The City of David', and occupation of a fine palace built specially for him. But David accepted also the responsibilities of king – to care for his people as he had once cared for his sheep and to rule them wisely for the common good.

> All the tribes of Israel came to David at Hebron and said, 'We are your own flesh and blood. In the past, while Saul was king over us, you were the one who led Israel on their military campaigns. And the LORD said to you, 'You shall shepherd my people Israel, and you shall become their ruler.'' ... And David knew that the LORD had established him as king over Israel and had exalted his kingdom for the sake of his people Israel.   **(verses 1 – 2 and 12)**

David's determination to honour God and fulfil his purpose was confirmed by steady progress and growing influence for good. A test of good leadership is the benefit which others receive.

† *Loving Father, thank you for every privilege I enjoy; may I never take them for granted. Instead, let me use your gifts responsibly, in the service of others and for your glory.*

GOD AT THE CENTRE

> David and the whole house of Israel were celebrating with all their might before the LORD, with songs and with harps, lyres, tambourines, sistrums and cymbals ... They brought the ark of the LORD and set it in its place inside the tent that David had pitched for it, and David sacrificed burnt offerings before the LORD. After ... he blessed the people in the name of the LORD Almighty.
> **(verses 5 and 17 – 18)**

The 'ark of God' symbolized God's presence with his people. It had been carried through the desert in their long journey from Egypt and kept for years at Kiriath Jearim; now David judged that the time had come to bring it to the capital city, Jerusalem. It contained precious souvenirs of God's provision for his people – a jar of manna, Aaron's staff, and the commandments inscribed on stone (*Hebrews 9.4*). By placing the ark in a central position, David reminded everyone that God was to be at the heart of the nation. Naturally, they rejoiced together at God's continuing presence and provision for his people. God occupies a central place in every true believer's life. He is a welcome and honoured guest who presides over all our activities in holiness and love.

† *Loving Lord, you are a welcome guest in every part of my life. Rule over my thoughts and actions, that I may please and honour you.*

Wednesday November 21   2 Samuel 7.1 – 17

BLESSED BY GOD   David's conscience pricked him. He had built a fine palace for himself, but the ark of God in Jerusalem was still kept in a tent. Should he have built a temple for God before completing his own palace? Nathan the prophet replied that he should perhaps do it, but God had chosen him and would continue to prosper his rule as king. David was not sinless and wrongdoing would be punished, but God's love for him would never cease.

'This is what the LORD Almighty says: I took you from the pasture and from following the flock to be ruler over my people Israel. I have been with you wherever you have gone, and I have cut off all your enemies from before you. Now I will make your name great ... I will be his father, and he shall be my son. When he does wrong, I will punish him ... But my love will never be taken away from him.'

(part of verses 8 – 9 and 14 – 15)

Experience of God's loving care does not permit sin to go unchecked. 'Those whom I love I rebuke and discipline' (*Revelation 3.19*). God's discipline is necessary for development of character and Christlikeness.

† *Help me, Lord, to receive your loving rebuke as willingly as I welcome praise, so that sin may be curbed and godliness encouraged.*

Thursday November 22   2 Samuel 7.18 – 29

THE KING AT PRAYER

Then King David went in and sat before the LORD, and he said: 'Who am I, O Sovereign LORD, and what is my

family, that you have brought me this far? ... How great you are, O Sovereign LORD! There is no-one like you, and there is no God but you ... And who is like your people Israel – the one nation on earth that God went out to redeem as a people for himself? ... Do as you promised, so that your name will be great for ever. Then men will say, 'The LORD Almighty is God over Israel!''

(part of verses 18, 22, 23 and 25)

David could not understand why he, of all people, had been chosen. But if this was God's sovereign will, both he and the nation would benefit from God's provision. He prayed that other nations also would acknowledge God and recognize his sovereign power. John Newton, who was once the captain of a slave ship, was converted and devoted the rest of his life to Christian ministry. He wrote, 'Amazing grace, how sweet the sound, that saved a wretch like me'. The benefits of God's grace are not given for private enjoyment alone. They are meant to be shared.

✝ *How incredible, Lord, that you have chosen to adopt me as your child! Grant that as others see your Spirit at work in me, they may glorify you.*

Friday November 23   **2 Samuel 8.15 – 9.13**

A KINDLY KING   King Saul's treacherous pursuit of David, long ago, had left no resentment. In fact, the warmth of his son Jonathan's friendship still lingered in David's memory.

The king asked, 'Is there no-one still left of the house of Saul to whom I can show God's kindness?' Ziba answered the king, 'There is still a son of Jonathan; he is crippled in both feet.' ... When Mephibosheth son of Jonathan, the son of Saul, came to David, he bowed down to pay him honour ... 'Don't be afraid,' David said to him, 'for I will surely show you kindness for the sake of your father Jonathan. I will restore to you all the land that belonged to your grandfather Saul, and you will always eat at my table.'

(verses 3 and 6 – 7)

Mephibosheth, crippled and ill provided for, suddenly and unexpectedly found himself the object of David's kindly provision. Top quality food and accommodation, with freedom of the palace, for the rest of his life – better than a pension! 'Be kind to one another' (*Ephesians 4.32*) is a Christian ideal.

Opportunities of doing kindness are often lost through lack of thought. Yet little nameless acts of kindness and love truly express the spirit of Christ.

† *Lord of all kindness, you treat me far better than I deserve. Help me also to be thoughtful and kind.*

Saturday November 24   **2 Samuel 11.1 – 27**

TEMPTATION AND DEFEAT   David should have known better. He was tempted by lust and yielded. Adultery, followed by attempted cover-up, led to murder.

> **One evening David got up from his bed and walked around on the roof of the palace. From the roof he saw a woman bathing ... the wife of Uriah the Hittite. Then David sent messengers to get her ... The woman conceived ... David wrote a letter to Joab ... 'Put Uriah in the front line where the fighting is fiercest. Then withdraw from him so that he will be struck down and die' ... After the time of mourning was over, David had [Bathsheba] brought to his house, and she became his wife and bore him a son. But the thing David had done displeased the LORD.**
> **(parts of verses 2 – 5, 14 – 15 and 27)**

Temptation is not sin. Yielding to temptation is. In spite of all David's fine qualities, and his admission that his action was wrong, his fall left a permanent scar on his character. Those who occupy a position of leadership and trust are especially vulnerable. Resistance at the start is essential. Dallying with temptation weakens resolve until it is too late.

† *Lord, I am weak in the face of temptation. Without your help I am defeated. Strengthen my will to resist. Give me courage to say 'No'. Should I fall, lift me up again. Show me the way to victory.*

For group discussion and personal thought

● Make a list of the good and bad aspects of King David's character and compare them with your own. What changes do you need to make?

PROFILE: KING DAVID 3
(Readings from 1 and 2 Samuel)

Notes by Charles F Makonde

based on the Good News Bible

Charles F Makonde is a minister from the Methodist Church in Kenya, currently serving as a Mission Partner in the World Church in Britain Partnership. He is stationed in the Edinburgh and Forth Circuit of the Methodist Church in Britain.

This week's readings give us an opportunity to recognize the main characteristics of King David, who was a remarkable man of God from the beginning of his career to the end of his life, probably from about 1040 to 970 BC. 'David was thirty years old when he became king, and he ruled for forty years' (*2 Samuel 5.4*). David was the greatest of Israel's kings and through him the ultimate king, the Messiah, eventually came: 'This is the list of the ancestors of Jesus Christ, a descendant of David, who was a descendant of Abraham' (*Matthew 1.1*).

Text for the week: 2 Samuel 12.13

Sunday November 25   **2 Samuel 12.1 – 15a**

GOD'S GRACE THROUGH A STORY   God sent Nathan to King David with a simple story about a rich man who had large flocks but who stole from a poor man his one and only little lamb and killed it. David was moved by the story but, because he had deceived himself so completely, he did not apply it to himself. Almost before the story ended, he burst out angrily:

> 'I swear by the living LORD that the man who did this ought to die! For having done such a cruel thing, he must pay back four times as much as he took.' 'You are that man,' Nathan said to David.   (part of verses 5 – 7a)

Nathan's message through a story challenged King David and exposed his lie. Everything came to an end. God's grace works round our resistance and makes us turn the spotlight on to our own darkness. He is always calling each and every individual to repent. This call could come to us today in the form of a story.

† Lord, help us to listen to those who share stories of your love. May our self-awareness draw us closer to you.

Monday November 26 2 Samuel 12.15b – 25

HOPE BEYOND DEATH In yesterday's passage, David confessed his sins to God. However, the prophet tells David what will happen to the child he has produced in adultery with Bathsheba. The child soon becomes ill, and the king fasts and prays to the Lord that the child will not die. But the child does die.

> **'Yes,' David answered, 'I did fast and weep while he was still alive. I thought that the LORD might be merciful to me and not let the child die. But now that he is dead, why should I fast? Could I bring back the child to life? I will some day go to where he is, but he can never come back to me.'** **(verses 22 – 23)**

The tragedy of human history shows us that it is not always the sinner who bears the evil effects of sin. Although David's plea was not granted, he did not forsake his God. He became more conscious of his failures, gained a hope which went beyond death and realized more clearly that there is one world of the dead and another world of the living. We can do very little to prevent our loved ones from dying; the living will one day go to the world of the dead, but not the other way round.

† Lord, in the midst of failure and death, give us strength to hear you more clearly, follow you more closely and love you more dearly.

Tuesday November 27 2 Samuel 18.1 – 18

SADNESS IN THE MIDST OF TRIUMPH In some villages in Africa, meetings are called by the sound of a horn used as a trumpet. In most African countries these meetings are called the chief's 'barazas'. In today's passage, we read that a similar trumpet was blown as a way of stopping a war:

> **David's army went out into the countryside and fought the Israelites in the forest of Ephraim. The Israelites were defeated by David's men; it was a terrible defeat, with twenty thousand men killed that day ... Joab ordered the trumpet to be blown to stop the fighting, and his troops came back from pursuing the Israelites.**
> **(verses 6 – 7 and 16)**

On Remembrance Day, when nations remember those who have died in war, trumpets are blown at the eleventh hour either in churches or at historic places of war, to signify the good news that the war is over. But the good news for Christians is that Christ has fought and victoriously won the spiritual war for us.

† *Lord, when forces of evil come our way, help us to fight with you.*

Wednesday November 28   **2 Samuel 18.19 – 33**

DILEMMA OF WAR   Despite the good news of victory over all who had rebelled against the king, the news of the death of his second son Absalom is too much to bear. The king wishes he had died in place of his son. Wars rob us of our young men and women. In war, no one is a winner. The results of war cause unbearable pain and grief. No grief is easy to bear.

> **The king was overcome with grief. He went up to the room over the gateway and wept. As he went, he cried, 'O my son! My son Absalom! Absalom, my son! If only I had died in your place, my son! Absalom, my son!'**   **(verse 33)**

David's anguish, his pitiful and helpless wail, shows us a deeper dimension of his grief. David wished he had died instead of Absalom because he knew he deserved to die. Guilt aggravates his grief. From the descendants of David will come a man of sorrows who will bear all our grief and carry our sorrows. God himself in Jesus Christ wipes away every tear from our eyes.

† *Lord, when we are faced with death and sorrow, help us to bear the grief.*

Thursday November 29   **2 Samuel 19.1 – 15**

REINSTATED IN LEADERSHIP Recently, an African country had a *coup d'état* which lasted for a day or so. It was a military take-over, but divisions arose among the soldiers and so the coup was suppressed and the president who had been overthrown was reinstated. The people of Judah were in a dilemma and, as often happens with people in this situation, they began to disagree among themselves.

> **All over the country they started quarrelling among themselves. 'King David saved us from our enemies,' they said to one another ... 'So why doesn't somebody try to bring King David back?' ... and they sent him word to return with all his officials.**   **(part of verses 9 – 10 and 14)**

The short-lived rebellion failed to gain its objective, and discontent spread throughout the country. However, with the help of the priests and David's gesture of reconciliation towards Amasa, God's providence brought them all to an agreement and reinstated David as king.

✝ *Lord, thank you that you always call us back to yourself.*

Friday November 30   **2 Samuel 22.1 – 7, 17 – 31**

PRAISE BE TO GOD   The theme of this psalm of praise also appears in the book of Psalms. It is a reflective piece, looking back over a period of salvation when God had delivered David from his enemies. God's people have often had many enemies and been in imminent danger of falling into their hands. The psalm shows us that David was a man loved by God, but not always by men. Many hated him and even sought to kill him. He did not take revenge, but always trusted in his God.

> The LORD is my protector;
>   he is my strong fortress.
> My God is my protection,
>   and with him I am safe ...
> He is my saviour;
>   he protects me and saves me from violence ...
> Praise the LORD! ...
> This God – how perfect are his deeds,
>   how dependable his words!   **(verses 2 – 4 and 31)**

David adores God and gives him glory for his infinite protection. He exults in his relationship with God, which is the foundation of all the benefits he has received from him. The many mercies we receive from God should lead us to praise him for them. Every new mercy given to us should put a new song into our mouths, a new song of praises to our God. We should not use difficulties as an excuse for turning away from God, but always be thankful to him.

✝ *Lord God, we praise and thank you for your love and providence, which we depend on.*

Saturday December 1   **2 Samuel 23.1 – 7**

FAREWELL   As a king, David is remembered for many things. Above all, he was an outstanding songwriter in the life and history of the people of Israel. His people loved him for the music that came from the inner depth of his heart. David's last words of farewell have a poetic form. They speak of the glory of God which will come in the rule of a righteous future king; this seals the covenant between God and David.

> **And that is how God will bless my descendants,**
>   **because he has made an eternal covenant with me,**
>   **an agreement that will not be broken,**
>   **a promise that will not be changed.**
> **That is all I desire;**
>   **that will be my victory,**
>   **and God will surely bring it about.**   **(verse 5)**

The Lord is a God who makes covenants with both individuals and nations. Although Israel failed to keep her side of the covenant, she did learn that God was always faithful.

✝ *Lord God, help us to remain faithful and always in a covenant relationship with you.*

For group discussion and personal thought

- Why do you think Nathan tells David a story rather than confronting him directly with his sin?
- Joab was extremely loyal to David but essentially did not submit to him. Could this be true of a Christian in relation to Christ?

GOD WITH US 1
David's descendant

Notes by Elina Templin

based on the New International Version

Elina Templin is both a musician and a Presbyterian pastor. After living in South Africa for many years, where she brought up her two children, she returned to her home country of Canada in 1998.

Our text for the first week of Advent reminds us that God so loved the world that he sent his only son to save it, not to condemn it. The Most High and the Holy One comes down to us, one of us, broken for us, not to condemn but to save.

Text for the week: John 3.16 – 17

Sunday December 2   **Jeremiah 33.14 – 16**

HOPING AGAINST HOPE   Like many parts of our world today, Jeremiah's world of 588 BC was a time of great storm and stress. God's people faced the powerful political giants of Assyria, Egypt and Babylon. In the midst of this turmoil, Jeremiah calls the people to stand firm in the faith. The people wanted to hear comfortable words, not doom and gloom. But Jeremiah continues to speak out about the coming destruction of the Kingdom of Judah and the end of an era. He warns that the corruption of the people and their leaders will bring God's wrath and judgement. But the day will also come when God will enter into a new covenant with his people.

> **'I will make a righteous Branch sprout from David's line:**
>   **he will do what is just and right in the land.**
> **In those days Judah will be saved**
>   **and Jerusalem will live in safety.'** (part of verses 15 – 16)

How often we feel tossed about by circumstances over which we have no control! Faith falters like a tree shaken at its roots. We need to remember that our salvation, our 'safety', rests not on our efforts or what we do, but on who God is.

† *Lord, may we trust in you with our whole heart and not rely on our own understanding.*

GOD'S LOVE STORY   In his history of Christian missions, Stephen Neill writes that the Bible is simply 'the background to God's love story with the human race'. This story does not begin with Jesus, but way back with Abraham, Isaac and Jacob. Like all of us, Jesus was not born in a vacuum. All that has happened in the past, the prophecies, the promises of God to save his people, are all caught up and brought together in the gift of God's very own life – Jesus Christ himself.

> **All this took place to fulfil what the Lord had said through the prophet: 'The virgin will be with child and will give birth to a son, and they will call him Immanuel' – which means, 'God with us'.   (verses 22 – 23)**

The genealogy of Jesus – a long list of mostly unfamiliar names! – has sometimes been used as a text for a sermon. Do you think the sermon was boring? Perhaps, but when we understand that the list of names sets the birth of Jesus within the framework of God's *whole* history of salvation with his people, this long, boring list begins to make sense. If you look up some of the names, you will discover that they were far from perfect, and they represent the broadest possible cross-section of humanity. God uses the whole world in his plan. Advent begins, not with the birth of Jesus, but with the genealogy of Jesus.

† *Lord, thank you for those who have gone before us in the faith.*

WHAT DO YOU THINK ABOUT THE CHRIST?   We may wonder today why people misunderstood Jesus and found him confusing; even those closest to him got it wrong. John the Baptist sends his disciples to ask Jesus, 'Are you the one or should we expect another?' People expected a political saviour to rescue God's people Israel from Roman domination. Jesus did not seem to fit their expectations. Indeed, frustratingly, Jesus did not seem to fit any formula. And so, when the religious leaders of the group are asked,

> **'What do you think about the Christ? Whose son is he?'**
> **'The son of David,' they replied.**
> **[Jesus] said to them, 'How is it then that David, speaking by the Spirit, calls him "Lord"? ... If then David calls him "Lord", how can he be his son?' No-one could say a word in reply.   (verses 42 – 43 and 45 – 46a)**

Our expectations about what something *should* be like, or how someone *should* act, may cloud our vision. Our prejudices often determine our expectations – we judge someone, and then we expect them to act in a certain way. We are disturbed when they do not fit our picture. Prejudice blinded the Pharisees (the religious leaders of the time) to the reality of Jesus.

† *Lord, let us not be deceived into thinking ourselves better than others, but help us constantly to search our hearts for any prejudice that may keep us from seeing the Christ in others.*

Wednesday December 5   John 3.1 – 17

THE GOD OF SURPRISES I never stop discovering new riches in this treasured story. Here is a man of power and position, very important. His world is under his control. He is a member of the religious ruling class. People like Nicodemus have most trouble coming to God. These are the ones who have managed life very well to get to the top, whether it is in the Church or in business. They have had to deny their own vulnerability and weaknesses. It is almost impossible for them to accept that they are accepted and loved by God not for what they have achieved, but simply for who they are – a child of God. So Jesus tells Nicodemus about the unpredictable nature of the Holy Spirit, and about being surprised by God.

> **'The wind blows wherever it pleases. You hear its sound but you cannot tell where it comes from or where it is going. So it is with everyone born of the Spirit.'   (verse 8)**

This is what Nicodemus most needs to hear – to let go and let God – but he cannot understand. His neat and tidy mind takes Jesus literally. But life is not neat and tidy. We make a mess. We are not, and can never be, perfect. But we can become more and more human. We need a saviour – someone who will 'keep humanity human'. We need to be born again from above, from God.

† *Lord, help us to become as free and open as a child to the movement of your Spirit.*

Thursday December 6   Colossians 1.15 – 20

ALL THE FULLNESS OF GOD IN CHRIST The church at Colossae was in danger of sliding back into old ways. Paul pleads with them to understand and distinguish between the shadow of

Old Testament ceremonies, human rules and ways of worship –
and the reality found in Christ (*2.13 – 23*). We are complete in
Christ. There is no need to add to God's work in Jesus Christ.

**For God was pleased to have all his fullness dwell in him,
and through him to reconcile to himself all things, whether
things on earth or things in heaven, by making peace
through his blood, shed on the cross.   (verses 19 – 20)**

This can be a hard lesson to learn. Do we think that something
more is needed? That Christ is not enough? Some Christians in
Paul's time felt that they needed to combine faith in Christ with
secret knowledge which belonged only to an élite group, not to
everyone. Others tried to fill up their faith with rules like
circumcision and not eating certain foods. Nonsense! we think.
But are we so different? Don't we try to fill up our faith with
anxiety, anger, depression and resentment? Paul calls us to the
glorious riches of Christ in us (*verse 27*). In Christ we can find all
the resources necessary for fullness of life. He has done it all.
Our part is only to reach out and grasp these riches of salvation
in both hands.

✝ *Lord, I do believe. Help me to overcome my unbelief.*

Friday December 7   **Romans 15.4 – 13**

GOD'S PURPOSE CONTINUES   Our values must change
once we accept that Jesus is Lord. The early Christians were
known as 'those people who have turned the world upside
down'. The values of God's Kingdom will never live
comfortably side by side with the values of the marketplace. To
live in the spirit of unity which Paul speaks about, we need to
deny self-interest and our personal agenda, as we struggle to
find and build on common ground. Without self-denial, we
cannot hope to praise and 'glorify God with one heart and
mouth'. We are not asked to agree or even to like one another.
When Jesus is Lord, we do commit ourselves to accepting and
loving one another in the sense that we want the best and not
the worst for others. In this way, we build up the Body of
Christ, so that we may glorify God more effectively.

**May the God who gives endurance and encouragement
give you a spirit of unity among yourselves as you follow
Christ Jesus, so that with one heart and mouth you may
glorify the God and Father of our Lord Jesus Christ.**

(verses 5 – 6)

Our lifestyle is a form of evangelism. Christians are watched more than they realize. Who we say we are must match what we do and how we live. So we look to Jesus for integrity of character: what you see is what you get. The best evangelism – message of hope – is yourself.

✝ *Lord, make me a message of your hope and peace and joy.*

Saturday December 8   Isaiah 2.1 – 5

GOD'S EARTHLY KINGDOM

> **They will beat their swords into ploughshares**
>   **and their spears into pruning hooks.**
> **Nation will not take up sword against nation,**
>   **nor will they train for war any more.**   **(verse 4)**

Like the time of Isaiah, we live in a time of upheaval, change and searching. We look for answers. What does the future hold? Jesus tells us that the future will take care of itself because it is God's future. Our task is to be accountable for the present. We may perhaps develop a more prophetic imagination by asking ourselves the following questions. Which voice speaks the truth in love? Which voice seeks justice, hears the cry of the powerless, stands for honesty, integrity and accountability? Who will lead us – and whom shall we lead – beyond the need to train for war any more? Who will show us – and whom shall we show – more godly, creative ways of dealing with conflict?

✝ *Lord, may I, too, be a fearless prophet and speak out for your justice and mercy.*

For group discussion and personal thought

- Where do you see a need to overcome prejudice? How could you become involved in helping to change this?
- Is there anyone for whom you believe Christ has not died? If so, why? Be honest. We say we believe that Christ died for all, but it is not always a belief we live out.

GOD WITH US 2
Words for today

Notes by Elina Templin

based on the New International Version

This week begins with Bible Sunday. The Word comes to us in so many ways. It can welcome us, trouble us, challenge, comfort – but it is always living and active, sharper than any double-edged sword. The living word of God cuts through all our pretensions and calls us to account for our lives. Most of all, God speaks his Word to us in Jesus – in his birth, life, suffering and death, and as risen Lord. In Jesus, we hear God's voice.

Text for the week: Isaiah 40.8

Sunday December 9   **Isaiah 52. 1 – 12**

A WELCOME WORD How beautiful are those who first brought to us the saving Word of God! After my baptism as an adult convert in my late 40s, I remember coming home and feeling so elated and joy-filled that I took a leap across the kitchen, totally convinced I could fly! This runner announces to Zion that her God has become king. I am convinced it must be a runner, because you would not just walk if you were bringing such exciting news – you would *run*!

> **How beautiful on the mountains**
>   **are the feet of those who bring good news ...**
> **who say to Zion,**
>   **'Your God reigns!' ...**
> **The LORD will lay bare his holy arm**
>   **in the sight of all the nations,**
> **and all the ends of the earth will see**
>   **the salvation of our God.**   **(part of verse 7 and verse 10)**

The Lord is coming! God's people will be restored to Zion. However, it is not the nation, the Temple, or a human being which is glorified, but the sovereign Lord who comes in power – with his arm 'bared' (*Isaiah 40.9 – 11*). In a sermon preached in 1529, the great Reformer Martin Luther wrote, 'Christians are a blissful people, who can rejoice at heart, sing praises, stamp and

269

dance and leap for joy. This is well pleasing to God, and does our heart good, when we trust God and find in him our pride and joyfulness.'

✝ *Lord, may the joy of salvation that we have received be a blessing to others.*

Monday December 10   1 Kings 18.17 – 39

YOU TROUBLER OF ISRAEL!   God's word can be welcoming and beautiful – a message we want to hear. But today brings a most unwelcome message from the prophet Elijah, bearer of trouble! A real disturber of peace, this one. He keeps challenging the people, challenging their gods, 'Baals'. These lifeless idols are powerless to speak a word to the people. Elijah mocks them as he compares them to the living Word, the living God. He challenges the people to choose.

'How long will you waver between two opinions? If the LORD is God, follow him; but if Baal is God, follow him.' But the people said nothing.   **(verse 21)**

The people said nothing – like their gods! People don't like to be disturbed. It can be threatening to have our beliefs questioned. The Pharisees might well have confronted Jesus with these words, 'You troubler of Israel!' Troublers can destroy and take away our capacity to grow; or they can be creative and shake up the comfortable way things are. They are critical of things that need to change and challenge us to grow, to choose – 'If the Lord is God...'

✝ *Living Lord, help us to obey your word, even when it is not comfortable.*

Tuesday December 11   Amos 5.4 – 15

LIFE UNDER GOD   One of the first things children say to each other is, 'It's not fair!' We seem to be born with an innate sense of fair play. But those who know the ways of the world will often say, 'Life is *not* fair – and that's just the way it is. The sooner you learn that, the better.' But life is meant to be fair. Amos says, 'Seek the Lord and *live*' (*verse 4*). Get your priorities right. Live real life under God. Then he exposes the true state of the people. Their lives are living proof that they have turned away from God and become self-seeking. Social responsibilities have broken down. Their relationships are in a mess, because their *first* love is neglected. Life is indeed unfair.

> You oppress the righteous and take bribes
>   and you deprive the poor of justice in the courts ...
> Seek good, not evil,
>   that you may live.
> Then the LORD God Almighty will be with you.
>
> (part of verses 12 and 14)

Hate evil. Love good. Do justice. This week we celebrate Human Rights Day. Let us not be afraid to speak out wherever the value and dignity of any person are threatened. Justice has been described as love in action. It is an attitude of heart and mind and mirrors God's compassion for the powerless. How does this 'love in action' work in your area?

† *Lord, make me a presence for good in my community.*

Wednesday December 12   **Jeremiah 7.1 – 15**

DO NOT TRUST IN DECEPTIVE WORDS   Deceptive words are false words that misrepresent, mislead and trick. Satan the devil is called the Great Deceiver. The people have been listening to false prophets. God sends Jeremiah to the Temple gates to face the people and tell them the truth: God will not protect the Temple (and Jerusalem and its people) from harm. False worship and bad behaviour have set the Lord against Israel. We are what we worship. When we worship false gods, our thinking and our words and actions become false. God's ways are no longer at the centre of our lives. Social injustices are allowed to continue and thrive. We no longer even recognize the false from the true and, above all, we lose a sense of life as a response to God, as obedience.

> While you were doing all these things, declares the LORD, I spoke to you again and again, but you did not listen: I called you, but you did not answer.   (verse 13)

During World War II the writer Victor Frankl met a man and a woman in a concentration camp who were close to suicide. Both expected nothing more from life. He asked them whether the question was 'What do we expect from life?' Or was the question really 'What does life expect from us?' It is not enough to hear the word. We must obey it.

† *Lord God, strengthen us to stand by the truth and obey your word.*

DRIVEN OR CALLED? The Bible teaches us about the sovereignty of God. It is *God* who has the first word and the last, who is 'alpha and omega' (*Revelation 1.8*). It is *God* who calls us and waits for an answer. Loving is not about us first loving God. Our love is an answer to the love of God (*1 John 4.10*). No one comes to Jesus unless the Father who sent him draws us (*John 6.44*). In Jeremiah 31.3, the Lord has '*drawn* you with loving-kindness'. All is grace. All begins with God.

> **For this is what the Sovereign LORD says: I myself will search for my sheep and look after them ... I will search for the lost and bring back the strays ... I will shepherd the flock with justice.** **(verse 11 and part of verse 16)**

It makes all the difference to see life as a series of choices. People who are driven are often their own worst enemy and rush through life causing damage. People who are called to wait – wait upon the Lord – wait quietly and confidently for the guidance of his Word. They know that there is calendar time – and there is the *kairos*, God's time. Their decisions and choices will be made in God's time and in God's way.

✝ *'The Lord is my Shepherd – I shall not want'.*

PREPARING THE WAY The people of Israel, God's people, cannot believe that they will ever be set free from exile in Babylon – let alone return to their homeland and national independence. But God is guiding history itself and preparing to come in person and lead them. The people are filled with fear when they think of the hard journey back home across the desert. But they are comforted by the promise that all barriers will be removed – valleys will be levelled, mountains lowered, rough ground made smooth. In this poetic way, Isaiah promises that all the uneven and rough places in their lives will disappear. God is marching to them and with them.

> **A voice of one calling:**
> **'In the desert prepare**
>   **the way for the LORD;**
> **make straight in the wilderness**
>   **a highway for our God.**
> **Every valley shall be raised up,**
>   **every mountain and hill made low;**

the rough ground shall become level,
    the rugged places a plain.
And the glory of the LORD will be revealed.'

(verses 3 – 5a)

The Bible uses the image of a desert to speak of life's troubles and suffering, especially when God seems absent. We all know this as part of our human condition. But we must also know that the Lord is both warrior and shepherd, the God of love and the God who can act. In the desert, we must not lose hope but prepare to see God work.

† *Lord, we trust in your power to lead us through the desert places in our lives.*

Saturday December 15   Matthew 3.1 – 12

ARE YOU FACING THE WRONG WAY? When an important speaker is coming to address a meeting, someone else comes forward first to introduce the speaker and to prepare us for his or her message. This is what John the Baptist did. The heart of John's message is repentance. Turn. Come back. Come home. Prepare for a radical change at the very root of your being. You are facing the wrong way. Do not think you can rely on another person's faith. Do not think you can escape from God's wrath. You are accountable. It matters how you live. Therefore ...

'Repent, for the kingdom of heaven is near' ... 'Produce fruit in keeping with repentance.'   **(verses 2 and 8)**

Jesus also comes preaching a message of repentance. But there is something new. Repent, says Jesus, and believe the good news. The Baptist warns of God's wrath and punishment. Jesus roots repentance in the love of God. Repent and believe the good news of God's saving love for us. In Jesus, the Kingdom of God's rule has begun. Some people still live in fear of God's judgement. Is repentance motivated by fear, or by love?

† *O God, search me and know my heart.*

For group discussion and personal thought

- Have you known real joy in your life as a Christian? Recently? If not, why not? If yes, has it been shared with others?
- How have you failed to seek or deepen your love for God?
- Are there areas in your life where you have carried on as if God had no word to say?

GOD WITH US 3

A voice in the wilderness

Notes by Elina Templin

*based on the New International Version and
the Contemporary English Version*

Here is a man for whom Jesus had such high praise. Yet John the Baptist points beyond himself to the One who is coming. He preaches a repentance for the forgiveness of sins and tells us to prepare to receive the Christ. How do we prepare? John said that he was not worthy to tie Christ's sandals, yet Jesus himself washed the feet of his disciples. It is those with a humble heart, the pure in heart, who will recognize Jesus, who will see God.

Text for the week: Luke 3.4

Sunday December 16   **Luke 1.57 – 66**

GOD'S BREAKTHROUGH   For the Jews, a name was much more than a label. Zechariah had to accept that his son would not be named after himself. This child needed to have a name that would show the kind of person he would become and the great work he was called to do for God. So Zechariah calls him John, which meant in Hebrew 'The Lord is gracious'.

> On the eighth day they came to circumcise the child, and they were going to name him after his father Zechariah, but his mother spoke up and said, 'No! He is to be called John'. They said to her, 'There is no-one among your relatives who has that name' ... to everyone's astonishment, [Zechariah] wrote, 'His name is John' ... Everyone who heard this wondered about it, asking, 'What then is this child going to be?' For the Lord's hand was with him.
> **(verses 59 – 61, part of 63, and verse 66)**

Zechariah's relatives cannot accept that a new name is introduced into their family. No-one has that name. It is not what we expect. Together with the family name goes a set of beliefs. The child must live out the expectations of the parents. We often think traditional customs will last for ever. But they can be shaped by human patterns of thinking and become idols, and God may be trying to break through this closed circle to bring in a new message for a new time.

✝ *Eternal God, help us to see that you alone are for ever.*

Monday December 17 Luke 1.67 – 79

GOD'S POWER BEYOND LIMITS Zechariah's first words to the angel – the messenger of God – were, 'How can I be sure?' (*Luke 1.18*). Where is the proof that God is able to do this? Now, in our text today, the Holy Spirit empowers Zechariah to confess God's mighty acts, and he can only praise and glorify God.

> **Zechariah was filled with the Holy Spirit and prophesied:**
> **Praise be to the Lord the God of Israel,**
> **because he has come and has redeemed his people ...**
> **(as he said through his holy prophets of long ago).**
> **(verses 67 – 68 and 70)**

This is indeed an act of conversion. God can change us. Zechariah had faith; he was upright in the sight of God and obedient to God's word (*Luke 1.6*). But he set limits on God's power. Zechariah had to learn how to be silent while God spoke his word. After the humbling experience of his ordeal, after he had learned that God is faithful to his Word, he could only praise God.

✝ *Almighty God, help us to trust that your power begins when we are still and willing to listen.*

Tuesday December 18 John 1.19 – 28

BEHOLD THE LAMB OF GOD! Because he had free will, John could have refused to give way to Jesus. He could have tried to keep all the attention on himself, to enjoy his fame. What would have happened then? But John faithfully represented God's righteousness and Jesus recognized his greatness. When the religious leaders, the Pharisees, keep asking him who he is, John can only point to Jesus.

> **'Who are you? Give us an answer to take back to those who sent us. What do you say about yourself?' John replied in the words of Isaiah the prophet, 'I am the voice of one calling in the desert, "Make straight the way for the Lord".'**
> **(verses 22 – 23)**

To make the way straight for the Lord, we ourselves must first become straight by repenting and turning back to God with a humble heart and broken spirit (*Psalm 51*). The only way to prepare is to get out of God's way. John was not perfect. But he was willing to perform the humblest task for Christ. When we understand who Christ is, pride and self-importance melt away. It does not matter who I am, John said. All that matters is who Jesus is.

† *Lord Jesus, may we fix our eyes on you alone, who begin and perfect our faith.*

Wednesday December 19   Luke 3.10 – 14, 18 – 20

THE COST OF TRUTH   John was firm and uncompromising in his faith. He was obedient to his calling to announce the coming of the Saviour King. But his way was not easy. Some react to the truth with repentance, others with resentment.

> **In many different ways John preached the Good News to the people. But to Herod the ruler, he said, 'It was wrong for you to take Herodias, your brother's wife'. John also said that Herod had done many other bad things. Finally, Herod put John in prison and this was the worst thing he had done. (verses 18 – 20, Contemporary English Version)**

Good news is not always good news for those who hide from the truth. John was not afraid to speak up when he saw things that were wrong. He attacked those who thought that their high positions gave them freedom to do what they wanted. John attacked greed: share with another, he said, be satisfied, don't take more than you need. But when he challenged the greed and corruption of King Herod and his court, he was imprisoned. The cost of speaking out was high, but sometimes the cost will be higher when we are silent. 'Evil thrives – and does well – when good people do nothing.' Christians are called by God to stand for justice and truth.

† *Gracious Lord, may we have eyes to see when things are wrong, and the compassion and courage and will to do something about it.*

Thursday December 20   Matthew 11.7 – 15

FROM HERE TO ETERNITY   Our Christian calendar begins with the birth of Jesus. Yet the history of our salvation really begins with the death and resurrection of Christ. The Christian way is marked with the cross. John lived in the time before the cross and the resurrection. He could not know what God would reveal to us on the cross. John gets high pràise from Jesus, yet he would only catch a glimpse, a hint, of God's plan.

'I tell you the truth: Among those born of women there has not risen anyone greater than John the Baptist; yet he who is least in the kingdom of heaven is greater than he.'

(verse 11)

Have you ever seen a small child run up to its mother or father, throw its arms out wide and say, 'I love you *this much*!'? How much? This much! For the child, what they embrace is the whole universe. They cannot describe a greater love than this wide embrace. How much does God love us? 'The eternal God is your refuge, and underneath are the everlasting arms' (*Deuteronomy 33.27*). God embraces us with a love that will never let us go. On the cross, we see a love so high, wide, long and deep that it is beyond all suffering, sin, evil and death. After the cross, things can never be the same again. So the least in the kingdom is greater than anyone who went before.

† *Loving Lord, thank you for your love that will never let us go.*

Friday December 21   **Matthew 11.16 – 19**

ANY EXCUSE WILL DO   You can never satisfy some people. John the Baptist was criticized for living in isolation. Jesus was criticized for mixing socially with all kinds of people. Whatever is said or done, some people always take the opposite view. It seems any excuse will do, if you don't want to hear the truth.

'For John came neither eating nor drinking, and they say, "He has a demon". The Son of Man came eating and drinking, and they say, 'Here is a glutton and a drunkard, a friend of tax collectors and "sinners".' But wisdom is proved right by her actions.'   **(verses 18 – 19)**

In the end, wisdom was indeed proved right by her actions. John brought many people to God. People found new life in Jesus, new direction and new power. Perhaps people do not recognize Jesus because they do not want to. Perhaps they sense that it would be too challenging to their comfort and security. So they make excuses. Putting God first may mean that we need to change.

† *Lord, help us to recognize when we are making excuses to put off doing what you want.*

AN UPSIDE-DOWN WORLD   Some people feel a need to prove that they are important. They need to show others that they are somebody and try to impress them with material success, power, influence. But riches often come at the cost of our humanity. Self-importance seems to grow at the same rate as our bank balance! The world honours riches and bows down to position and power, yet we preach Christ crucified. The values of the Kingdom of God are radical and revolutionary.

> **And Mary said:**
>   **'My soul praises the Lord**
> **and my spirit rejoices in God my Saviour,**
> **for he has been mindful of the humble state of his servant ...**
>   **he has scattered those who are proud in their inmost thoughts.**
> **He has brought down rulers from their thrones**
>   **but has lifted up the humble.**
> **He has filled the hungry with good things**
>   **but has sent the rich away empty.**
>   **(verses 46 – 48a and 52 – 53)**

All that we have and are is a gift. A gift is given to be given. God gives different gifts to each of us. But the gift is not as important as what we do with it. Being a servant is about sharing. Perhaps you think you are too poor to share. I have seen that those who have the least share the most. But faith is the greatest gift of all – and the greatest gift of all to share.

✝ *Lord, strengthen me as I seek to serve in your name.*

For group discussion and personal thought

- Do you experience fear, hero-worship of a person or addiction in your life? Are there things, people or traditions that you cannot live without, which challenge your commitment to God?
- Do you have a picture of yourself as spiritually weak and limited? Does this picture make it possible for you to avoid discovering your strengths, the gifts that the Holy Spirit wants you to use to serve your community?

GOD WITH US 4
Born of God

Notes by Elina Templin

based on the New International Version

The season of Advent/Christmas reminds us that life is meant to be lived in expectant hope. The love of God is making all things new. There can never be a dull moment when we walk with Christ. All things become possible. Each day becomes an advent – an adventure when we can say with Mary, 'Let it be to me according to your Word'.

Text for the week: John 1.12 – 13

Sunday December 23   **Isaiah 7.10 – 16**

A TIME OF CRISIS   Ahaz has been called the Judas of the Old Testament, because he abandoned God when he gave his loyalty to the highest bidder – the world power of the time, Assyria. The name Immanuel was a sign. It was meant to assure Ahaz that God could rescue him from his enemies.

> **'The Lord himself will give you a sign: The virgin will be with child and will give birth to a son, and will call him Immanuel.'**   **(verse 14)**

But Ahaz chose not to trust God. He preferred his own understanding of the critical situation with the enemy. He pretended he wanted God's help, but did not really want to hear the message. But he gets it anyway: one day a child called Immanuel, God with us, would come from the very heart of God. Who do you pay attention to in times of crisis?

✝ *Lord Jesus, in your strength I shall live in obedience to your Word.*

Monday December 24   **Luke 1.26 – 45**

LET GOD!   Zechariah's question to the messenger of God, 'How can I be sure?' is one that all Christians know only too well. But I hope we have all known the other side of the coin as well – the faith of Mary. We see in Mary all the loveliness of Advent lit up by faith – she is the obedient servant, most prepared to receive the Lord. Her response seems in the end so simple, so quiet and, in a way, so easy! Compare Zechariah's response with Mary's:

> **'I am the Lord's servant,' Mary answered. 'May it be to me as you have said.' Then the angel left her.** (verse 38)

Sometimes the closer we come to God, the greater is our struggle with doubt, because the devil does not bother with those who are already far from God. But he will be most active when a Christian takes God seriously and wants to serve his kingdom. It is easy to believe when we are sure and have proof. True faith is faith that is tested in the storms of life and survives the test (*1 Peter 1.6, 7*).

✝ *Lord Jesus, help us to keep going in faith even when things don't turn out exactly as we thought they would.*

Tuesday December 25   **Luke 2.1 – 20**

GOD'S POWER FOR OUR WEAKNESS   In his book, *The God Who Comes*, Carlo Carretto compares the Church to Mary and Joseph travelling from Egypt to Nazareth on a donkey. They hold the weakness and poverty of the child Jesus in their arms: God incarnate. All human achievement and life are vulnerable. They will always have their weak spots, however strong and advanced they may appear to be. That is the nature of being human. But in the weakness and poverty of the baby Jesus, in that vulnerability, lies the hidden power of God. This is the true message of Christmas.

> **'Today in the town of David a Saviour has been born to you; he is Christ the Lord. This will be a sign to you: You will find a baby wrapped in cloths and lying in a manger.'** (verses 11 – 12)

Paul hears the word of the Lord saying to him: 'My grace is sufficient for you, for my power is made perfect in weakness' (*2 Corinthians 12.9*).

✝ *Lord, help us to find true satisfaction in your kingdom and not in the things of this world.*

Wednesday December 26   **Titus 2.11 – 14**

WORKING AND WAITING   The heart of the Christian gospel is good news about something that has happened in the past. 'The grace of God has appeared' (*verse 11*). Today, we are tempted to say in despair, 'Look what the world has come to! How terrible it all is!' Compare this with the first Christians as they shouted with joy, 'See what has come to the world!' God has come to save all people. Yet we wait – for the coming again of Christ. There is still work to be done. We still have to become more and more like Jesus.

> **The grace of God that brings salvation has appeared ... It teaches us to say 'No' to ungodliness ... to live self-controlled, upright and godly lives ... while we wait for ... Christ, who gave himself for us ... that are his very own.**
> **(part of verses 11 – 14)**

There is an old Scottish saying, 'The one who has something to look forward to is never tired'. The grace of God trains us to live a godly life in this world. Looking ahead empowers the present. Life is going somewhere. Our task is to do everything truly for Christ's sake and the coming of God's kingdom on earth. Then we can be certain and confident that he will be beside us to guide our steps.

† *Lord, let me not be frozen either by the past or the present. Keep alive in me the forward look and the high hope, to live like Jesus.*

Thursday December 27   John 1.1 – 18

STAMPED BY GOD

> **The Word became flesh and lived for a while among us. We have seen his glory, the glory of the one and only [Son], who came from the Father, full of grace and truth.**
>
> **(verse 14)**

How lovely these words are! It is good to memorize key Bible readings such as this one, so that they sink deep within your soul. The Word became flesh ... God in person ... the very life of God in our midst. The entertainment world sometimes introduces famous people 'in person'. Such excitement flows from the crowd. The name suddenly becomes so real. What does it all mean? It means that God becomes like us so that we might become like him. You put a stamp on a letter or a parcel to show that it has been approved, it is authentic. The incarnation of Jesus means that God has put his very own stamp on human beings.

† *Almighty God, loving Father, thank you for who I am.*

WORTHY OF WORSHIP Many people would like to know the future. Predicting the future, or trying to, seems to be part of human nature. Yet we remember the words of our Lord, 'No one knows about that day or hour' (*Matthew 24.36*). The book of Revelation is a fascinating book, but it is not easy to understand. It is the last book of the Bible and witnesses to God's final victory, when God's work of salvation will be finished. Meanwhile, only the Lamb is worthy to open the scroll which is the book of the future. Because of the sacrifice of the Lamb (Christ), he is the only one who holds the key to the future and therefore the only one worthy of worship.

> **'Worthy is the Lamb, who was slain,**
> **to receive power and wealth and wisdom and strength**
> **and honour and glory and praise!'** (verse 12)

Our answer to God's grace can only be praise and worship. Worship is at its best in community. A Christian writer said that when we worship we should remember that God is the audience. We share in the ongoing drama by declaring his glory.

✝ *Lord God, may you truly be at the centre of all I think, and do, and feel.*

NOW IS ALL WE HAVE Why do we worry about the future? The future belongs to God! I can do nothing to bring it closer or to change it in any way. Jesus said that each day is enough for us to cope with and we are not to worry about tomorrow (*Matthew 6.34*). But we can do something about today. One Christian writer has written, 'Christian faith always lives "as if" the second coming were just around the corner'. If I believe 'Christ will come again', if I believe that all life is marching towards that time, then I will live *now* in that expectation. That hope will be a light for my path. I must become *now* what I want to be *then*.

> **'Behold, I am coming soon! My reward is with me, and I**
> **will give to everyone according to what he has done. I am**
> **the Alpha and the Omega, the First and the Last, the**
> **Beginning and the End.'** (verses 12 – 13)

How can we be sure? Jesus commands us to 'Watch!' (*Mark 13.35, 37*). Be alert! Keep your eyes and ears open! Why? For what? For the daily, hourly, every moment coming of Christ into my life: in the preached Word, in the bread and wine of communion, in worship with my brothers and sisters, in the face of everyone I meet, especially those in need of bread or justice or love. Our Christian hope is indeed in the coming in glory of Christ. But for today, there is work to be done for God.

† *Lord, help me to let go of the past and the future, and to live and rest in your presence now.*

Sunday December 30 1 John 3.16 – 24

LOVE IN TRUTH AND ACTIONS The word 'command' is not one we usually think of when we speak of love. This is because our world today is often confused about what love is. Sadly, we have only one word in English for 'love'. In Greek, there are several words, including love between friends, between a man and a woman, and *agape* – God's love for us, who do not deserve it. Love is not a feeling but a decision. We prefer to like those who are like us, but we are called to be like Jesus. God does not suggest that we love others; he commands us to do so. We truly have no choice. The poet W H Auden said, 'We must love one another or die'.

> **This is his command: to believe in the name of his Son, Jesus Christ, and to love one another as he commanded us. Those who obey his commands live in him, and he in them. And this is how we know that he lives in us: We know it by the Spirit he gave us. (verses 23 – 24)**

We believe in the name of Jesus when we *do* his word. People need to be shown love – and we need to show it.

† *Heavenly Father, help us to be more caring and loving, especially to those we don't like.*

Monday December 31 1 John 4.7 – 21

LOVE IS THE SIGN Love goes out, love does not hold life to itself. Love gives freely of itself, not counting the cost. Love gets back many times over what it gives – but it does not see the reward. Love only sees the other. Love always bears fruit. 'By their fruit you will recognize them' (*Matthew 7.16*

> **This is love: not that we loved God, but that he loved us and sent his Son as an atoning sacrifice for our sins. Dear friends, since God so loved us, we also ought to love one another. (verses 10 – 11)**

A Christian worker tells the following story. In the bush in Botswana in Africa was a small, simple hospital. Outside stood a wheelbarrow with two very clean pillows. A woman came out of the clinic, walking in pain, and her husband helped her to the wheelbarrow. The worker writes how moving it was to see the tall, thin African slowly lifting his sick wife into the wheelbarrow, where she lay in comfort on the pillows. Then, proudly lifting the handles of the wheelbarrow, he looked around at everyone and off they went into the bush. The doctor said, 'There's a miracle – that a man cares enough to wheel his sick wife in his barrow for twenty miles. He's been here before. He'll come again and again until she's better!' That is the kind of love we are called to show to all people – whoever they are.

† *Loving Lord, make me a channel of your love and peace in the world.*

For group discussion and personal thought

- Do you look down on other religions or traditions? If so, why?
- Are you prepared to let God change your mind? Do you pray to be open to his light?

INTERNATIONAL BIBLE READING ASSOCIATION

– a worldwide service of the National Christian Education Council at work in five continents.

HEADQUARTERS

1020 Bristol Road
Selly Oak
Birmingham
Great Britain
B29 6LB

http://www.ncec.org.uk
ibra@ncec.org.uk

and the following agencies

AUSTRALIA

Uniting Education (previously The Joint Board of Christian Education)
PO Box 1245 (65 Oxford Street)
Collingwood
Victoria 3066

GHANA

IBRA Secretary
PO Box 919
Accra

INDIA

All India Sunday School Association
PO Box 2099
Secunderabad – 500 003
Andhra Pradesh

NEW ZEALAND

Epworth Bookshop
PO Box 6133, Te Aro
75 Taranaki Street
Wellington 6035

NIGERIA

IBRA Representative
PMB 5298
Ibadan

SOUTH AND CENTRAL AFRICA

IBRA Representative
Box 1176
Sedgefield 6573

Scheme of readings for 2002

1. Becoming disciples (Matthew)
God with us – Strangers – Child of Abraham – Testing – New teaching – Integrity – Clear choice

2. Lenten encounter
In sin and in forgiveness – In danger and in safety – In doubt and in faith – In darkness and in light – In death and in life – In rejection and in recognition

3. Easter people, Easter places
Women – Men – Church communities – Easter places

4. Breaking the mould
Breaking Traditions – Breaking Expectations – Breaking and Shaping – Breaking Bread

5. Rough passage to the Promised Land (Numbers)
The Route to Moab – Balaam and the Israelites – Getting ready to arrive

6. Different ways of learning
From each other – From the past – Through stories – Through precepts – By doing – Through worship

7. Uncomfortable words
Difficult texts – Difficult sayings

8. From glory to glory
The glory of God the Almighty – The glory of God, the Creator and Rescuer – The glory revealed – Changed into his likeness – The glory to come

9. Philippians
The mind of Christ – The life of Christ

10. Life together
God's party

11. Amos
The challenge of justice – The cost of true discipleship

12. Mission
Gathering in – Going out – Proclaiming the Good News – Hearing the Good News

13. Advent: The coming Kingdom (Mark)
Watch and wait – The Baptist – The Holy Family – Christmas Feasting – Kingdom come

The themes and books studied each year are linked to the **Revised Common Lectionary.**

Facing the challenges of being Christian in today's and tomorrow's world

Publications now available

Family and all that stuff
TRUE stories by over 20 well-known Christians about their family lives: fascinating stories, illustrating some impressive mental and faith journeys.

Never mind the gap
Explore the challenge and adventure of being a grandparent in today's society. Includes activities, reflections and ideas to help you make the most of this significant relationship.

Tell it again!
Explore story-telling and creative games with young children. Offers advice, background and a comprehensive set of resources including games, rhymes and stories.

Happy ever after
Explore the ways of nurturing and sustaining a marriage. This book also considers the similarities and differences between formal marriages, recognized by Church and State, and informal marriages or committed cohabitation.

Breaking up is hard to do
A source of support and information for those who come to the moment of breaking up. Discover the positive elements of the experience, beyond the pain and loss.

Godparents
Support and advice for parents, godparents, godchildren and churches. Written by respected authorities on family life.

Facing the challenges of being Christian in today's and tomorrow's world

Order form

Please send me the following books:

Title of book	Quantity	Unit price	Total
Breaking up is hard to do		£6.00	
Family and all that stuff		£10.00	
Godparents		£6.00	
Happy ever after		£6.00	
Never mind the gap		£6.50	
Tell it again!		£6.00	
	Total cost of books		
	Postage and packing (see below)		
	Donation to *Faith in the Future* project		
	TOTAL DUE		

*Payments in **Pounds Sterling**, please.*

Postage and packing: In the UK, add 15p in the pound.
Overseas, add £3.00 airmail per book.

❑ I enclose a cheque (*payable to NCEC*)

❑ I wish to pay by Visa, Mastercard or Switch:

Card number: _____

Expiry date: _____ *Issue no. (Switch):* _____

Name: _____

Address: _____

_____

_____

Postcode: _____

Signature: _____

National Christian Education Council
1020 Bristol Road, Selly Oak,
Birmingham B29 6LB